DATE RAPE
DRUGS

BY KATE CONLEY

CONTENT CONSULTANT

R. E. GAENSSLEN, PHD

PROFESSOR EMERITUS, FORENSIC SCIENCE
UNIVERSITY OF ILLINOIS AT CHICAGO

Essential Library

An Imprint of Abdo Publishing | abdopublishing.com

Published by Abdo Publishing, a division of ABDO, PO Box 398166, Minneapolis, Minnesota 55439.
Copyright © 2019 by Abdo Consulting Group, Inc. International copyrights reserved in all countries.
No part of this book may be reproduced in any form without written permission from the publisher.
Essential Library™ is a trademark and logo of Abdo Publishing.

Printed in the United States of America, North Mankato, Minnesota.
042018
092018

THIS BOOK CONTAINS
RECYCLED MATERIALS

Cover Photo: Doug McLean/Shutterstock Images
Interior Photos: Kseniia Yeskova/Shutterstock Images, 5; iStockphoto, 7, 26, 38–39, 41, 63, 64–65, 66; Mark Ralston/AFP/Getty Images, 11; Ellen Creager/Detroit Free Press/Tribune News Service/Getty Images, 14–15; Kevin Link/Science Source, 16–17; Red Line Editorial, 19, 31, 51, 83; Merja Ojala/AFP/Getty Images, 20; Wave Break Media/iStockphoto, 23, 72; Theo Heimann/Getty Images News/Getty Images, 25; Bernard Bodo/iStockphoto, 29; Daniel Acker/Bloomberg/Getty Images, 32; Mark Boster/Los Angeles Times/Getty Images, 35; Shutterstock Images, 43, 44; Katarzyna Bialasiewicz/iStockphoto, 46, 70; Light Field Studios/Shutterstock Images, 50; Eric Risberg/AP Images, 52–53; Bryan Chan/Los Angeles Times/Getty Images, 57; Graeme Robertson/Getty Images News/Getty Images, 58; Izabela Habur/iStockphoto, 60; Juan Monino/iStockphoto, 69; Sundry Photography/Shutterstock Images, 75; DEA/Science Source, 76–77; Jim West/Alamy, 78; Tim Brakemeier/picture-alliance/dpa/AP Images, 82; Boris Roessler/picture-alliance/dpa/AP Images, 84; Mark J. Terrill/AP Images, 86; Paul Warner/AP Images, 88–89; Chris Walker/Chicago Tribune/Tribune News Service/Getty Images, 90–91; People Images/iStockphoto, 94; Carolyn Cole/Los Angeles Times/Getty Images, 97; Riccardo Savi/Getty Images Entertainment/Getty Images, 98

Editor: Susan E. Hamen
Series Designer: Laura Polzin

Library of Congress Control Number: 2017961351

Publisher's Cataloging-in-Publication Data

Names: Conley, Kate, author.
Title: Date rape drugs / by Kate Conley.
Description: Minneapolis, Minnesota : Abdo Publishing, 2019. | Series: Drugs in real life | Includes online resources and index.
Identifiers: ISBN 9781532114151 (lib.bdg.) | ISBN 9781532153983 (ebook)
Subjects: LCSH: Date rape drugs--Juvenile literature. | Sexual assault--Juvenile literature. | Dating violence--Juvenile literature. | Drug control--United States--Juvenile literature.
Classification: DDC 362.883--dc23

CONTENTS

CHAPTER ONE
SECRETLY DRUGGED
4

CHAPTER TWO
THE BIG THREE
16

CHAPTER THREE
OTHER DANGERS
28

CHAPTER FOUR
BRAIN AND BODY
40

CHAPTER FIVE
#NOTINMYDRINK
52

CHAPTER SIX
A DOUBLE CRIME
64

CHAPTER SEVEN
THE LAW
76

CHAPTER EIGHT
CONTROVERSY
90

ESSENTIAL FACTS   100   SOURCE NOTES   106
GLOSSARY   102   INDEX   110
ADDITIONAL RESOURCES   104   ABOUT THE AUTHOR   112

SECRETLY DRUGGED

"When victims drink this dopey stuff they get talkative, walk around in a restless manner, and then fall into a deep sleep and you can't arouse them until the effect of the drug wears off," said Mary "Gold Tooth" Thornton.[1] She was speaking against her employer, an infamous pickpocket and bar owner named Mickey Finn.

Thornton worked at Finn's Lone Star Saloon in Chicago, Illinois. It was in a rough neighborhood, and Thornton witnessed numerous crimes while working there. Many of those were committed by her own boss. Thornton kept quiet for years as

For more than a century, unscrupulous bartenders have mixed drugs into drinks in order to rob or assault customers.

Finn drugged patrons and then robbed them. Fearing for her life, she finally quit her job in the fall of 1903 and went to the police.

According to Thornton, Finn had sought out the services of a man known as Dr. Hall. Hall sold love potions, charms, and drugs—including cocaine and morphine. Hall sold Finn a large bottle filled with a white powder, most likely chloral hydrate. It was the first synthetic substance used as a sedative-hypnotic drug. This type of drug relaxes muscles, reduces anxiety, and brings on sleep. Mixing it with alcohol amplifies the drug's effects.

Finn served Dr. Hall's powder mixed in a blend of raw alcohol and tobacco-soaked water. He called the drink the Mickey Finn Special. Customers who drank it would fall into a deep sleep, and saloon staff would take them to a back room. There, Finn would strip victims and search for money and valuables. Then he'd throw the victims in the alley. They often woke confused, with no memory of being drugged or robbed or how they came to be in the alley.

Based on Thornton's testimony, the city revoked

SEDATIVE-HYPNOTIC DRUGS

Sedative-hypnotics are a class of drugs that reduce anxiety and bring about sleep. For many years, alcohol and opium were the only substances that could produce these effects. Today, a variety of synthetic drugs, such as Valium and Xanax, have taken their place. They are intended only for short-term use under a doctor's care. People who abuse these drugs may develop a tolerance or become addicted.

Finn's saloon license in late 1903. By that time, however, Finn had already sold his secret drink recipe to barkeeps across the city. Any drink secretly spiked with knockout drugs quickly became known as a Mickey Finn or simply a mickey.

A PROBLEM BEGINS

More than 100 years later, today's predators covertly slip drugs into drinks to make their victims helpless. The drugs make it easier for perpetrators to commit a crime, often rape or sexual assault, without resistance from the victims. Law enforcement officials call this type of crime a drug-facilitated sexual assault (DFSA). The substances used to commit DFSAs are called date rape drugs.

DFSAs began to pose a serious threat in the 1990s. At that time, all-night parties called raves became popular among

In the 1990s, teens who got caught up in the atmosphere at raves didn't fully understand the dangers of the club drugs they encountered at these parties.

teenagers and young adults. Raves featured high-energy techno music and elaborate laser light shows. Many ravers used illegal drugs to enhance their experience. These drugs decreased inhibitions and provided energy that allowed the user to dance all night. The drugs ravers used became known as club drugs, and many of them have also become date rape drugs.

Rohypnol, one of the most common date rape drugs, came to the attention of police officers in 1993. That year, the first reports of Rohypnol use appeared among high school students in Miami, Florida. Though the drug was illegal in the United States, it quickly spread to other parts of the country. Other club drugs used for DFSAs, such as gamma-hydroxybutyric acid (GHB) and ketamine, also began to spread.

A TREND EMERGES

By 1995, doctors at the Rape Treatment Center at the Santa Monica campus of the University of California noticed a startling trend. When victims reported a rape, they also reported that they had been drugged. The drugs were often added to drinks without the victim's knowledge or consent. Since the drugs had had no taste, no smell, and no color, they were undetectable to the victim.

Within 15 to 30 minutes of sipping their drinks, victims would feel dizzy, confused, and sick. "I felt as if someone had stuffed my brain with cotton and strapped me to a tilt-a-whirl," recalled one victim.[2] Because the drugs took effect so quickly and mimicked symptoms of heavy alcohol consumption, many victims did not realize what had happened to them.

In most cases, less than an hour after being drugged, victims would become unconscious. When they woke up the next morning, they had no memory of the night before. Or, if victims did have some memories, they were often fragmented and hard to understand. Many woke up partially dressed, in an unknown location with a stranger, or with other signs of sexual assault.

In December 1997, US Attorney General Janet Reno asked a Department of Justice (DOJ) committee to assess the problem. It was a difficult assignment because no single

CLUB DRUGS

Club drugs are the dangerous and unpredictable substances people use recreationally at dance clubs, raves, concerts, and parties. The most commonly used club drugs are ecstasy, GHB, Rohypnol, ketamine, meth, and LSD. Alone or combined with alcohol, these drugs can produce hallucinations, euphoria, and out-of-body experiences.

Many users believe club drugs are safer than other drugs, such as cocaine or heroin, but emergency department doctors disagree. Dr. Philip Fagan Jr. saw the dangers firsthand when he treated a number of severely ill patients after a rave at the Los Angeles Memorial Coliseum. According to Fagan, raves and the drugs present at them pose a more serious health threat than people realize. "We don't have as many people that are comatose and medically compromised" at other events, said Fagan. "I don't know anybody dying at USC football games from drugs and alcohol."[3]

agency collected information about DFSAs. And many women did not report these crimes at all. However, the DOJ committee studied the law enforcement data on DFSAs that did exist. It also looked at scientific studies and media reports on date rape drugs.

While verifying the number of cases was nearly impossible, the DOJ was able to make three important recommendations in its 1998 report. The first centered on educating potential victims of date rape drugs, especially women in high school and college. The second focused on coordinating efforts between the doctors and police officers who work with DFSA victims. The third and final recommendation was to establish clear guidelines to identify victims who may not even realize they had been drugged.

DRINK SPIKING

The term *drink spiking* is closely related to date rape drugs. Drink spiking is the act of putting any type of drug or alcohol into another person's drink without the person's knowledge or permission. Most drink spiking occurs with the intent to sexually assault the victim. Theft, physical violence, and kidnapping can also be reasons for drink spiking.

THE COSBY TRIALS

In light of these recommendations, college campuses began campaigns to educate students about the dangers of drink spiking. They recommended that students avoid drinking out of cans and bottles they had not opened themselves. They also advised students never to leave their

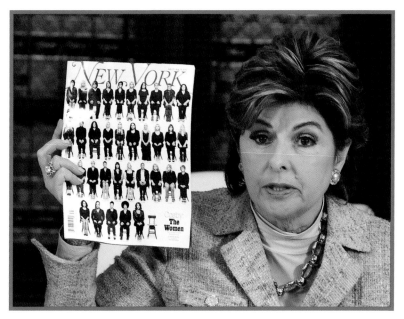

Attorney Gloria Allred holds a copy of *New York* magazine depicting a number of women who alleged comedian Bill Cosby drugged and assaulted them.

drinks unattended. While dozens of news stories alerted the public to DFSAs, the problem was largely regarded as limited to young people.

Then, in 2005, the face of DFSAs changed. In a civil suit that year, a woman named Andrea Constand alleged that actor and comedian Bill Cosby had drugged and sexually assaulted her. Cosby had been a well-respected community leader, and people followed the case closely. It was one of the first high-profile celebrity cases of DFSA. At the trial, Cosby admitted to drugging Constand in order to sexually assault her. In November 2006, the case was settled for an undisclosed amount of money.

While it appeared the Cosby case had come to a conclusion, new allegations surfaced in late 2014. Most of the incidents had happened decades earlier and could no longer be brought to trial because the statute of limitations had expired. One exception to this was Constand, who brought criminal charges against Cosby just before the time on the statute of limitations would have run out. The case went to court and resulted in a mistrial in 2017.

The accusations against Cosby had a far-reaching impact. They drew attention to date rape drugs and the crimes associated with them for more than a decade. They opened up a platform where victims could speak about their experiences. While it does not erase the pain associated with DFSAs, this new atmosphere provides victims with an opportunity to be heard and believed in ways that did not exist earlier.

THE CASE OF ABBEY CONNER

As the Cosby case played out in US courts, Americans vacationing south of the border encountered their own problems with surreptitious drugging. In January 2017, Abbey Conner, a 20-year-old college student, traveled to Mexico with her mom, stepdad, and brother, Austin. The family had hoped for a relaxing vacation, but instead they faced a tragedy. While at the resort, Abbey died. Abbey's official cause of death was listed as an accidental drowning, but her family believes this is not the whole story. They believe she may have been drugged or given tainted alcohol.

On the night in question, Abbey and her mom had been shopping for souvenirs around 5:45. Abbey then went to the pool with Austin, and they all agreed to meet again at 7:00 for dinner. While at the pool Abbey and Austin each took a shot of tequila with another group of vacationers. That is the last thing Austin remembers before waking up in a hospital bed with a concussion. Abbey was in a coma and relying on a ventilator to breathe. Doctors could not detect any brain activity.

Toxicology reports showed that Abbey and Austin had blood-alcohol levels nearly three times above the legal limit. But it seems unlikely that they could have consumed enough alcohol to reach those levels in the short time between when Abbey said goodbye to her mother and the time she drowned. "Somebody had to slip them some type of drug," said Bill Conner, Austin and Abbey's father.[4]

When news of Abbey's death reached media outlets in the United States, something unexpected happened. People reported more than 140 similar

#METOO MOVEMENT

In October 2017, the hashtag #MeToo went viral as a rallying cry against sexual misconduct. That fall, a wave of sexual misconduct accusations against high-powered men in news and entertainment flooded the press. The high-profile #MeToo movement and the Cosby trials have shined a new light on these crimes, as more victims gain the confidence to tell their stories.

The US State Department has warned travelers to Mexico about the threat of resort bars serving tampered-with drinks, which can cause victims to black out and become easy targets for crime.

experiences at resorts in Mexico. The common thread in these stories was that the victims had all ingested some type of substance without their consent. Like Austin, they reported drinking an alcoholic beverage, blacking out, and waking up confused. Some also reported being robbed, injured, or sexually assaulted.

American officials had difficulty getting all the data they wanted on these cases because the alleged crimes took place on foreign soil. Most evidence, however, points to drink tampering. The US State Department issued a warning for

Americans traveling to Mexico. "There have been allegations that consumption of tainted or substandard alcohol has resulted in illness or blacking out," warned the state department.[5]

Conner's death, the Cosby trials, and hundreds of other high-profile cases have raised the awareness of surreptitious drugging to new levels. People across the world are more aware than ever of date rape drugs and drink spiking. It has become a new threat to protect against. When socializing and drinking, people have changed their habits in ways that would have been unimaginable just three decades earlier.

CHAPTER TWO

THE BIG THREE

The threat of date rape had existed for many years, but the idea that perpetrators would use drugs as a weapon to commit the crime was a new idea in the 1990s. Before 1995, no major newspapers in the United States had printed any articles about date rape drugs. That quickly began to change as club drugs gained popularity and spread across the country.

By 1996, 231 articles about Rohypnol had appeared in newspapers across the United States.[1] Americans wanted to know what the drugs were and how they could protect themselves. Articles often featured sobering warnings that teenagers and young adults had

Ketamine, one of the most common date rape drugs, was developed to be used to start and maintain anesthesia in surgery patients.

rarely heard in the past. For example, an October 1996 *Newsweek* article entitled "'Roofies': The Date-Rape Drug" ended with a warning to readers: "don't take your eye off your drink."[2] While this may seem like common sense today, it was novel advice to young people facing a frightening new crime.

Newspapers were not the only media outlets to highlight this new danger. Women's magazines, talk shows, and television news programs were covering the topic. Popular television dramas, such as *Beverly Hills 90210* and *ER*, featured story lines about characters who had been given Rohypnol and then raped. With all the media attention around this issue in the late 1990s, three drugs stood out as the most common offenders: Rohypnol, GHB, and ketamine.

Referred to as "The Big Three," Rohypnol, GHB, and ketamine share several traits. In the 1990s, they were cheap and relatively easy to obtain. They can be slipped into a drink without altering its taste, color, or smell. The drugs take effect quickly, generally in less than

KURT COBAIN

One of the earliest high-profile stories about Rohypnol in the United States appeared in 1994, though the event did not involve drink spiking. That March, Kurt Cobain, the lead singer of the grunge rock band Nirvana, had been found unconscious at his hotel in Rome, Italy. According to Cobain's wife, Courtney Love, the night before they had been eating and drinking champagne together. Love also noted that Cobain had taken an alarming amount of Rohypnol pills. Cobain received medical help and recovered from the overdose, but he died of a self-inflicted gunshot wound just a month later.

STREET NAMES		
ROHYPNOL	**GHB**	**KETAMINE**
Circles	G	Cat Tranquilizer
Forget-Me-Pill	Georgia Home Boy	Cat Valium
Lunch Money	Goop	Jet K
Mexican Valium	Grievous Bodily Harm	Kit Kat
Roofies	Liquid Ecstasy	Special K
Roach	Liquid X	Super K
Roapies	Scoop	Vitamin K

Rohypnol, GHB, and ketamine each have a long list of street names. These are the names the drugs go by outside of a medical setting.

30 minutes, rendering the victims unconscious and unable to resist an attack. As the drugs wear off, victims have little to no memory of what happened, making it hard for them to identify the predator later.

ROHYPNOL

Rohypnol, commonly known as a "roofie," is the trade name for the drug flunitrazepam. It is a sedative, which is a drug that makes people feel calm and drowsy. Rohypnol is related to other types of sedatives known as benzodiazepines. Some benzodiazepines, such as Valium and Xanax, are legal for medical use in the United States.

Rohypnol is ten times more powerful than Valium, which is the strongest medication in its class approved for medical use.

The Swiss company Hoffman-La Roche developed Rohypnol in the 1970s. The Food and Drug Administration (FDA) has never approved it for medical use in the United States. It is classified as an illegal substance. However, Rohypnol is not illegal everywhere. More than 60 countries across Europe, Latin America, and Asia have approved it for medical use. Doctors prescribe it to treat insomnia. Some patients also receive it before surgery to reduce anxiety.

Though Rohypnol is illegal in the United States, it is still fairly easy to buy. Some people smuggle it across the border from Mexico, where Rohypnol is legal. In other cases, Rohypnol is sent to the United States through international mail or couriers. When it arrives in the United States, it is commonly sold as a club drug.

Rohypnol comes in capsules filled with powder or pills that can be crushed, making it easy to add to drinks.

It is also used to reduce side
effects after bingeing on other
illegal drugs, such as cocaine
and heroin.

As Rohypnol use spread,
predators saw its advantages. It
was cheap, often less than five
dollars a pill. It was easy to slip
into a drink unnoticed, because
it has no taste, smell, or color.
It also works quickly, rendering
victims helpless within 15 to 20
minutes after ingestion. In 1997, manufacturer Hoffman-La Roche
responded to concerns of Rohypnol's use in DFSA. The company
added a dye to the pill that turns liquids bright blue. However,
many predators know about this safeguard. They get around it
by putting Rohypnol into alcohol that is already blue in color,
such as curaçao. And illegally manufactured pills do not contain
any dye at all.

ROHYPNOL AT RAVES

While Rohypnol has earned
a reputation as a date rape
drug, some people take it
voluntarily while at raves,
parties, and clubs. Users are
able to feel drunk quickly
without consuming expensive
and calorie-filled alcoholic
beverages. However, people
who use Rohypnol can
become addicted to it easily,
requiring larger and larger
doses to feel its effects.

GAMMA-HYDROXYBUTYRIC ACID

Gamma-hydroxybutyric acid (GHB), also known as sodium
oxybate and Xyrem, was first manufactured in the 1920s. In the
1960s, researchers explored its potential use as an anesthetic.
However, they stopped their trials upon an alarming discovery.

Tests revealed that GHB slowed a patient's heart rate and breathing to dangerous levels.

Despite this, drug companies marketed GHB as a safe dietary supplement. They claimed it could increase muscle mass, produce deep sleep, and suppress appetites. GHB could be purchased at health-food stores without a prescription. As its popularity grew, so too did the number of adverse effects reported. These included seizures, coma, and even death. In response, the FDA banned over-the-counter (OTC) sales of GHB in 1990.

Users began to look for GHB substitutes, known as GHB analogs. They found them in two chemicals: gamma-butyrolactone (GBL) and 1,4-butanediol (BD). Both of these chemicals convert into GHB when consumed. However, neither one is meant for human consumption. They are both

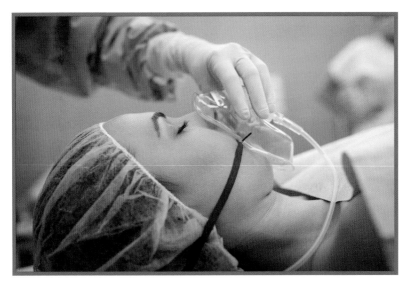

It was believed in the 1960s that GHB could be used as an anesthetic until research showed it was too dangerous for humans.

industrial solvents used to make products such as paint thinners, glue removers, and herbicides.

By the early 1990s, GHB and its analogs had become popular club drugs. Users would drink a capful (approximately 1 teaspoon) to achieve a feeling similar to being drunk. Some users claim that a single capful gives the same feeling of intoxication as 12 beers. This quality made it popular among young people, but they often underestimated its dangers. GHB's effects on users are highly unpredictable. These effects are heightened by the fact that GHB is often made in secret home labs. Each batch of GHB is different, and every lab has its own recipe. "The dose that might make a 150-pound girl high could kill a 300-pound man," said former narcotics detective Trinka

Porrata. "And the dose that made you high yesterday might kill you today."[3]

GHB quickly caught on as a date rape drug. It was easy for predators to slip into a victim's drink. It is clear and odorless. And though it tastes salty, alcohol or soda can easily mask the flavor. Perpetrators fill small vessels—commonly food coloring bottles, tiny vanilla bottles, or eye droppers—with the GHB. The small bottles fit easily into a perpetrator's pocket, where he or she can easily pull it out and drop the GHB in a drink without anyone noticing. Within minutes, a victim can become mentally and physically paralyzed, unable to resist an attack by the predator.

KETAMINE ON THE BATTLEFIELD

Soon after the FDA approved ketamine, military doctors began using it on wounded soldiers in the Vietnam War (1954–1975). It was especially useful because doctors could administer it easily in challenging settings, such as on battlefields. It quickly took away a wounded soldier's pain during the wait for further medical treatment. Today, battlefield medics still use ketamine for these reasons.

KETAMINE

In 1962, Dr. Calvin Stevens was researching drugs to replace phencyclidine (PCP) as a general anesthetic when he discovered ketamine. It dulled pain and made patients fall asleep quickly. Even more promising, ketamine was safe in surgeries because it did not slow a patient's breathing. And it caused short-term memory loss. This meant a patient would not have any memory of pain or of surgery. In 1970, the FDA approved ketamine for medical use.

Approximately 90 percent of legal ketamine sales in the United States are for veterinary use.

Over time, doctors began to notice ketamine's alarming side effects. Patients reported strange hallucinations, such as talking to angels, meeting dead relatives, or having out-of-body experiences. As the reports grew, doctors stopped using ketamine to treat patients. Veterinarians, who did not notice any negative effects, continued to use it in treating animals. In the 1990s, veterinarians reported a rise in ketamine theft. The Drug Enforcement Administration (DEA) linked these thefts to ketamine's growing popularity as a club drug.

Ketamine is routinely used to induce and maintain anesthesia in animals such as horses, cows, camels, and even cats.

As a club drug, ketamine may be ingested in a few different ways. Users may swallow its liquid form or use a needle to inject it directly into a muscle. Some people heat ketamine until it forms crystals, grind the crystals into powder, and then snort the powder. No matter how they take it, users are looking for a ketamine trip, which is an extended period of hallucinations. They are often of a visual nature, such as seeing objects appear to melt into each other or morph into other objects. Some people also report hearing sounds that are not really there.

High doses of ketamine may bring on what people have dubbed the "K-Hole." According to the National Institute on Drug Abuse, people who land in the K-Hole "report experiencing terrifying feelings of almost complete sensory detachment likened to a near-death experience."[4] Upon regaining awareness after the K-Hole, people may not remember their identity or know where they are. Users report that it often takes 24 to 48 hours after a K-Hole experience before they feel like themselves again.

As ketamine's popularity as a club drug grew and the range of its effects became known, predators saw its potential as a date rape drug. Like GHB and Rohypnol, ketamine can be easily mixed into a drink without a change in color, smell, or taste. Ketamine's effects make a victim unable to move. As a result, the victim may be aware of the attack but unable to fight back.

CHAPTER THREE

OTHER DANGERS

Rohypnol, GHB, and ketamine grab much of the media attention surrounding date rape drugs. But in truth, any drug that alters a person's judgment, coordination, or memory has the potential to be a date rape drug. This includes everything from the exotic Colombian date rape drug known as devil's breath to more common substances such as alcohol and OTC medications. They all have the potential to make a person vulnerable and helpless, especially when they are given surreptitiously or in large doses.

ALCOHOL

When people think of date rape drugs, alcohol is often overlooked in favor of more glamorous or headline-grabbing substances. In reality, alcohol is much more common than any other drugs when it comes to DFSAs. "Quite honestly, alcohol is

the number one date rape drug," said Mike Lyttle, a supervisor in the crime lab at the Tennessee Bureau of Investigation. "Roofies are very rarely—if ever—seen in real life."[1]

In 2015, the *Washington Post* and the Kaiser Family Foundation conducted a poll about college drinking habits and sexual assault. The results showed that heavy drinking is the most common predictor of sexual assault.[2] Other studies indicate that alcohol is involved in at least 50 percent of college sexual assaults, though that percentage could actually be much higher.[3]

Many young people downplay the dangers of alcohol, focusing on date rape drugs as the real threat to safety. Alcohol is legal to consume, easy to obtain, and socially acceptable. But in truth, these are also the qualities that make it the most dangerous date rape drug.

Christopher Krebs, a social research scientist who has studied sexual assault on college campuses, said it's important to reinforce the message that young women can reduce their risk of being assaulted by drinking in moderation. "I'm not saying a woman is responsible

BINGE DRINKING

In 2004, the National Institute on Alcohol Abuse and Alcoholism created an official definition of binge drinking for the federal government. Binge drinking is an event in which a person's blood alcohol concentration rises to 0.08 percent or higher. This amounts to an average of five drinks in two hours for a man, or four drinks in two hours for a woman.[4] Binge drinking is most common among adults ages 18–34, which is also the most common age range for victims of DFSAs.

for being sexually victimized,"

Krebs said. "But when your

judgment is compromised,

your risk is elevated of having

sexual violence perpetrated

against you."[5]

In a 2007 study of perpetrators of DFSA, 16 percent admitted adding extra shots to drinks to increase the victim's intoxication.[6]

Alcohol plays a complex role in sexual assaults. In most cases,

both the victim and the perpetrator are drinking willingly. The

spiking can occur when a predator adds more alcohol to the

victim's drink than she realizes. Or he may pay a bartender to

add the extra shots so he does not look suspicious to the victim.

Double and triple shots of alcohol can add up quickly, leaving

A study by the Medical University of South Carolina's National Crime Victims Research & Treatment Center showed that a larger percentage of DFSA cases involved strictly alcohol rather than drugs.

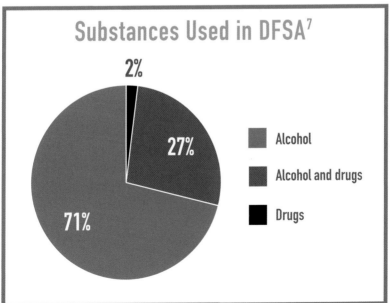

Substances Used in DFSA[7]

2%

27%

71%

- Alcohol
- Alcohol and drugs
- Drugs

a victim incapacitated. Or the perpetrator may encourage a victim to drink with him. He may give the illusion that he, too, is drinking heavily. But in reality, the predator intends to make the victim drunk in order to carry out an assault.

OTC MEDICATIONS

Like alcohol, OTC medications are legal and easy to obtain. This combination makes them a useful tool for people looking to commit DFSA. An OTC antihistamine called Benadryl has recently gained a reputation as a new type of date rape drug. Its active ingredient is a drug called diphenhydramine. The drug is a sedative and its most common side effect is drowsiness, which is why perpetrators use it.

Benadryl is commonly used for allergy symptoms, but when used incorrectly, it can amplify the effects of alcohol.

When perpetrators add diphenhydramine to a victim's drink, the result is what has been nicknamed the Benadryl Cocktail. Usually it is the liquid form of the drug that is added to an alcoholic drink. When alcohol combines with diphenhydramine, it increases the effects of the drug. Rather than just getting drowsy, the victim passes out and becomes vulnerable to sexual assault.

Two other OTC medications are also commonly screened for when victims report a DFSA. One is a sleeping pill called Unisom. The other is a cough medicine called Dimetapp. Like Benadryl, the active ingredients in Unisom and Dimetapp are sedatives. When taken in high doses combined with alcohol, they can render a victim unconscious.

PRESCRIPTION SLEEP AIDS

Prescription sleep aids are another common type of drug that perpetrators use to spike drinks. According to the Centers for Disease Control and Prevention, more than nine million American adults use prescription sleep aids. This

OVER-THE-COUNTER MEDICINES

Over-the-counter (OTC) medicines are drugs that can be purchased without a doctor's prescription. The FDA determines which medications fall into the categories of prescription or OTC. Drugs that are safe and effective to use without the care of a doctor are approved as OTC medicines. These medicines can treat a variety of common health problems, from headaches to athlete's foot.

large pool of users means the drugs are fairly easy for predators to obtain—they may even hold a legal prescription for these powerful drugs in their own name.

Prescription sleep aids are sedative-hypnotics. They quickly slow down the central nervous system to bring on sleep. One of the most prescribed sleep aids in the United States is Ambien, which is the trade name for the drug zolpidem. It ranks as the fifteenth most commonly prescribed drug in the United States, with 4.3 million prescriptions written annually.[8]

The widespread use of Ambien led people to think of it in the same way they think of OTC medications such as Tylenol or Advil. But Ambien is much more dangerous. At high doses, it can cause symptoms similar to drunkenness. Some users report walking, eating, and even driving while completely asleep. And since memory loss is a side effect, a person may not remember anything the next morning.

Ambien was at the center of a high-profile case of DFSA in 2012. Retired professional football player Darren Sharper reported sleeping problems to his doctor, who then prescribed Ambien. Sharper used Ambien frequently, sometimes going through 70 pills in less than two months. Sharper had 20 Ambien pills in his possession when police arrested him on charges of sexual assault on January 17, 2014. Sharper's victims alleged that he had slipped Ambien into their drinks to make them unconscious before raping them.

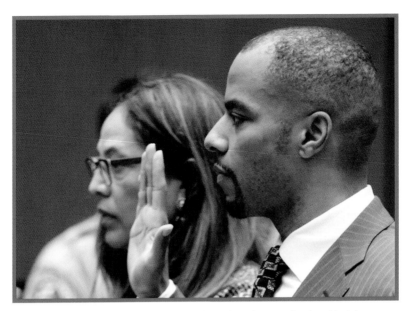

During Darren Sharper's sentencing hearing, he apologized to his victims and said his parents hadn't raised him to act in the way he had.

In November 2016, Sharper received a 20-year prison sentence for drugging and sexually assaulting nine women in multiple states. At the sentencing, one of Sharper's victims spoke out about her experience. "I can only imagine myself lying there like a vegetable while he took advantage of my body without my permission," she said. "I have lost every bit of self-confidence I've ever had and am always in fear while alone. . . . I feel lost in this world."[9]

OTHER PRESCRIPTION MEDICATIONS

Like Ambien, another class of commonly prescribed drugs has been cited as a source of date rape drugs. Rohypnol belongs to this class of drugs, which are called benzodiazepines. They are some of the most commonly prescribed drugs in the world. So, like prescription sleep aids, they are relatively easy for perpetrators to obtain. Commonly prescribed benzodiazepines include Valium, Xanax, and Ativan. They are used to treat anxiety, but when added to alcohol they can lead to memory loss and unconsciousness. They are also commonly used in DFSAs.

In rarer instances, other types of prescription drugs have also been used as date rape drugs. When testing victims of DFSA, toxicology tests routinely screen for prescription painkillers such as OxyContin, Vicodin, and codeine. Victims are also typically tested for a class of prescription sedatives called barbiturates. Illegal drugs, such as marijuana, cocaine, and heroin, are also included in many DFSA toxicology screens as well. This fact can prevent some victims of sexual assault who are using illegal drugs from consenting to drug screens that look for drugs used in DFSAs because they are afraid their intentional illegal drug use will be uncovered.

TOXICOLOGY

Toxicology is a branch of science that studies the effects of chemicals on living creatures. Toxicologists work in labs, testing bodily tissues and fluids for the presence of chemicals and drugs. They can work on a variety of cases. Toxicologists can test athletes for performance-enhancing drugs. If a town experiences a chemical spill, toxicologists can determine if the chemical is making residents ill. And if a person has been involved in a crime, toxicologists can test to see if the person was under the influence of drugs or alcohol at the time.

DEVIL'S BREATH

In other parts of the world, lesser-known drugs are also used without a person's consent to commit crimes. In 2012, American journalist Ryan Duffy traveled to Colombia to begin work on a documentary about what has been dubbed the world's scariest drug: scopolamine. Known by many nicknames— *burundanga*, hyoscine, devil's breath—the drug takes away a person's free will. "You're like a complete zombie," said one victim.[10] Another person Duffy interviewed described it by saying, "You can guide [victims] wherever you want. It's like they're a child."[11] Victims can walk and talk normally. But they will do whatever the criminal asks of them.

These qualities make scopolamine an attractive drug to criminals who use it to commit robberies, kidnappings, and sexual assaults. Like other date rape drugs, scopolamine can be given to the victim by mixing it

THE BORRACHERO TREE

Scopolamine is made from the seeds of a plant called *Brugmansia arborea*. It is more commonly known as Angel's Trumpet due to the shape of its large, fragrant flowers. In Colombia, people also call it the borrachero tree, which loosely translated means drunken binge tree in Spanish. The plant is native to South America, where people have been using it in religious ceremonies and as a medication for untold generations. To make the modern version of the drug, manufacturers grind the plant's seeds into powder and treat the powder with chemicals. In this form the drug is extremely potent. Just a small whiff of the powder can make a person high, and it is easy to overdose on even small doses.

The beautiful, trumpet-shaped *Brugmansia arborea* flower is used to make the powerful drug devil's breath.

with food or beverages. But it can also be administered in other, more unusual ways. Just blowing a small amount of scopolamine powder into a victim's face can transform him into the zombielike state. Even coating scopolamine on a small paper, such as a business card, and then waving it under a victim's nose can trigger this reaction.

While using scopolamine to commit crimes is rare in the United States, reports of its use are turning up in many other countries. Criminals using the drug to rob victims have been reported in France and Spain. In 2011, the US State Department issued a warning about the drug to Americans traveling to Colombia. The report warned that an estimated 50,000 cases of scopolamine-facilitated crimes take place each year.[12] In these cases, women often target wealthy men, drugging them and then ordering them to disclose bank account numbers and other valuable information. Males also target female victims, often with the intent of committing a DFSA.

CHAPTER FOUR

BRAIN AND BODY

Simon Garcia, a businessman from California, was working in Hong Kong, China, when he went out for drinks on a Friday night with coworkers. "The next thing I knew, it was 2 a.m. on Sunday, and I was lying on my bed, butt-naked," recalled Garcia. "My cell phone, wallet, and $3,000 Omega watch were gone."[1]

Garcia is one of many wealthy businessmen whom female thieves, often referred to as "bar girls," have targeted in Hong Kong. The women offer to buy the men drinks. They spike the drinks with Rohypnol or GHB and then take the men to ATMs. There, they force the drugged men to give out their passwords, allowing the thieves to take as much money from bank accounts as they dare. The women also steal other valuables, such as jewelry and electronics.

Date rape drugs can be used to incapacitate victims and rob them.

The female thieves see it as a nearly perfect crime. The men blame themselves for drinking too much and are too embarrassed to file a report with the police. Even if they do report it, the men cannot remember the events of the night clearly or at all. The ways these drugs play on the mind and body of the victims are what make them so appealing to criminals.

MEMORY LOSS AND THE BRAIN

Memory loss is a common side effect of date rape drugs. Humans form memories through a complex process among the brain's neurons. Neurons are nerve cells. The human brain contains roughly 100 billion neurons. Each neuron is made up of three major parts: a cell body, an axon, and group of dendrites. All of the parts play an important role in memory formation.

The cell body's job is to process information accurately. To do this, the cell body must communicate with other cells. Neurons are separated by small gaps called synapses. To send messages across the synapses, the cell body relies on its axon and dendrites. The axon

WHY SPIKE A DRINK?

In a 2016 study of college students, 1 percent admitted to spiking another person's drink. Of those, nearly half—43 percent—did it for fun.[2] Respondents stated that they did it as a joke or because it would be hilarious. In truth, the outcome is rarely ever fun. The most common experience for women after being drugged is sexual assault, and for men it's theft or physical violence. In other, less common circumstances, criminals may use date rape drugs to facilitate a kidnapping.

NEURON

Cell body

Dendrite

Axon

Synapse

Neurons can transmit nerve signals to and from the brain at speeds of 200 miles per hour (320 kmh).

sends information from the cell body. It does this by releasing a chemical called a neurotransmitter. The dendrites receive neurotransmitters from other cells and deliver them to the cell body.

When a chemical change occurs during the transmission of information between neurons, a memory forms. The first step in the process of memory formation is encoding. This means the brain recognizes the information it is taking in. The second step is storage, where the brain is able to record the incoming information. The final step is retrieval. The brain is able to access the information it recorded. As this process takes place,

Psychology professor Paul Reber at Northwestern University calculated that the human brain can store roughly 2.5 petabytes of data and memories, which is the equivalent of 2.5 million gigabytes, or 300 years' worth of television shows.[3]

a new pathway forms to create the memory. A person can recall a memory by activating its pathway.

Date rape drugs disrupt the process of memory formation. Rohypnol, GHB, and many date rape prescription medications such as Ambien are depressants. They affect a neurotransmitter called gamma-aminobutyric acid (GABA). The GABA neurotransmitter's job is to slow

Drugs such as Rohypnol disorient victims and often leave them with no memory of the assault.

communication between brain cells. Depressants make the GABA neurotransmitter work especially well. This means communication between brain cells grinds to a halt. When this happens, memory loss often occurs.

The type of memory loss date rape dugs cause is called anterograde amnesia. It begins shortly after a person ingests the drug, and it ends hours later when the drug has left the body. During that time, the victim's brain is not encoding or storing any of the events taking place as memories. In some cases, people do form a few memories. Because the drugs disrupt the process, the memories they are able to recall are usually hazy and disconnected. This effect is why many people refer to Rohypnol as the Forget-Me-Pill. It is also why criminals like these drugs. Victims have a hard—if not impossible—time remembering any details of the attack.

ALTERED REALITY

Ketamine is the only one of the Big Three date rape drugs that is not a depressant. Instead, it is classified as a hallucinogen. This type of drug alters a person's perceptions and moods. It happens when the hallucinogen changes the brain's ability to use the neurotransmitter called glutamate. Glutamate is a powerful neurotransmitter. It regulates the way information flows between the brain and the body.

While ketamine can cause a feeling of relaxation and calm in some people, others experience a complete detachment that can feel like a near-death experience.

Ketamine can cause people to hallucinate or experience feelings of floating or being detached from their bodies.

When ketamine enters the brain, it effectively turns off the glutamate neurotransmitter. When this happens, messages that are associated with the senses appear differently than normal. Sights and sounds become distorted in the victim's mind. Time and space take on a different quality, and people may have the feeling that they are detached from their own body.

This type of distorted sensory perception is called a hallucination. Ketamine hallucinations might make victims feel as though their bodies are made of strange materials such as wood, foam, or plastic. Body parts distort in perceived size. A person's hands or feet may seem much too large or too small. The room a person is in may become colorful or filled with glowing, geometric patterns. People also commonly report feelings of floating or flying.

THE CENTRAL NERVOUS SYSTEM

Date rape drugs act powerfully on a victim's brain, but they also affect the entire central nervous system, which is made up of the brain and spinal cord. The system forms a crucial link between a person's surroundings and the way he or she reacts to those surroundings. The brain receives input from the body's sensory organs—eyes, ears, nose, tongue, and skin. The spinal cord acts as the link between the brain and the body. As information passes through the brain, the spinal cord sends out messages to the body to react.

When the central nervous system is working properly, a person has coordinated reactions that usually appear logical. For example, when a person hears a

JOHN C. LILLY

People who take date rape drugs recreationally may develop an addiction to the substances. One of the most famous cases of ketamine addiction occurred with a scientist named John C. Lilly (1915–2001). He worked in various scientific fields, and one of his great interests was understanding how the brain functioned. This led him to experiment with the effects of hallucinogenic drugs, such as ketamine and LSD.

Lilly thought researchers should undergo the same treatments they subjected their patients to. This included not only taking hallucinogenic drugs but also spending time in a sensory deprivation device—a dark, soundproof tank filled with warm salt water. As a result of this belief, Lilly tried ketamine and the sensory deprivation tank and quickly became addicted. During the worst moments of his addiction, Lilly was injecting himself with 50 milligrams of ketamine several times a day.

phone ring, presses a button to answer it, and then says "hello,"
that is the central nervous system working as it should. It reacts
to sensory input (the ringing), coordinates movement (pushing a
button), and then organizes a spoken response ("hello").

Date rape drugs prevent this type of reaction from occurring normally. The transmission of information between the brain and body is disrupted. When this happens, a person may have difficulty walking, blurred vision, and slurred speech. Impaired judgment and loss of inhibitions are also common. Other symptoms include dizziness, loss of muscle control, and an inability to feel pain.

EFFECTS ON THE BODY

The brain is not the only organ date rape drugs affect. Often a person's entire body suffers the effects. And when these drugs are combined with other depressants, including alcohol,

THE SPINAL COLUMN

The spinal column is made up of 33 small bones called vertebrae. The bones' job is to protect the body's spinal cord. Scientists divide the spinal column into four regions. Each one is responsible for coordinating movements in a different area of the body. The top seven vertebrae are called the cervical area. They protect the part of the spinal cord that controls the neck, diaphragm, shoulders, wrists, triceps, and fingers. The next 12 vertebrae are the thoracic area. They protect the part of the spinal cord that controls the hands, trunk, and abdomen. The next five vertebrae are part of the lumbar area. This part of the spinal cord controls the hips, quadriceps, hamstrings, knees, and feet. The bottom set of vertebrae form the sacral area. These bones protect the part of the spinal cord that controls the bowels and bladder.

they can cause severe sedation. A person loses consciousness. The heart slows to a dangerously low rate. Breathing slows, too, sometimes down to six breaths per minute. In some people, the gag reflex stops working, and victims can choke on their own vomit. All of these effects can lead to coma or death.

Date rape drugs have other dangerous effects, too. High doses of GHB cause seizures, coma, and liver damage. They can also lower a person's body temperature. When this happens, the body's organs start to shut down. If the person is not treated in time, this can cause death.

Ketamine has a unique effect on the body. When ketamine was developed as an anesthetic, it had two qualities that made it successful. It made patients temporarily paralyzed and unconscious. When ketamine is used as a date rape drug, these two qualities often split. So, victims may be conscious but unable to move their body or react in any way. Predators like this quality because a victim is unable to fight back.

AFTEREFFECTS

When a victim regains consciousness after being drugged, the drug's effects on the body are far from over. Victims can experience vomiting, dizziness, headaches, and confusion for days. One victim of a Rohypnol drugging explained the physical effects the next day, explaining, "My body had never felt like that before. I was dizzy, I had blurred vision, I still felt loopy, and I was generally confused about everything that was going on. This feeling was different than a hangover; it was 10 times worse. I knew something was wrong."[4]

Men are also at risk of being drugged by a perpetrator who intends to sexually assault or rob them.

EFFECTS ON THE MIND AND BODY

	ROHYPNOL	GHB	KETAMINE
EFFECTS BEGIN	20 to 30 min. after ingestion	15 to 30 min. after ingestion	5 to 20 min. after ingestion
EFFECTS LAST	4 to 6 hours	3 to 6 hours	Up to 90 min.
EFFECTS ON THE MIND	Drowsiness Lowered anxiety Memory loss Unconsciousness	Drowsiness Lowered anxiety Hallucinations Memory loss Confusion Euphoria Unconsciousness	Hallucinations Memory loss Agitation Unconsciousness
EFFECTS ON THE BODY	Slurred speech Headache Shallow breathing Loss of coordination Weakness	Slowed heart rate Shallow breathing Coma Seizures Nausea Vomiting	Temporary paralysis Dilated pupils Salivation Tear production Stiff muscles
DETECTABLE IN THE BODY	Up to 60 hours	Up to 12 hours	Up to 48 hours

Date rape drugs have other, less dangerous effects on the body as well. People often experience blurred vision or slurred speech. They may have trouble with coordination, or their muscles may feel weak. Headaches, nausea, and vomiting are common, too. While these symptoms are less serious, their sudden onset can alert people to the possibility that their drink has been spiked. Knowing these signs can allow people to seek help for themselves or their friends before the drug takes full effect.

CHAPTER FIVE

#NOTINMYDRINK

A college student was standing outside as he watched his fraternity brother take a woman to the house. The woman was so drunk that she needed help making it up the stairs. This worried the student. He sensed something might not be right, and he decided to intervene. "Hey, dude, your car is getting towed!" he yelled.[1] The fraternity brother went to investigate, and the drunk woman's friends swooped in and took her out of the potentially dangerous situation.

The distraction technique the student used was something he had learned during a training session on bystander intervention. It is just one of the new and creative ways people can work to prevent DFSAs. In Scotland, the Castle Leisure Group, which runs entertainment venues, has an awareness campaign

In 2002, a company in Sausalito, California, developed a beverage coaster that could detect the presence of date rape drugs in a beverage.

in which servers put a stir stick that says "be aware" in any unattended drinks.[2] Hashtags such as #NotInMyDrink, apps that use GPS so friends can keep tabs on each other at parties, and new gadgets that tell when drinks have been spiked have put a new spin on preventing date rape drugging.

BYSTANDER INTERVENTION

Bystander intervention programs have become popular at schools and businesses in recent years. They teach that every bystander has the power to defuse potentially dangerous situations ranging from bullying to sexual assault. This approach helps bystanders overcome their own barriers, such as peer pressure or fear of embarrassment, so that they can step in and help.

A bystander intervention in May 2016 made headlines when it stopped a potential DFSA. Sonia Ulrich and two friends were at a restaurant in Santa Monica, California, enjoying appetizers and drinks. They noticed a man at the next table drop something into his companion's glass while she was in the bathroom. After a quick discussion, the women agreed they had to do something.

Ulrich headed for the bathroom to warn the woman. "Hey! Um, this is kind of weird, but, uh, we saw the guy you were with put something in your drink," said Ulrich.[3] The woman was shocked but went back to

The Rape, Abuse & Incest National Network reports that bystanders may be reluctant to step in to prevent a sexual assault from occurring because they don't want to cause a scene or because they believe someone else will step in and do something.

the table. Ulrich and her friends alerted the manager, who called authorities. While waiting for the police to arrive, the staff stalled on giving them the bill by saying the computer was down.

"The poor woman had to sit through 40 more minutes," said Ulrich. "She played it cool. Mostly, I believed, just stunned. Then, in walks [the police.] They say 'Come with us' and he doesn't protest. Doesn't ask why. Doesn't seem surprised. The head of security came by and said that because we notified them immediately, they were able to go back and review the footage from the security camera. They got him on tape. They had proof of him drugging this girl."[4]

WHAT WOULD YOU DO?

The woman whom Ulrich alerted was lucky. Even when people see a potential drugging situation, they may be reluctant to step in. In the ABC program *What Would You Do?*, journalist John Quiñones sets up pretend situations that force people to act. In a 2015 episode called "College Kids Drug Girl's Drink," he tackled the idea of bystander intervention and date rape drugs.

On the episode, a female and two male actors pretended to be college students at a bar. They set up the situation to make it look as though the men were putting date rape drugs into the girl's drink while she was in the bathroom. The actors made sure to be relatively obvious about what they were doing to attract the attention of other patrons at the bar. They repeated the charade several times to see how a variety of people would react. Would they warn the girl? Or would they ignore what they had seen?

GREEN DOT

Many schools, colleges, and businesses have adopted a bystander intervention program called Green Dot. A green dot is any choice, behavior, word, or attitude that communicates intolerance for personal violence and promotes safety. Green dot actions are often actions taken by bystanders to prevent violent actions by others. Red dots represent these violent actions. The goal is to create as many green dots in a community as possible. The program teaches bystanders to prevent violence by following the 3 Ds:

- Directly intervening in a situation to prevent violence

- Delegating someone else to intervene if you feel uncomfortable doing so

- Distracting people in a potentially violent situation to defuse the conflict

Going to parties and bars with a group of trustworthy friends is one way young adults avoid becoming victims of date rape drugging.

Nearly all the college-age girls who witnessed the attempted drugging stepped in. One girl directly confronted the men, saying, "Hey, stop! Get out of here right now. I will call the police, get out of here." When they ignored her, she sat back and waited for the female actor to return and then told her not to take a sip of her drink because the men had drugged it. Then she told the men, "She's going to sit with us now" and made room for the female at a seat next to her, putting a physical barrier between her and the men.[5]

Many other people were willing to step up and aid her. One called 911, and another told the waitress and offered a ride. One college-age woman physically removed the glass from the actress's hand when she was about to drink it. Another older woman took charge of the situation, telling the men she was gathering the actress's things to take her home. "As a woman, I felt like I had to protect another woman. And I would hope that somebody would do that for me," she explained.[6]

Not everyone was quite so willing to intervene, though. A middle-aged woman watched the pretend drugging and addressed the men directly, saying, "Guys, I didn't see that did I? You put something in that girl's drink. I just saw you—you're stirring it!" While she was stunned, she watched as the actress sipped from the drugged drink. When asked about it later, she said, "I was afraid of them. If the cops come, what will they do to me? That was my fear, as a

RAISING AWARENESS

Social media has become a new platform to raise awareness of drink spiking. In March 2016, actress Rebel Wilson shared her experience with her 2.45 million Twitter followers. While at a club, Wilson began to feel tired and confused after a few sips of her drink. She got home safely, but she knew not everyone is so lucky. "Hey guys, but especially to all the girls out there, please be super careful about what you drink when out at clubs and bars at night. I never thought it would happen to me," she tweeted.[7]

Less than a year later, in January 2017, actress Mischa Barton shared a similar experience on Twitter. While celebrating her birthday with friends, her behavior became erratic and worsened throughout the night. After being hospitalized, she learned her drink had been spiked with GHB. Like Wilson, Barton drew awareness to the problem, saying, "This is a lesson to all young women out there, be aware of your surroundings."[8]

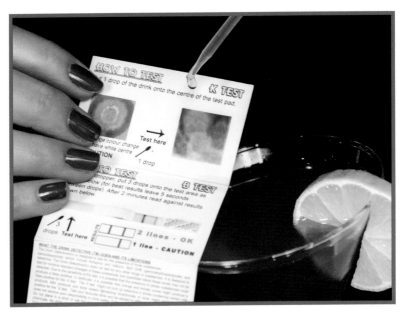

Small kits have been developed that allow people to test drinks for the presence of date rape drugs.

woman. But that's awful. I will toss and turn about this for a long time."[9]

DETECTION GADGETS

Bystander intervention is just one way to curb date rape drugging. A number of young entrepreneurs have also been busy working on the problem. In 2017, three high school students from Miami, Florida, invented a straw that can detect Rohypnol, GHB, and ketamine. The straw has two chemical strips on it. When the straw is placed in the drink, the strips turn dark blue if they come in contact with a date rape drug.

The detection straws are just the beginning when it comes to safe drink technology. Specially designed coasters allow people to discreetly place a drop of their beverage on test strips to check for date rape drugs. Silicone lids that fit over several different cup sizes deter drink tampering. And developers are working on new products, too. A high-tech nail polish could detect date rape drugs when a fingernail is dipped into a drink. And the cups themselves could change color when a drug is added.

These drug-testing gadgets have been created with the best of intentions, but it is unclear how accurate they are. If the drug is not evenly distributed throughout the drink, the testing could provide a false negative. And no studies have been done regarding how often the products test positive for drugs in error.

IF IT HAPPENS...

Making smart choices and using gadgets can cut the risk of drink spiking, but these things cannot prevent it entirely. Even the most vigilant person can be distracted or deceived. Date rape drugs take effect quickly. Still, knowing the early signs can give a victim enough time to ask for help before he or she is completely impaired. Being aware of these signs can also help a person notice when a friend may have been drugged. The bystander can watch over the friend and get him or her to medical care.

As the drug enters a victim's system, a feeling of drunkenness may hit quickly. If the victim has not consumed any alcohol or has had only a small amount of alcohol, this is a sign that a predator may have slipped date rape drugs into the victim's drink. Victims may feel light-headed, nauseous, or dizzy or have blurred vision. Sudden changes in body temperature—either sweating or shivering—can also be a sign. Some drugs, especially ketamine, may give a person a distorted feeling of reality.

This is what happened to Kristina King, a 24-year-old living in New York, who wrote about her experience being drugged while out with a coworker one evening. As the two were dining out, a man at the table next to them offered to buy them shots to make up for accidentally bumping King. Minutes after taking the shot, King blacked out and lost all memories of the rest of the night. Her coworker reported she was acting a bit drunk, but nothing too alarming. King then left and took a cab home. "My next memory is waking up in the hospital, covered in vomit, with an IV in and no recollection of how I got there," she said.[10] She had no memory of what had happened to her after she left the bar, but she knew she had been drugged.

Victims of date rape druggings often report waking up with only hazy memories of the night before. Some claim to have a

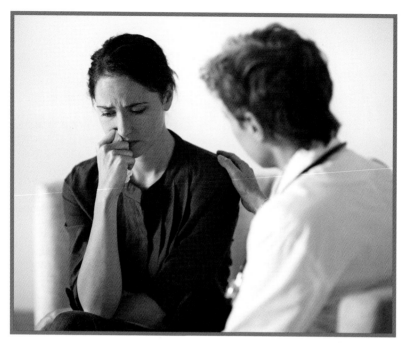
Hospitals employ doctors, nurses, and counselors who are trained and experienced in helping patients following a DFSA.

gut feeling that something is not right. These are all common signs of a DFSA.

If you or a friend find yourself in this situation, getting medical care right away is important. The sooner a victim has a medical examination, the more likely it is that lab work can detect any drugs in the person's system. Some date rape drugs stay in the body for mere hours, so getting tested right away is vital. A test from a doctor is the best way to find out what drugs may have been consumed. And the drug test is a key piece of evidence when prosecuting a predator.

CHAPTER SIX

A DOUBLE CRIME

"I feel humiliated all the time. Other people out there know what happened to me. They watched. I will never know what they saw. For me, not knowing is worse than knowing," said a victim of DFSA. "It's like the rapist gets to take something more from me and keep it forever."[1]

This victim's reaction helps explain why DFSA is referred to as a double crime. The sexual assault is the first crime; the second is surreptitious drugging. These two violations leave victims with the task of trying to understand a crime they cannot remember.

OBSTACLES TO REPORTING

When victims reported DFSAs in the mid-1990s, they faced a number of obstacles. The biggest challenge was the victim's

Feelings of fear, embarrassment, or shame prevent some victims of DFSA from seeking medical treatment.

Date rape drugging can be difficult to prove because of how quickly the drugs leave the victim's system.

lack of memory. As one officer told a victim, "He has his memory. You don't have yours. There's no evidence. The case is closed."[2] Indeed, finding any kind of empathy was difficult. One victim of DFSA remembers being told, "You're lucky you can't remember, you won't suffer as much as other [sexual assault] victims."[3]

As more victims of DFSA came forward, the reaction from law enforcement and doctors began to change. They realized that the date rape drugs impacted the victim's experience of the crime. The aftereffects of date rape drugs—nausea, vomiting, headaches, and confusion—often linger with victims. Several days may pass before they feel well enough to realize what happened and consider reporting it to the police.

At that point, so much time has passed that it is typically too late to collect any useful evidence. Date rape drugs leave the bloodstream quickly, sometimes in a matter of hours. This makes it impossible to obtain proof of the drugging days after the fact. Lack of evidence combined with memory loss leaves many victims of DFSA feeling powerless to seek justice.

THE VICTIM'S EXPERIENCE

DFSAs are different than other sexual assaults because victims often have no sense of danger before the attack occurs. They have no awareness that they are being made powerless. By being drugged surreptitiously, they are robbed of any opportunity to scream, fight back, or even remember the face of the attacker. "Rape is never a fair fight, but I didn't even have a chance to defend myself," said one victim of DFSA.[4]

In some cases, perpetrators may actually look as though they are helping the victim. Many symptoms of date rape drugs mimic drunkenness. Perpetrators may step in when they see their victim acting drunk and offer to help. They may suggest walking the person home or finding the person a quiet place to lie down.

HAIR ANALYSIS

Hair analysis is a new way to test for date rape drugs. "Hair is like a diary, it preserves information over time," says forensic toxicologist Dr. Walter Martz.[5] If a victim was drugged, small molecules of the drug will show up in the segment of the hair at the root. By analyzing the hair, toxicologists can determine what drug a victim ingested. Hair analysis may be useful in cases of date rape drugging because it can be done weeks after the assault occurred.

Bystanders may see the perpetrator as a kind person caring for a friend. The victim may go with the perpetrator willingly, because the drugs have impaired the victim's judgment and sense of danger.

The experience of the attack is different for victims of DFSA, too. Unlike other sexual assault victims, victims of DFSA are not witnesses to the crime against them. They are often unable to remember the key elements of the attack—the identity of the attacker, the type of assault committed, and the time and location of the crime. While other victims of sexual assault may be tormented by flashbacks and nightmares, victims of DFSA are often haunted by their lack of information.

When reporting any type of sexual assault, victims may find speaking about the event to officials is difficult. However, many victims who were assaulted but not drugged may also find the process a relief. Speaking to authorities who are supportive and helpful can be therapeutic. Victims of DFSA often have a different experience. They struggle to answer questions about the assault due to memory loss. Instead of feeling relief, they may feel anxious and revictimized.

When discussing DFSAs, it's important to remember that both women and men can be victims. Date rape drugs also play a role in same-sex assaults. Keith Cowen, a spokesman for the gay rights charity Outright Scotland, said, "[Date rape drug usage] is a

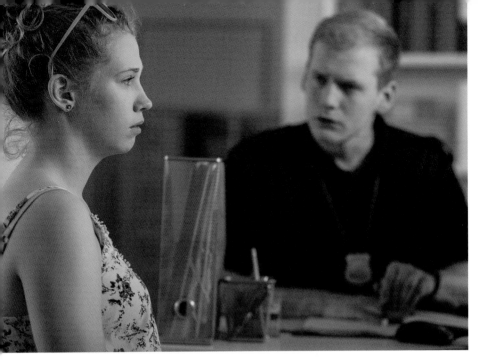

Only 20 percent of female college students report sexual assaults to the police.[7]

huge problem for everyone. We spoke to people at sexual health clinics and they are telling us it happens all the time—among heterosexuals and among gay people. . . . The fact is anyone who drinks is potentially a victim."[6]

A LACK OF REPORTING

Many victims of DFSA choose not to file a report with police. This happens for many reasons. Victims may feel as though the drugging was their own fault. They may blame themselves for voluntarily drinking alcohol. Victims may assume if they hadn't been drinking in the first place, they wouldn't have been drugged.

Most sexual assaults are not committed by strangers. Seventy-four percent of victims of sexual assault know their attackers.[8]

The situation may be complicated by the age of people who were drinking. In the United States, consuming alcohol is illegal for anyone under age 21, but many young people ignore this law. If a person under age 21 is given a date rape drug, she may not want to report it for fear of drawing attention to her own illegal act of drinking while underage.

Additionally, some victims were using illegal drugs voluntarily when their drink was spiked. If they report the DFSA to police or doctors, they will be asked to provide blood, urine, and hair samples. These samples will show evidence of all drug use, not just the date rape drugs. Victims may fear legal trouble or embarrassment for using illegal drugs in the first place.

Victims may choose not to report their DFSA for social reasons, too. Most DFSAs are not committed by strangers. The perpetrators are often friends, significant others, or acquaintances. Victims may fear that if they report the DFSA, their friends may get in legal trouble—not only for the drugging, but also for the assault. Since victims can't

DRINKING DEFENSIVELY

Students on college campuses have always had to be aware of their safety. In the past, this meant carrying pepper spray, going out in groups, or calling for campus escorts at night. The use of date rape drugs has added a new item to the list: drinking defensively. Women now routinely refuse drinks from strangers. They carry drinks onto the dance floor and to the bathroom rather than leaving them unattended. These precautions, which would have been unheard of a generation ago, are now common practices.

remember the assault clearly, they may not feel confident enough to report it and potentially damage a relationship.

Gender also affects self-reporting. While most date rape drugging involves men as the perpetrators and women as the victims, that is not always the case. According to the US Department of Justice, approximately 1 out of every 10 rape victims is male.[9] Males who are victims of date rape drugging are even less likely than females to report the assault to authorities.

Many obstacles stop men from reporting DFSAs. If the victim is gay, he may be unready to reveal this fact to his family and friends. For others, the idea of reporting a same-sex DFSA may seem like a way of being disloyal to the gay community. And for those who do decide to report the crime, they may discover that rape crisis centers are geared toward women, with few resources for male victims. For others, they feel it is

REPORTING ESTIMATES

According to the Rape, Abuse & Incest National Network, a majority of rapes are not reported to police.

- For every 1,000 rapes, only 310 are reported to police.
- Of the 310 reported rape cases, only 57 lead to arrests.
- Of the 57 arrests, only 7 lead to a conviction.
- Of the 7 convictions, only 6 perpetrators serve jail time.
- That means 994 perpetrators of rape go unpunished.[10]

Because DFSAs are reported even less than other rapes, it is likely that thousands go unreported each year.

a black mark against their identities as men. Rape survivor Fred Pelka explains this notion by saying, "To see rape as a women's issue is a form of male privilege most men would prefer not to surrender."[11]

FIGHTING BACK

For some victims, reporting the crime is not an option—they are forced to face it because of social media. The ease of taking and sharing photos online has added a new dimension to DFSAs. In 2014, a 16-year-old girl from Texas named Jada found herself in that situation. She had been at a party where her drink was spiked. She woke up the next morning with her underwear on backward, bruises on her face, and no memory of the previous night.

A few weeks later, Jada received a text with a photo of herself from the party. It showed her passed out and unclothed. The photo soon went viral, and people started mocking her by posting images of themselves looking like her and tagging them #jadapose. Jada was angry—not only had she been

PLACES WHERE DRINK SPIKING MAY OCCUR

Drink spiking is most likely to occur in a social setting but not in public places such as restaurants, clubs, or bars. A 2016 survey of college students revealed that 37 percent of druggings took place in a home or apartment. Fraternity and sorority houses combined made up almost 35 percent of drugging sites. Only 15 percent of drugging took place in bars, while 13 percent took place in dorms.[12]

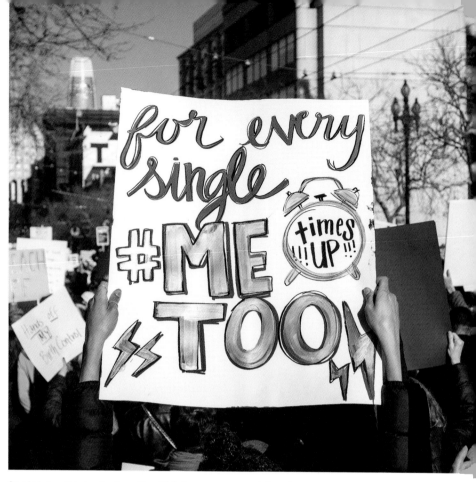

Social media, including the #MeToo movement, has become a powerful tool in spreading awareness about sexual assault.

drugged and assaulted, but people were making fun of her, too. She decided to fight back.

Soon, the social media that had allowed thousands of people to mock her became her greatest weapon. Jada started her own hashtag, #iamjada, and began speaking to local news outlets. Thousands of online supporters took pictures of themselves with their fists held up in solidarity and the hashtag #iamjada. "There's no point in hiding," she said. "Everybody has already seen my face and my body, but that's not what I am and who I am."[13]

CHAPTER SEVEN

THE LAW

In the 1990s, the majority of Rohypnol entered the United States through Mexico. Mexican cities that border the United States were brimming with pharmacies—the city of Tijuana, Mexico, had 700 pharmacies alone. Americans could walk in and obtain any number of powerful drugs easily. Mexico's government controlled the prices on drugs to keep them affordable. This set up a potentially dangerous situation. Americans could walk across the border and buy drugs without a prescription at rock-bottom prices—often at least 50 percent less than US prices. One of the most popular drugs at the pharmacies was Rohypnol.[1]

Rohypnol was a growing problem in states close to the Mexican border. In February 1995, US customs made

Rohypnol cannot legally be manufactured in the United States, but it is smuggled in from other countries.

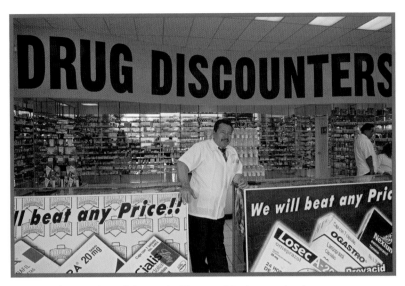

Pharmacies, such as this one in Tijuana, Mexico, cater to American tourists looking to purchase prescription medications, including Rohypnol.

the largest Rohypnol seizure in history. On February 13, state police officers in Louisiana confiscated 52,000 Rohypnol tablets. They had been loosely placed in plastic bags, which were then stuffed inside a car door. The next day, the US border patrol in McAllen, Texas, confiscated 57,000 Rohypnol tablets in a car attempting to cross from Mexico into the United States.

As more Rohypnol pills entered the United States, police officers and rape crisis counselors began to hear from a growing number of drugging victims. By the end of 1995, law enforcement officials had seized 164,534 doses of Rohypnol.[2] Crimes and injuries related to Rohypnol began to rise. Police officers began arresting a growing number of high school and college students on charges of Rohypnol possession.

In March 1996, the federal government banned Rohypnol. It had never been approved for sale in the United States. But visitors from other countries who held valid prescriptions for Rohypnol were allowed to bring a three-month supply into the United States. After the ban took effect, customs officials were ordered to seize any Rohypnol that arrived in the United States.

Hoffman-La Roche, the manufacturer of Rohypnol, made changes in its distribution in response to the abuse of its drug. Two hundred distributors in Mexico had been authorized to sell the drug. In 1996, Hoffman-La Roche reduced that number to 16 distributors. And the company offered free drug testing for victims who believed they had been given Rohypnol surreptitiously.

BRINGING DRUGS OVER THE BORDER

During the early 1990s, many people took advantage of buying drugs such as Rohypnol in Mexico and then reselling them in the United States. In a 1996 interview, a man named Robert explained how the process worked. He would drive across the Texas border into Nuevo Laredo, Mexico. Once there, Robert said, "you have kids running up to you, asking 'pharmacy,' 'pharmacy.'"[3]

Once inside the pharmacy, Robert could obtain various prescriptions from the doctor there. Robert would take them to be filled on the other side of the building. Federal law at the time allowed a person to bring a three-month supply of up to seven different drugs across the border, as long as the drugs were accompanied by a valid doctor's prescription. Despite the fact that the Rohypnol he had purchased was not approved for use in the United States, US customs officials let Robert bring it in because he had a valid prescription. Upon arriving home, Robert would resell the drugs at a profit.

HILLORY J. FARIAS

Stories about Rohypnol and other date rape drugs had been making headlines on and off for much of the early 1990s. Then, on August 4, 1996, a story broke that outraged the nation. That night, Hillory J. Farias, a 17-year-old girl from La Porte, Texas, went with friends to a teen dance club. She had just returned from a weeklong volleyball camp, and she was excited to be back home and reconnect with her friends before school started.

A 2015 study reports that 15 percent of college freshmen women report having been raped while incapacitated by alcohol or drugs.[4]

While at the club, Farias danced and drank a couple of Sprites. Before the evening was over, Farias complained to her friends of a headache. Farias was not a drinker or a smoker, and her friends had no reason to believe she may have been intoxicated. Thinking Farias must have been tired or coming down with a cold after the volleyball camp, they took her home. She took some aspirin and went to bed. The next morning, Farias's grandmother found her unconscious. She was rushed to the hospital where she later died.

Toxicology reports confirmed that Farias had no drugs or alcohol in her system. Her death remained a mystery. Two months after Farias's death, medical examiners used a different lab test. It detected a new type of date rape drug, GHB. The tests came back positive. Authorities believed someone put the GHB in her Sprite and she died from an overdose.

A NEW LAW

Less than two months after the death of Farias, federal lawmakers addressed the problem of date rape drugs. Representative Gerald B. H. Solomon of New York sponsored a bill in the US House of Representatives. The bill stiffened penalties for people who committed crimes by spiking drinks. "It seems to me that this kind of manipulative drug use is as dangerous and loathsome as holding a knife to someone's throat—and should be dealt with accordingly," said Solomon.[5]

On October 13, 1996, Solomon's bill, the Drug-Induced Rape Prevention and Punishment Act, became a federal law. It added up to 20 years of prison time for perpetrators who secretly drugged their victims with the intent to commit a crime. The law also increased penalties for people who possessed Rohypnol. The possession of 1 gram or more could get a person up to three years in prison.

THE DRUG ENFORCEMENT AGENCY

The DEA was created in 1973. Its role in the government is to make sure all federal laws regarding controlled substances are followed. The agency brings cases against criminals who have broken these laws. The DEA has 222 offices in the United States and 91 offices in 70 other countries.[6]

CONTROLLED SUBSTANCES

The DEA places regulated substances into five categories, which are called schedules. A drug is placed on a schedule based on its medical use, potential to be abused, and safety. The schedule categorizes thousands of drugs, but alcohol and tobacco are not included. If new information about patterns of use or abuse arises, drugs may be moved to a new schedule.

In 1970, President Richard Nixon signed into law the Controlled Substances Act, which created the drug classification schedules and made narcotic drug crimes federal offenses.

	EXAMPLES OF DRUGS	PENALTIES FOR FIRST OFFENSE
SCHEDULE I • High potential for abuse • No accepted medical use • Lack of accepted safety for use	GHB Heroin Ecstasy	Up to 20 years in prison Fine up to $1 million
SCHEDULE II • High potential for abuse • Currently accepted medical use • Abuse may lead to dependence	Meth Fentanyl Oxycodone	Up to 20 years in prison Fine up to $1 million
SCHEDULE III • Lower potential for abuse • Currently accepted medical use • Abuse may lead to moderate dependence	Ketamine Anabolic steroids Codeine	Up to 10 years in prison Fine up to $500,000
SCHEDULE IV • Low potential for abuse • Currently accepted medical use • Abuse may lead to limited dependence	Rohypnol* Valium Xanax	Up to 5 years in prison Fine up to $250,000
SCHEDULE V • Low potential for abuse • Currently accepted medical use • Abuse unlikely to lead to dependence	Robitussin AC Motofen Lyrica	Up to 1 year in prison Fine up to $100,000[7]

*Rohypnol is a Schedule IV drug, but it is subject to penalties for Schedule I drugs.

The act also required the DEA to complete a study on Rohypnol. Specifically, the DEA was tasked with deciding if Rohypnol should have its status as a controlled substance changed. It was a Schedule IV drug, but officials wondered if it should be a Schedule I drug. Schedule I drugs are associated with much more severe punishments. The result of the study kept Rohypnol as a Schedule IV drug but made its use a Schedule I offense.

ROOFIE ROMEOS

Though awareness of date rape drugs was growing, the problems continued. Rohypnol made national headlines again in 1998, when identical twin brothers George "Gino" and Julian "Stefan" Spitzer were charged with drugging and sexually assaulting victims. Police officers armed with a search warrant raided the Spitzer home. There, officers found and confiscated seven boxes of Rohypnol, as well as other evidence of DFSAs.

At the trial, victims shared similar stories. They believed they had taken proper safety precautions for dating by meeting the brothers in public during daylight. But the victims also described them as smooth-talking, handsome men who claimed to have powerful careers in Hollywood. The women reported feeling strange during their dates with the brothers and then blacking out, often waking up hours later amid signs of sexual assault.

The Spitzer brothers were found guilty of drugging and sexually assaulting women in California in the 1990s.

The Spitzer brothers, whom members of the press had nicknamed the Roofie Romeos, maintained their innocence. A jury convicted both men—George of eight felonies and Julian of seven. The judge, Richard Neidorf, gave the Spitzers the maximum sentence. George received 60 years in prison, while Julian received 37 years and 2 months. One of the victims, identified only as Kimberly B., was relieved to finally have justice. "I'm really just numb right now, but my faith is back, definitely, in the system," she said. "There are two more evil people off the street, and because of us ladies they can't hurt anyone else."[8]

SAMANTHA REID

High-profile cases, such as that of the Spitzer brothers, drew attention to DFSAs, but the crime continued to claim victims. It wasn't long before news stories focused on another death from date rape drugs. On January 16, 1999, 15-year-old Samantha Reid of Grosse Ile, Michigan, met up with friends. They went to watch movies at an apartment with four young men. The men served Reid and her friends Mountain Dew spiked with GHB. Within 24 hours, Reid vomited, lost consciousness, and died.

Reid's story, along with that of Hillory J. Farias, inspired a new law that targeted GHB. In February 2000, Congress passed the Hillory J. Farias and Samantha Reid Date-Rape Drug Prohibition Act. It changed the status of GHB to a Schedule I drug. It also called for the Department of Health and Human Services to educate students, health-care workers, and police officers on the dangers of date rape drugs.

A month after the new law took effect, the men who had served Reid the GHB went on trial. They faced a number of charges ranging from felony poisoning to manslaughter. During the trial, a number of disturbing details came out. The men had been smoking marijuana and drinking alcohol before giving the girls GHB, which may have led to their poor judgment. And when the girls became ill, the men refused to call an ambulance. Precious time for medical intervention slipped away as Reid lay passed out on the floor. It was not until Reid had trouble

MAKING GHB

One of the reasons that GHB is so dangerous is that it is often made in homes. The recipe for GHB is easy to find on the internet. Creating the drug requires only a few chemicals, which can be found in cleaners and solvents. The making of homemade GHB often results in drugs that have unknown potencies.

Charles Reid, *right*, listened to opening arguments in the trial of Joshua Cole, *left*, one of the men found guilty of drugging his daughter Samantha Reid.

breathing a few hours later that they sought medical help, but by then it was too late.

During the proceedings, the case's prosecutor, Doug Baker, reminded jurors that "the weapon in this case . . . was not a knife, not a gun, but a drug just as fatal as any other weapon."[9] The men were found guilty on charges in connection with Reid's death, and they all served time in prison. This was one of the nation's first convictions connected to GHB poisoning. "It's the right message sent by jurors: When you mix and mingle GHB, you will go to jail," said Reid's mother, Judi Clark, after hearing the convictions.[10]

CHAPTER EIGHT

CONTROVERSY

The dangers of date rape drugs are well known, but just how often DFSA happens is a matter of debate. Gathering statistics on DFSAs is difficult. Many victims choose not to report the assault to authorities because of memory loss or embarrassment. Other cases are dismissed due to lack of evidence. Date rape drugs pass out of a victim's system quickly. By the time a victim reports a DFSA, the drug is often no longer detectable in blood or urine.

"We get a huge array of anecdotal reports—people contacting the National Sexual Assault Hotline and reporting that they were drugged," said Scott Berkowitz, president of the Rape, Abuse & Incest National Network. "But as far as how common it is, the honest answer is, we don't know. It certainly seems to be more prevalent than the number of prosecutions

Northwestern University student Becca Schwartz marched on campus in support of rape survivors on February 10, 2017.

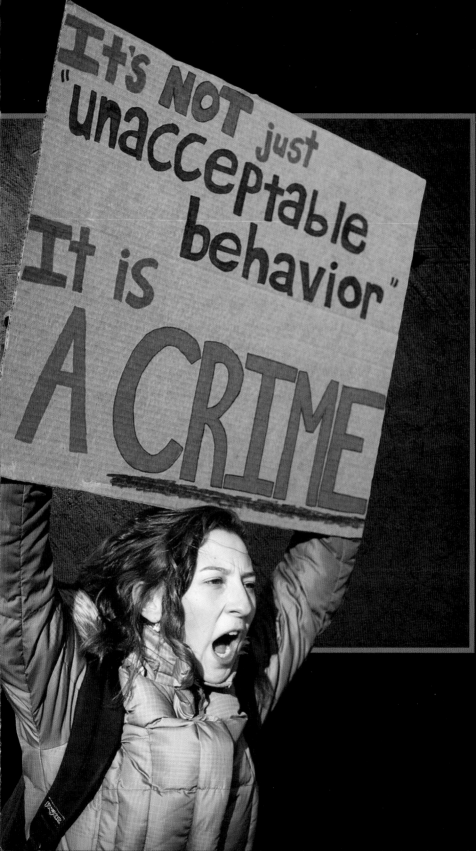

would suggest, based on reports from victims, but we have no good way to quantify just how many cases there are."[1]

THE DIFFICULTIES WITH DATA

With no official statistics to rely on, the prevalence of date rape drugging is hard to pinpoint. Many victims choose not to go to law enforcement after a DFSA. Lack of memory, guilt, embarrassment, and fear keep many victims away. And victims who had been voluntarily drinking alcohol underage or taking illegal drugs at the time of the DFSA may worry about getting in trouble with the law.

As a result, researchers must rely heavily on self-reporting by respondents. Self-reporting is not highly reliable. People often underestimate how much alcohol they have consumed. Their levels of intoxication may alter their perceptions of the crime. Another problem is that toxicology tests cannot determine if a victim consumed drugs and alcohol recreationally or not. This means that unless a bystander witnessed a perpetrator spiking a victim's drink, it may be nearly impossible to prove. The short window of time in which these drugs show up in drug tests compounds these problems.

AN URBAN LEGEND?

While many victims claim they were drugged, the number of confirmed cases of Rohypnol, GHB, ketamine, and other drugs are quite low. As a result, a growing number of law enforcement officials, doctors, and professors are skeptical about the perceived prevalence of date rape drugging. They believe that fears over drink spiking have become overinflated. Dr. Adam Burgess studied attitudes about drink spiking among students in the United States and the United Kingdom. He released his findings in a 2009 article in *The British Journal of Criminology.*

Burgess discovered students have a high awareness of the danger of date rape drugs. But in their haste to prevent drink spiking, they are overlooking the much larger danger of rapid and heavy alcohol consumption. One female respondent said a strategy she uses is to "drink as fast as possible" so no one has time to spike her drink.[2] But this type of caution may backfire.

According to Burgess, "The recommendation that one drink 'as fast as possible' in order not to leave a drink unattended might allow one to evade the drink spiker, but it also, ironically opens up a much more significant set of risks associated with rapid alcohol consumption."[3] And that risk of overindulging

GETTING ROOFIED

A 2016 study found that nearly half of people who believed they had been drugged thought they had been given Rohypnol, or roofies. But experts estimate that Rohypnol, GHB, and ketamine—the three classic date rape drugs—are used at much lower rates, probably in about 5 percent of cases.[4] So why do so many people think they've been roofied? It has become a catchall term to mean a person has been drugged unknowingly.

in alcohol, according to Burgess, is much more common than drink spiking.

As a result of this hyperawareness, many students assume that if they have blackouts, memory loss, nausea, and dizziness after a night of drinking, it must be due to drink spiking rather than the amount of alcohol they consumed. This appears to account for the discrepancy between the large number of people who claim to be victims of drink spiking and the small number of cases prosecuted. This has led many experts to wonder if drink spiking is an urban legend.

Some people take date rape drugs recreationally to quickly obtain effects similar to heavy alcohol consumption. They argue that compared with alcohol, the drugs work faster and cost less.

Drinking alcoholic beverages too quickly can also put people in danger of becoming inebriated and thus at risk for assault.

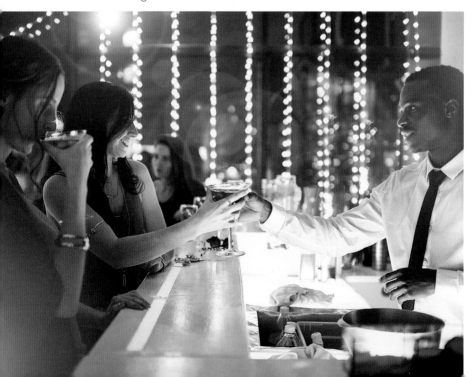

THE MEDIA'S ROLE

People who question high rates of date rape drugging cases often point to the media as part of the problem. While many journalists believe they are helping young people by spreading information, critics are not so sure. Some have even gone so far as to say that all the media information is teaching people how to commit drugging. They also argue that media coverage may lead people to think that any time they have too much to drink, the resulting symptoms are from a date rape drug rather than just alcohol.

In 2005, forensic scientists Michael Ham and Fiona Burton examined this idea. They tested blood and urine samples from 1,014 cases of suspected DFSA in the United Kingdom. The most common finding was alcohol. After that were recreational drugs such as marijuana and cocaine. In only 21 of the total cases did the scientists find evidence of date rape drugs. It is impossible to know if these

A MISLEADING MONIKER

Some people who think date rape drugging has been overreported even take issue with the term *date rape drugs*. Author Pamela Donovan expressed this perspective in her book *Drink Spiking and Predatory Drugging*. "The term 'date rape drug' is probably the most misleading moniker a class of drugs could possibly get," said Donovan. "As American drug scares go, the date-rape drugs scare that emerged in the 1990s, and continues through today, had unusual elements. This was the first time that a drug managed to pick up a core identity related to its occasional (and it turns out, not all that common) role in a violent crime."[5]

drugs were ingested voluntarily or not. Studies in the United States, Australia, and Wales produced similar results.[6]

These numbers suggest that the media may be overhyping the problem. In a 2009 article that appeared in the *British Journal of Criminology*, authors reported on this idea. "Drug-facilitated sexual assault is a culturally embedded crime fear . . . and there seems to be widespread acceptance that it is a prevalent form of 'date rape.'" According to the authors, so many variables must fall into place that the chances of this crime actually happening are low. "Routinized DFSA is improbable as a widespread crime: it involves a stranger extracting an individual from her social group unnoticed, administering a substance undetected, precisely controlling drug effects, and reliably erasing memory of the experience."[7]

THE CRIMINAL MIND-SET

According to law enforcement officers, a DFSA perpetrator generally looks for four elements. First, the perpetrator must have access to drugs and know how to administer them to the victim. Second, the perpetrator must have a setting where he or she can carry out the crime without being discovered. Third, the perpetrator must have the opportunity to spike the drink without anyone noticing. Finally, the perpetrator must have a plan to avoid getting caught—for example, the perpetrator may persuade the victim that she or he is not remembering the night correctly.[8]

LOOKING FOR THE TRUTH

Complicating the problem further, no agencies officially track the number of reported DFSAs. Even if they did, the

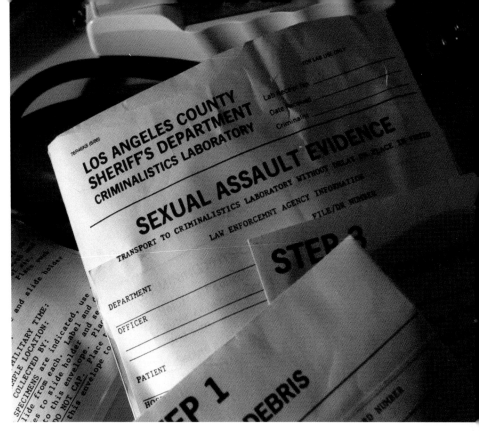

A backlog of sexual assault rape-kit evidence that has not been tested in busy police precincts further adds to the lack of information on sexual assaults in the United States.

number would likely be inaccurate because so many DFSAs go unreported. To learn more about how widespread the problem truly is, the US Department of Justice funded a nationwide study about sexual assaults. Researchers interviewed 5,000 women from across the country and released their findings in 2007.

Researchers discovered that 70 of the women interviewed had reported being victims of DFSA. This accounts for approximately 2.3 percent of the total group. Researchers then multiplied that percentage by the total number of adult women in the United States, which was a little more than 112 million.

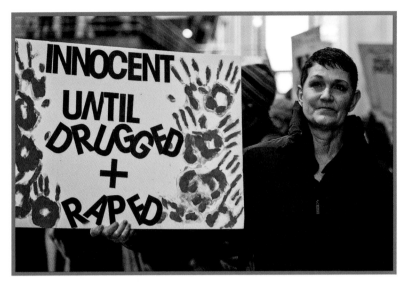

Beth Ferrier, an alleged rape victim of Bill Cosby, protests date rape drugging and assault with others in Denver in 2015.

Based on these estimates, researchers believe that approximately 2.6 million women may have been victims of DFSA.[9]

Other independent studies have found similar results. A 2016 survey published in *Psychology of Violence* revealed the numbers might even be higher than previously thought. The study included more than 6,000 college students at three major universities. Of those, 8 percent believed they had been drugged.[9] While studies in which people self-report drugging are not always accurate, the results of the 2016 study are consistent with other studies completed in the United States, Australia, and the United Kingdom.

The study's lead author, professor Suzanne Swan of the University of South Carolina, thinks the focus needs to switch from victims to perpetrators. She and many others would like to see outreach to the people who do the drugging. "We've been telling people to watch their drinks since the 90s. I think we need to do more than that," said Swan. "There needs to be a targeted message to people who say their motives are [to spike drinks] to have fun. They need to understand that they might be hurting someone with this behavior."[10]

The crime of DFSA has become more visible in society as victims have come forward and shared their stories. Meanwhile, the technology to detect date rape drugs before and after their ingestion has improved. As potential victims learn behaviors to better protect themselves, society continues its push on one hand to ensure perpetrators are punished and on the other hand to educate children so they do not grow up to commit these crimes.

ESSENTIAL FACTS

EFFECTS ON THE BODY

- Some date rape drugs make a victim unable to move, leaving him or her unable to fight back against an attacker. Many cause blurred vision, slurred speech, and the loss of inhibitions. When these drugs are combined with alcohol, these symptoms can become more pronounced.

- Date rape drugs can take effect very quickly, altering a victim's judgment, coordination, or memory. Some date rape drugs, such as Rohypnol, can leave a person helpless in as little as 15 minutes. A teaspoon of liquid gamma-hydroxybutyric acid, or GHB, can make a person feel drunk. But it also slows a person's heart rate and breathing to dangerously low levels. When too much is taken, death may occur. Ketamine, another popular date rape drug, causes strange hallucinations. All three of these drugs disrupt the process of memory formation, leaving the victim with hazy or disrupted memories, or no memories at all about what happened until hours later when the drug has left the body. High doses of GHB can cause seizures, coma, and liver damage.

LAWS AND POLICIES

- In the 1990s, a large number of illegal date rape drugs entered the United States through Mexico. US customs officers seized record amounts of Rohypnol. Crimes and injuries related to the illegal date rape drug began to rise. In 1996, after the death of 17-year-old Hillory J. Farias, who had been drugged with GHB, lawmakers decided to address the problem of date rape drugs. In October, the Drug-Induced Rape Prevention and Punishment Act became federal law. It added up to 20 years of prison time for perpetrators who secretly drugged their victims in order to commit a crime.

- In 1999, following the death of 15-year-old Samantha Reid from ingestion of Mountain Dew that had surreptitiously been spiked with GHB, Congress passed the Hillory J. Farias and Samantha Reid Date-Rape Drug Prohibition Act. This recategorized GHB to a Schedule I drug. Since that time, national campaigns have educated people on the dangers of drugs and how to avoid becoming a victim.

IMPACT ON SOCIETY

- Drug-facilitated sexual assault (DFSA) is considered a double crime. In addition to the sexual assault itself, victims are also drugged without their knowledge. Many struggle to remember the details of what has happened once the effects of the drug have ended. This lack of memory can make reporting the crime, as well as prosecuting, very difficult. Additionally, by the time a victim reports the crime, often too much time has passed for accurate evidence collection. Because date rape drugs leave the bloodstream quickly, by the time victims are conscious, too many hours have passed. No agencies officially track the number of reported DFSAs. But even if they did, with the vast number of crimes that go unreported, it would be difficult to arrive at an accurate number of DFSAs that occur annually.

- Often, victims feel as though the drugging was their own fault. Perhaps they blame themselves for drinking too much, or for not being more on guard. Victims who are under the legal drinking age are even less likely to report a DFSA out of fear of getting in trouble. Embarrassment also causes a number of victims to choose not to report the crime. Celebrity cases involving date rape drugs have drawn attention to the problems recently.

QUOTE

"My body had never felt like that before. I was dizzy, I had blurred vision, I still felt loopy, and I was generally confused about everything that was going on. This feeling was different than a hangover; it was 10 times worse. I knew something was wrong."

—*A Rohypnol drugging victim*

GLOSSARY

ALLEGE
To claim or assert.

ANESTHESIA
A drug given to a person to cause loss of consciousness and block pain, such as in surgery.

ANTIHISTAMINE
A drug used to treat allergies.

ANXIETY
A feeling of fear about a future event.

CONSCIOUS
Alert, awake, and aware of one's surroundings.

EMPATHY
Being able to understand and share another person's thoughts and feelings.

ENTREPRENEUR
A person who organizes and operates a business or businesses.

EUPHORIA
A feeling of joy, elation, or happiness.

HALLUCINATION
Something that is sensed but isn't actually there.

INCAPACITATED
Lacking mental or physical powers or awareness.

INHIBITION
A mental restraint on a person's behavior or speech.

INSOMNIA
The inability to fall asleep and stay asleep.

INTERVENTION
The act of stepping into a situation to prevent something from happening.

MONIKER
A nickname.

PERPETRATOR
Someone who is responsible for an act.

SEDATIVE
A drug used to induce calm.

SEIZURE
A sudden attack that results in the body shaking violently.

SURREPTITIOUS
Done secretly.

SYNTHETIC
Made by combining chemicals, typically to imitate a natural product.

ADDITIONAL RESOURCES

SELECTED BIBLIOGRAPHY

Donovan, Pamela. *Drink Spiking and Predatory Drugging*. London: Palgrave Macmillan, 2016. Print.

"Drugs of Abuse: A DEA Resource Guide." *DEA*. DEA, 2017. Web. 6 Feb. 2018.

Fitzgerald, Nora, and K. Jack Riley. "Drug Facilitated Rape: Looking for the Missing Pieces." *National Institute of Justice Journal*, April 2000: 8–15. Print.

FURTHER READINGS

Amstutz, Lisa J. *Alcohol*. Minneapolis: Abdo, 2019. Print.

Hawkins, Cordelia T. *Club Drugs*. Minneapolis: Abdo, 2019. Print.

Rissman, Rebecca. *Rape Culture and Sexual Violence*. Minneapolis: Abdo, 2018. Print.

ONLINE RESOURCES

Booklinks
NONFICTION NETWORK
FREE! ONLINE NONFICTION RESOURCES

To learn more about date rape drugs, visit **abdobooklinks.com.** These links are routinely monitored and updated to provide the most current information available.

MORE INFORMATION

For more information on this subject, contact or visit the following organizations:

RAPE, ABUSE & INCEST NATIONAL NETWORK (RAINN)
800-656-4673
rainn.org

RAINN is the largest organization in the country dedicated to working against sexual violence. It operates the National Sexual Assault Hotline, works with local organizations, and offers services to people who are victims of sexual assault.

US DRUG ENFORCEMENT ADMINISTRATION
8701 Morrissette Drive
Springfield, VA 22152
202-307-1000
dea.gov

The Drug Enforcement Administration is the US government's lead agency in the war on drugs. Its site has up-to-date news on drug problems, fact sheets on drugs, and information on programs to prevent drug abuse.

US FOOD AND DRUG ADMINISTRATION
10903 New Hampshire Avenue
Silver Spring, MD 20993
888-463-6332
fda.gov

The Food and Drug Administration is the US government agency charged with making sure the food and drugs available in the United States are safe. The agency regulates a wide variety of products including food, dietary supplements, prescription drugs, OTC drugs, and vaccines.

SOURCE NOTES

CHAPTER 1. SECRETLY DRUGGED

1. Herbert Asbury. *Gem of the Prairie*. New York: Knopf, 1940. Print. 174.
2. Sophia Carroll. "Testing for Date Rape Drugs." *Huffington Post*. Oath, 17 Nov. 2011. Web. 1 Oct. 2017.
3. Rong-Gong Lin II. "ER Doctors: Drug-Fueled Raves Too Dangerous and Should Be Banned." *Los Angeles Times*. Los Angeles Times, 10 Aug. 2015. Web. 1 Oct. 2017.
4. Raquel Rutledge. "A Mexican Vacation, a Mysterious Death, and Now Endless Questions for Wisconsin Family." *Milwaukee Journal Sentinel*. USA Today Network, 11 July 2017. Web. 1 Oct. 2017.
5. Faith Karimi. "US Warns Travelers about Tainted Alcohol in Mexico." *CNN*. Cable News Network, 27 July 2017. Web. 1 Oct. 2017.

CHAPTER 2. THE BIG THREE

1. Nora Fitzgerald, et al. "A Report to the Attorney General from the Department of Justice Drug-Facilitated Rape Working Group." *US Department of Justice*. US Department of Justice, 26 June 1998. Web. 20 Oct. 2017.
2. "'Roofies': The Date-Rape Drug." *Newsweek*. Newsweek, 25 Feb. 1996. Web. 15 Oct. 2017.
3. Tamar Nordenberg. "The Death of the Party." *FDA Consumer* 34.2 (2000): 16. Print.
4. "What Are the Effects of Common Dissociative Drugs on the Brain and Body?" *National Institute on Drug Abuse*. NIH, Feb. 2015. Web. 1 Oct. 2017.

CHAPTER 3. OTHER DANGERS

1. "Alcohol Most Common 'Date Rape' Drug, Law Enforcement Officials Say." *Partnership for Drug-Free Kids*. Partnership for Drug-Free Kids, 29 Oct. 2013. Web. 15 Oct. 2017.
2. Emma Brown, et al. "Drinking Is Central to College Culture—and to Sexual Assault." *Washington Post*. Washington Post, 14 June 2015. Web. 15 Oct. 2017.
3. Antonia Abbey. "Alcohol and Sexual Assault." *National Institute on Alcohol Abuse and Alcoholism*. NIH, n.d. Web. 15 Oct. 2017.
4. "National Institute on Alcohol Abuse and Alcoholism Newsletter." *National Institute on Alcohol Abuse and Alcoholism*. NIH, Winter 2004. Web. 15 Oct. 2017.
5. Emily Yoffe. "College Women: Stop Getting Drunk." *Slate*. Slate, 15 Oct. 2013. Web. 26 March 2018.
6. Suzanne Swan, et al. "Just a Dare or Unaware? Outcomes and Motives of Drugging ('Drink Spiking') among Students at Three College Campuses." *Psychology of Violence* 7.2 (2017): 255. Print.
7. Dean G. Kilpatrick, et al. "Drug-Facilitated, Incapacitated, and Forcible Rape: A National Study." *National Crime Victims Research & Treatment Center*. US Department of Justice, July 2007. Web. 15 Oct. 2017.
8. Brent Schrotenboer. "Darren Sharper Case Spotlights Sleep Drug's Dark Side." *USA Today*. USA Today, 26 Mar. 2014. Web. 15 Oct. 2017.
9. Corina Knoll. "Ex-NFL Star Darren Sharper Sentenced to 20 Years in Prison as Rape Victims in L.A. Speak Out." *Los Angeles Times*. Los Angeles Times, 29 Nov. 2016. Web. 15 Oct. 2017.
10. VICE. "World's Scariest Drug (Documentary Exclusive)." YouTube video, 35:43. Posted 11 May 2012. Web. 15 Oct. 2017.

11. Beth Stebner. "The Most Dangerous Drug in the World: 'Devil's Breath' Chemical from Colombia Can Block Free Will, Wipe Memory and Even Kill." *Daily Mail*. Daily Mail, 2 Feb. 2016. Web. 15 Oct. 2017.

12. "Colombia 2011 Crime and Safety Report." *United States Department of State Bureau of Diplomatic Security*. OSAC, 4 Mar. 2011. Web. 15 Oct. 2017.

CHAPTER 4. BRAIN AND BODY

1. Abigail Haworth. "Dangerous Liaisons." *Marie Claire*. Marie Claire, 7 Jan. 2009. Web. 15 Oct. 2017.

2. Suzanne Swan, et al. "Just a Dare or Unaware? Outcomes and Motives of Drugging ('Drink Spiking') among Students at Three College Campuses." *Psychology of Violence* 7.2 (2017): 255–259. Print.

3. Paul Reber. "What Is the Memory Capacity of the Human Brain?" *Scientific American*. Nature America, 1 May 2010. Web. 15 Oct. 2017.

4. "Her Story: I Was Roofied." *Her Campus*. Her Campus Media, 8 Mar. 2015. Web. 15 Oct. 2017.

CHAPTER 5. #NOTINMYDRINK

1. Beth Howard. "How Colleges Are Battling Sexual Violence." *US News and World Report*. US News and World Report, 28 Aug. 2015. Web. 15 Oct. 2017.

2. Anushka Asthana. "Men Fall Prey to Date Rape Drug Gangs." *Guardian*. Guardian News and Media, 20 Dec. 2003. Web. 15 Oct. 2017.

3. Thomas Dexter. "'That Guy Just Put Something in Her Drink.' Women Say They Stopped a Date Rape Attempt at Santa Monica Restaurant." *Los Angeles Times*. Los Angeles Times, 31 May 2016. Web. 15 Oct. 2017.

4. Dexter, "'That Guy Just Put Something in Her Drink.'"

5. "'What Would You Do?': College Kids Drug Girl's Drink." *ABC News*. ABC News Network, n.d. Web. 15 Oct. 2017.

6. "'What Would You Do?'"

7. Maria Puente. "Rebel Wilson Tweets: 'My Drink Was Spiked' at Trendy Club." *USA Today*. USA Today, 11 Mar. 2016. Web. 15 Oct. 2017.

8. Jayme Deerwester. "Mischa Barton Says Spiked Drink Spurred Hospital Stay." *USA Today*. USA Today, 28 Jan. 2017. Web. 15 Oct. 2017.

9. "'What Would You Do?'"

10. Melissa Kravitz. "What Every Woman Needs to Know about Being Roofied." *Refinery29*. Refinery29, 9 Nov. 2017. Web. 15 Oct. 2017.

SOURCE NOTES CONTINUED

CHAPTER 6. A DOUBLE CRIME

1. Marc A. LeBeau. *Drug-Facilitated Sexual Assault: A Forensic Handbook*. San Diego, CA: Academic, 2001. Print. 29.
2. Nora Fitzgerald and K. Jack Riley. "Drug Facilitated Rape: Looking for the Missing Pieces." *Journal*. National Institute of Justice, Apr. 2000. Web. 15 Oct. 2017.
3. Fitzgerald and Riley, "Drug Facilitated Rape."
4. LeBeau, *Drug-Facilitated Sexual Assault*, 25–26.
5. Denise Ryan. "Hair Test Portends Dramatic Shift in Date-Rape Trials." *Vancouver Sun*. Vancouver Sun, 4 Nov. 2010. Web. 15 Oct. 2017.
6. Anushka Asthana. "Men Fall Prey to Date Rape Drug Gangs." *Guardian*. Guardian News and Media, 20 Dec. 2003. Web. 15 Oct. 2017.
7. "Campus Sexual Violence: Statistics." *RAINN*. RAINN, n.d. Web. 20 Oct. 2017.
8. LeBeau, *Drug-Facilitated Sexual Assault*, 258.
9. "Victims of Sexual Violence: Statistics." *RAINN*. RAINN, n.d. Web. 20 Oct. 2017.
10. "The Criminal Justice System: Statistics." *RAINN*. RAINN, n.d. Web. 20 Oct. 2017.
11. "When Men Are Raped." *Ohio Department of Health*. ODH, n.d. Web. 20 Oct. 2017.
12. Suzanne Swan, et al. "Just a Dare or Unaware? Outcomes and Motives of Drugging ('Drink Spiking') among Students at Three College Campuses." *Psychology of Violence* 7.2 (2017): 259. Print.
13. Alicia W. Stewart. "#IamJada: When Abuse Becomes a Teen Meme." *CNN*. CNN, 18 July 2014. Web. 20 Oct. 2017.

CHAPTER 7. THE LAW

1. Mary Beth Sheridan. "Americans Fuel Tijuana Drugstore Boom." *Los Angeles Times*. Los Angeles Times, 5 July 1996. Web. 16 Oct. 2017.
2. "21 Amazing Roofies Statistics." *Health Research Funding*. HAS, 8 Dec. 2014. Web. 16 Oct. 2017.
3. Steve Bannister. "Drug Flow Is Traced to Mexico." *Town Talk* (Alexandria, LA), 29 Feb. 1996.
4. Adam Burgess and Pamela Donovan. "Embodying Uncertainty: Understanding Heightened Risk Perception of Drink 'Spiking.'" *British Journal of Criminology* 49.6 (2009): 852. Web.
5. "Congress Adds to Penalty for Using 'Date-Rape' Drugs." *Los Angeles Times*. Los Angeles Times, 5 Oct. 1996. Web. 20 Oct. 2017.
6. "DEA Offices." *US Drug Enforcement Agency*. US Department of Justice, n.d. Web. 16 Oct. 2017.
7. "Drugs of Abuse: A DEA Resource Guide." *Drug Enforcement Administration*. US Department of Justice, 2017. Web. 15 Oct. 2017.
8. Sue McAllister. "Jury Convicts Twin Brothers in Date Rape Drugging Case." *Los Angeles Times*. Los Angeles Times, 18 June 1998. Web. 15 Oct. 2017.
9. "Trial Begins for Three in Date-Rape Drug Death." *Lansing State Journal*. Lansing State Journal, 10 Feb. 2000. Web. 16 Oct. 2017.
10. "3 Teens Guilty in Date-Rape Case." *CBS News*. CBS News, 14 Mar. 2000. Web. 16 Oct. 2017.

CHAPTER 8. CONTROVERSY

1. Cara Tabachnick. "The Scary Future of Date-Rape Drugs—and Why Their Perpetrators Are So Hard to Bring to Justice." *Marie Claire.* Marie Claire, 20 Oct. 2015. Web. 15 Oct. 2017.

2. Adam Burgess and Pamela Donovan. "Embodying Uncertainty: Understanding Heightened Risk Perception of Drink 'Spiking.'" *British Journal of Criminology* 49.6 (2009): 857. Web.

3. Burgess and Donovan, "Embodying Uncertainty."

4. Suzanne Swan, et al. "Just a Dare or Unaware? Outcomes and Motives of Drugging ('Drink Spiking') among Students at Three College Campuses." *Psychology of Violence* 7.2 (2017): 262. Print.

5. Pamela Donovan. *Drink Spiking and Predatory Drugging.* New York: Palgrave Macmillan, 2016. Print. 123.

6. "Alcohol Is by Far the Most Dangerous 'Date Rape Drug.'" *Guardian.* Guardian News and Media, 22 Sept. 2014. Web. 15 Oct. 2017.

7. Burgess and Donovan, "Embodying Uncertainty."

8. Dean G. Kilpatrick, et al. "Drug-Facilitated, Incapacitated, and Forcible Rape: A National Study." *National Crime Victims Research & Treatment Center.* US Department of Justice, July 2007. Web. 15 Oct. 2017.

9. Linda Carroll. "Drink Spiking at College May Be More Common Than Thought." *NBC News.* NBC News, 28 May 2016. Web. 15 Oct. 2017.

10. Carroll, "Drink Spiking at College May Be More Common Than Thought."

INDEX

alcohol
    addiction to, 22
    binge drinking, 30
    as date rape drug, 28–31, 92
    and sexual assault, 6, 9, 10, 13, 30–33,
        42, 92, 94, 95
    underage drinking, 71
Ambien, 34–35, 44
Ativan, 36

Baker, Doug, 88
Barton, Mischa, 59
Benadryl, 32–33
benzodiazepines, 19, 35–36
Berkowitz, Scott, 90
Beverly Hills 90210, 18
Brugmansia arborea, 37
Burgess, Adam, 93–94
Burton, Fiona, 95

Castle Leisure Group, 52–54
chloral hydrate, 6
Clark, Judi, 89
Cobain, Kurt, 18
cocaine, 6, 9, 21, 36, 95
Conner, Abbey, 12–14, 15
Conner, Austin, 12–13
Conner, Bill, 13
Constand, Andrea, 11–12
Cosby, Bill, 11, 13, 15
Cowen, Keith, 68–70

depressant, 44–45, 48
detection kits, 60–61
devil's breath, 28, 37–38
Dimetapp, 33
diphenhydramine, 32–33

drink spiking, 7, 10, 13–15, 18, 21, 24, 31, 33,
    34, 40, 42, 51, 54, 59, 61–62, 71, 74, 81,
    87, 92–94, 96, 99
Drink Spiking and Predatory Drugging, 95
Donovan, Pamela, 95
Drug Enforcement Administration (DEA),
    25, 81–82, 85
drug-facilitated sexual assault (DFSA)
    aftereffects of, 66, 68
    cases, 10–15, 34–35, 40, 80–81, 85–89
    as a double crime, 64
    drugs used in, 20–21, 23–25, 27, 31–33,
        35–39
    earliest known occurrences, 7–9
    intervention of, 52–60
    portrayed on television, 18
    reporting of, 64, 68, 70–71, 73, 90, 92
    same-sex, 68–70, 73
    symptoms of, 62–63, 66
Drug-Induced Rape Prevention and
    Punishment Act, 81
Duffy, Ryan, 37

ecstasy, 9, 19, 83
ER, 18

Fagan, Phillip Jr., 9
Farias, Hillory J., 80–81, 87
Finn, Mickey, 4–7
flunitrazepam, 19
Food and Drug Administration (FDA), 19,
    22, 25, 33
Forget-Me-Pill, 19, 45

gamma-hydroxybutyric acid (GHB), 8–9,
    18–19, 21–24, 27–28, 40, 44, 49, 51,
    59–60, 80–81, 83, 87, 89, 92–93
Garcia, Simon, 40
glutamate, 45–46
Green Dot, 56

hair analysis, 67
Hall, Dr., 6
hallucinogen, 45–47
Ham, Michael, 95
heroin, 9, 21, 36, 83
Hoffman-La Roche, 19, 21, 79

Jada, 74–75

Kaiser Family Foundation, 30
ketamine, 8–9, 18–19, 24–28, 45–47, 49, 51,
    60, 62, 83, 92–93

Lilly, John C., 47
Lone Star Saloon, 4
Love, Courtney, 18
LSD, 9, 47
Lyttle, Mike, 30

marijuana, 36, 87, 95
Martz, Walter, 67
memory loss, 24, 34, 36, 42–45, 51, 67–68,
    90, 94, 96
methamphetamine, 9, 83
morphine, 6

National Crime Victims Research &
    Treatment Center, 31
National Institute on Alcohol Abuse and
    Alcoholism, 30
National Institute on Drug Abuse, 27
National Sexual Assault Hotline, 90
neurons, 42–43
Nixon, Richard, 83

Pelka, Fred, 74
phencyclidine (PCP), 24
Porrata, Trinka, 23–24
prescription sleep aids, 33 –34, 36
Psychology of Violence, 98

Rape, Abuse & Incest National Network,
    55, 73, 90
Rape Treatment Center, 8
rave, 8–9, 21
Reber, Paul, 44
Reid, Samantha, 86–89
Reno, Janet, 9
Rohypnol, 8–9, 16, 18–21, 27–28, 35, 40,
    44–45, 49, 51, 60, 76, 81, 83, 85, 92–93
"Roofie Romeos," 85–86

Schedule drugs, 82–83, 85, 87
scopolamine, 37–39
sedative-hypnotics, 6, 34
sexual assault, 7, 9, 10–11, 14, 30–37, 42,
    54–55, 64, 67–68, 70, 85, 96–97
Sharper, Darren, 34–35
Solomon, Gerald B. H., 81
Spitzer, George "Gino," 85–86
Spitzer, Julian "Stefan," 85–86
Stevens, Calvin, 24
Swan, Suzanne, 98–99

Thornton, Mary "Gold Tooth," 4, 6
toxicology, 13, 36, 80, 92
Tylenol, 34

Ulrich, Sonia, 54–55
Unisom, 33

Valium, 6, 19, 36, 83

What Would You Do?, 56–60
Wilson, Rebel, 59

Xanax, 6, 19, 36, 83
Xyrem, 21

zolpidem, 34

ABOUT THE AUTHOR

Kate Conley has been writing nonfiction books for children for more than ten years. When she's not writing, Conley spends her time reading, sewing, and solving crossword puzzles. She lives in Minnesota with her husband and two children.

Everybody's Got Something

By Robin Roberts
with Veronica Chambers

GRAND CENTRAL
PUBLISHING

LARGE PRINT

Grand Central Publishing
Hachette Book Group
237 Park Avenue
New York, NY 10017

HachetteBookGroup.com

Printed in the United States of America

RRD-C and RRD-H

First Edition: April 2014
10 9 8 7 6 5 4 3 2 1

Grand Central Publishing is a division of Hachette Book Group, Inc.
The Grand Central Publishing name and logo is a trademark of Hachette Book Group,
Inc.

The Hachette Speakers Bureau provides a wide range of authors for speaking events. To
find out more, go to www.hachettespeakersbureau.com or call (866) 376-6591.

The publisher is not responsible for websites (or their content) that are not owned by the
publisher.

Library of Congress Cataloging-in-Publication Data
Roberts, Robin.
  Everybody's got something / by Robin Roberts with Veronica Chambers. — First
edition.
     pages cm
  ISBN 978-1-4555-7845-0 (hardcover) — ISBN 978-1-4555-8199-3 (large print
hardcover) — ISBN 978-1-4555-7843-6 (ebook) — ISBN 978-1-4789-7963-0 (audiobook)
— ISBN 978-1-4789-7962-3 (audio download) 1. Roberts, Robin. 2. Roberts,
Robin—Health. 3. Breast—Cancer—Patients—United States—Biography. 4.
Myelodysplastic syndromes—Patients—United States—Biography. 5. Women television
news anchors—United States—Biography. 6. Life change events. 7. Faith. 8. Hope. 9.
Encouragement. I. Chambers, Veronica. II. Title.
  RC280.B8R586 2014
  362.19699'4490092—dc23
                              2014002792

This book is dedicated to my sister Sally-Ann for saving my life. And to all donors: your gifts are the definition of selflessness.

Everybody's Got Something

Before We Begin

The great Southern writer Zora Neale Hurston once said, "There are years that ask questions and years that answer." For me, 2012 was a year that asked a lot of questions. Many of you who are reading this book followed my journey that year. Many of you are experiencing or caring for a loved one with a life-threatening illness. You know the questions that I asked in 2012. *What's that funny bump in my neck? What exactly is wrong with me? How will I find a donor who will be a match? Will the match take? Am I going to lose my momma? How will I survive without my mother? Will this illness kill me? The pain, the pills, the fatigue. Lord, please, give me strength, show my body—which is just falling apart—some mercy, because I don't know how much more I can take.*

I'm writing this book because I want you to know how—during the most difficult time in my life—I lived the questions. I want to share with you the people and experiences that helped me make it through, day by day and sometimes moment by moment. In the church of my childhood we were urged to find the good and praise it. I promise you I will not sugarcoat my journey, but I do want to sing a praise song for the love that carried me through. This is a story about the genius of my doctors and nurses and the warmth and generosity of my colleagues. It's about the kindness of strangers and the strength, humor and comfort of old friends. In Mississippi, where I'm from, there's an understanding that hard times do not discriminate. My mother used to say, "Everybody's got something." This is the story of my something and my road to something better. And my hope is that you will find your better, too.

CHAPTER I

The Oscars

I was nine years old when my family moved from Izmir, Turkey, to Biloxi, Mississippi. To say it was a culture shock would be the understatement of the year. Even as a child, I took cues and comfort in the images that I saw on TV. There used to be a commercial, some of you are probably old enough to remember it: It was for RC Cola, and I loved the image of the little kid ambling down to the corner store to buy his bottle of soda pop. I remember clutching a shiny dime and doing the same thing. Those first few months in Mississippi, I was often lonely but not alone. It was me and my RC, and I don't even like cola.

The Gulf Coast slowly but surely became home. I was the youngest of four children. Old enough to remember our travels abroad, young enough to become acclimated to our new life in the South. My parents bought a home in Pass Christian. It's a small town, about twenty miles from Biloxi, with beaches as far as the eye can see. The Pass is just fifteen square miles, but there's the Gulf of Mexico to the south, the Bay of Saint Louis to the west and to the north, the bayou just goes on and on.

The house that I will always think of as home has four bedrooms, a screened-in sun porch, a piano in the living room and a basketball hoop over the driveway. When we bought the house in 1975, Mom insisted on having a fireplace built in the family room. A beautiful stone fireplace that we never used. After all, it doesn't get that cold on the Mississippi Gulf Coast. But Mom always wanted a fireplace, and a fireplace we had. Mom was like that. She'd get her mind set on something and that was that.

For as long as I can remember, I've gone home to the Pass for the holidays. It's just not Christmas until I open the door and hear the little bell ring. I brought that bell back home for my mother after I covered the Lillehammer Olympic Games. The jingle it makes when the door opens is one of the sweetest sounds I know. Momma taught me to always treasure a memento from my world travels. Our home in the Pass is filled with beautiful pieces, reminders of all the places we lived when my dad was in the Air Force.

I welcomed in 2012 with Momma at our family home in the Pass. Usually when I entered the house, the first thing that greeted me after a warm hug from Momma was the aroma of something she was whipping up in the kitchen. Not this time. That was the first sign that Momma wasn't feeling well. She had battled illnesses for as long as I could remember. High blood pressure, heart disease, arthritis and most recently seizures. Momma had begun to suffer TIAs (transient ischemic attacks). That's when blood flow to a part of the brain stops for a brief period of time. Momma would have strokelike symptoms for an hour or two but then, thankfully, return to normal. It was always so scary when that would happen.

Momma wasn't the only one feeling ill. I was, too. I didn't want to worry her, but I had been experiencing a bone-weary tiredness for a couple of months. I kept thinking I'd shake it off and that I would be feeling better soon. I'd been through worse. Or so I thought at the time. Plus I had the Oscars to get ready for the following month.

For the past few years, I've been the host of the *Oscars Red Carpet Live*. It's like the pregame for Hollywood's biggest night. Lots of glitz, glamour and movie stars. In 2012, I arrived in Los Angeles feeling a little more tired than usual. Covering the Oscars is exhausting. I usually fly out Friday after *Good Morning America*. I stay at the hotel that is attached to the theatre where the Oscars are held. This makes it more convenient to go to rehearsals for the show. Plus I don't have to worry about wrinkling my Oscar dress in the car. I just walk from my hotel room to the Red Carpet.

That year I flew out to LA a day early to do a story on Janne Kouri. Janne was told he would never walk again. A freak accident in the ocean in 2006 left him paralyzed from the neck down. His then-girlfriend, Susan, told me the doctor looked her right in the eye and said: "You need to prepare for him never to walk again." Before the accident, the six-four, 285-pound Kouri was a star defensive tackle on the Georgetown University football team with NFL prospects. His friends gave him the nickname "The General" for his take-charge attitude. His spinal cord was fractured in two places. During the two months he was in intensive care, Janne developed pneumonia and almost died twice. Susan told me there were many times he said to her, "You don't need to do this. You don't need to be here." Susan told me, "I promised him that as long as his heart and his mind stayed the same that I would love him."

The couple moved to Louisville to work with Dr. Susan Harkema. She helped develop a cutting-edge therapy known as "locomotor training." The late actor Christopher Reeve, someone I was fortunate to meet, was among her first test subjects. The training teaches the spinal cord how to control motor functions like walking by using repetitive motion. After two months of intensive training, Janne had his first milestone, a little toe wiggle. And in May 2009, Janne took his first steps in three years with the assistance of a walker.

Always thinking of others, "The General" had an idea. He wanted to make this training available near his home in California. With the help of many, Janne raised the funds to start NextStep Fitness, a nonprofit rehab center in Los Angeles where anyone could get locomotor training at an affordable price. Janne was doing something my mom taught me: Make your mess your message. I went to conduct the interview at NextStep, and my jaw dropped when I walked through the door. First of all, it was a large automatic sliding door, and people in wheelchairs were working out in the gym.

I never stopped to think that the fitness centers I go to are not wheelchair-friendly environments. I was there for Janne's most recent milestone: standing for the first time, on his own, without his walker. I loved when he jokingly told me, "I forgot how tall I was." I and many others did not know what else was about to happen. He and my producer, Rich McHugh, had a little—make that a huge—surprise for us. Especially Susan, who is now Janne's wife. They married a year and a half after his accident. After Janne stood one more time, he asked Susan to help him. Then their wedding song, "Better Together," started to play, and they did something they couldn't do at their wedding. They danced. I melted into tears of happiness. It was so beautiful to witness. This is the moment I treasure most from that Oscars, not chatting up the stars on the Red Carpet.

Spending time with Janne was uplifting. It actually made me stop thinking about how exhausted I was. How could I complain about being tired after witnessing his strength and courage?

Also with me this time at the Oscars was my wonderful girlfriend, Amber. We've been together for nearly a decade. Mutual friends set us up on a blind date. I liked the fact that she had no idea who I was. She rarely followed sports, so she never saw me on ESPN, and her office mates at the time watched a different morning show…ouch! She's originally from Northern California and is extremely laid-back, no drama, no fuss. The main thing we have in common is positive energy. She sees the good in everyone and everything.

When we met in 2005, she worked in the fashion industry. It was a great opportunity for her, and she adored her bosses, Alana and Jackie. Amber has an eye for fashion, but she wasn't passionate about it in the way the other people she worked with were. I'll never forget when I was in the middle of treatment for breast cancer in 2007, she announced at dinner: "I quit my job today!" I had only two hairs on my head as a result of chemo, and I just stared at her. She said watching my battle up close inspired her to make changes in her life. She had a front-row seat witnessing how precious life is, and she'd decided she could no longer wait to pursue her dreams. She had hopes of being a contemporary dancer, but before she moved to New York she was in a terrible car accident. A chiropractor and a massage therapist healed her, and she wanted to do the same for others. So she enrolled in the Swedish Institute's Massage Therapy program, earned her associate's degree and is now a licensed massage therapist. She has a nurturing spirit and has never been happier.

When it comes to relationships, my parents set the bar very high. They didn't have to publicly display their love and affection for one another. You knew how they felt about each other by simply being in their presence. What made such a lasting impact on me was how equal they were. Yes, Dad was a career military man and the breadwinner in the family, but he knew that Mom's contributions were every bit as important. When Mom stepped up and became more active in the various organizations she was involved with, Dad was happy to let her shine. It was her turn, and she had his full support. Amber simply is not interested in the spotlight. We don't attend many events. As my former *GMA* colleague Charlie Gibson once said: "When you're on a morning show, you're invited to every event but too tired to go to any of them." True dat! When we do go out, Amber is supportive and proud of me, but in reality we are content to be homebodies.

She lovingly stood with me through the death of my beloved dad, Hurricane Katrina destroying my hometown of Pass Christian, Mississippi, and my battle with breast cancer.

In 2011, when I asked Amber what she wanted for Christmas, she said, "I want to go to the Oscars." She rarely asks for anything like that. As part of my compensation for hosting *Oscars Red Carpet Live*, the thoughtful people involved with the Oscars give me two tickets to the show. I always have to turn them down, because after being on the Red Carpet I run backstage to begin my work for *GMA*. In 2012, I was thrilled to be able to give my tickets to Amber, who planned on attending with her good friend Jason.

*   *   *

It was a little different having Amber with me during that Oscars broadcast, because I wanted to make sure she was taken care of. She's very low maintenance, which I greatly appreciate. She knows when I'm on assignment I have to concentrate and focus my energy on work. That's why she doesn't often ask to accompany me on trips like this. She has a lot of great friends on the West Coast, so she entertained herself while I worked.

I don't have a lot of downtime when I'm in LA. I'm meeting with *GMA* producers and producers for the Red Carpet show. We have many rehearsals and run through the show a few times. But I do manage to have lunch or dinner with friends out there. The day after the Oscars I did an extra shoot with *Real Housewives of Beverly Hills* star Lisa Vanderpump and, of course, her adorable dog, Giggy. Lisa is such a lovely person inside and out. She has a commanding presence, oozing beauty and femininity. The interview took place at her gorgeous new home. It's a grand setting: No detail is overlooked or spared. I was impressed that Lisa did all the decorating herself. The master bedroom closet alone is as large as my first apartment, yet this massive house still feels like a warm home. The interview was for an ABC *20/20* special I anchored called "Pet Crazy." It's well known how crazy I am for my Jack Russell, KJ (that's Killer Jack). After the interview, Lisa graciously invited me and my crew to join her and her husband at their restaurant, Villa Blanca, in Beverly Hills. Lisa and her handsome husband, Ken Todd, are so down-to-earth. They included everyone in their lively conversation. Their restaurant is spectacular, sexy and stylish (words I long to be used to describe me one day!).

At Ken's insistence, I had the English Sticky Toffee Pudding for dessert. It's a family recipe, straight from his grandma Edith. It was my first time trying the British dessert, which consists of a very moist sponge cake and finely chopped dates, all covered in toffee sauce. It doesn't hurt that it's also served with a scoop of vanilla ice cream. Actually it did hurt my waistline, but who cares. It is one of the most delectable dishes I have ever eaten.

Between my extra shoots and rehearsals I go to the hotel gym as much as possible; gotta look good in that Oscar dress! I usually have the dress picked out before I get to LA. I'm fortunate that designers like to work with me. One year, GMA viewers voted online and picked the dress I would wear. They selected a gorgeous orange gown from J.Crew. I was so proud to wear it among the stars wearing more expensive gowns. After my workout, I like to sit out by the pool for a bit to soak up a little LA sun. I also get a mani-pedi in the hotel spa the day before the Oscars.

My Team Beauty, Elena George and Petula Skeete, travel with me, and that makes it all extra fun. Elena, my makeup artist, has won three Emmys and worked with many A-list celebrities. She sees her journey as being more than about physical beauty. She says, "Every day I ask God to give me the creativity and innovation to make women more beautiful than they were the day before."

Petula, who does my hair, is a little taller than me and is originally from Nevis. Her singsong accent always transports me to a warmer place. Both Petula and Elena love going to the Oscars.

The looks they get to create for the Red Carpet are on a whole other level than what they can do for morning TV. Elena enjoys the extra makeup she gets to use on me: longer fake eyelashes, the more dramatic colors. We are a true team. We spend a lot of time together and trust that we always have each other's best interests at heart.

In 2007, when I was diagnosed with breast cancer, they were both on vacation. It's rare that that happens. They felt so bad that one of them was not there with me. They vowed right then and there never to be off at the same time. One of them is always with me.

It was all so much fun, but my exhaustion was off the charts. I was so tired, I could barely focus. Truth be known, when I was backstage at the Oscars, I noticed a little lump in my neck. I even asked my producer, Emily, to check it out. When I felt the nodule in my neck, I really wasn't too concerned. I had a couple of nodules biopsied in recent years and it always turned out to be nothing. I may not have even bothered to have it checked if Amber had not been there. She was the one who insisted something wasn't quite right with me.

I was about to go on the air for the Red Carpet show when I spotted Amber and Jason. They made such a stunning couple. They made several passes so they could see me in action. It was an incredible year for movies: from Meryl Streep in *The Iron Lady* to Octavia Spencer and Viola Davis in *The Help*, from George Clooney in *The Descendants* to the miraculous underdogs, the cast and crew of *The Artist*, who helped make a silent film a smash. Angelina Jolie, dressed in a high-cut black Atelier Versace gown, boldly flashed her right leg, and the resulting memes nearly broke the Internet. I knew, even before I set a single high-heeled foot on that Red Carpet, that it would be a wonderful show, full of moments and memories that I would carry home with me.

I had been told that one day I would wake up and not even think about cancer. When I woke up that Sunday morning before the Oscars, cancer was the furthest thing from my mind. As far as I was concerned it was in my rearview mirror.

CHAPTER 2

Snowballs

The first thing that hits you when you come back to New York after being in Los Angeles is the weather. No matter how mild the winter is, it's never as warm and sunny as LA. If the temps are below freezing, you're lucky if your plane lands without danger or delay. If you're *really* lucky, though, when you get back, New York is at its show-off Winter Wonderland best: It's cold, but not frigid, and the air is filled with big, plump snowflakes that land and rest for a second before melting on your nose or in your hand. On those days, the city is like a movie set or the inside of a snow globe, and when you walk down the street, grown-ups and kids alike are grinning as if Christmas has come all over again. I was lucky when I came back from the Oscars in 2012. It was one of those picture-perfect New York winter days.

Two snowy days after I was back from LA, I went to see Dr. Ruth Oratz, the oncologist who had carefully guided me through breast cancer. Ruth has a calm, soothing style. But there is also a fire in her eyes. She's passionate about her work. She wants the absolute best for her patients, and she travels the world attending conferences to gain the latest information. I did a lot of research and had visited a lot of hospitals before deciding on Ruth, primarily because she treats only patients with breast cancer. Her office is a warm, inviting setting, not located in a hospital. Her chemotherapy rooms are small and intimate, equipped to hold only two patients. Other places I saw were large, cold, sterile environments. I always opt for warm and cozy.

Ruth checked out the lump in my neck and determined it was nothing to worry about. But since I was there, she wanted to draw blood. I had done that on a regular basis, but it had been six months since my last test. Usually after a blood test, I get a call from one of Ruth's stellar nurses like Beth, telling me that all is fine. But one day passed and no nurse called. Then it was two days. By the third day, I was willing the phone to ring. Then Ruth finally called. "Your counts are a little lower than usual," she said. "I'm not too concerned. It could be from all the travel, or maybe you picked up a little virus. Let's wait a couple of weeks and then have more blood drawn."

Honestly, I didn't think too much about it. I had a few minor scares since completing my breast cancer treatment in 2008. Thankfully, it always turned out to be nothing. For the first couple of years, I was worried my cancer might return. But eventually, the fear subsided. I just wanted to live life to the fullest, and that was exactly what I was doing.

* * *

Before I joined *GMA*, I spent nearly fifteen years at ESPN, the worldwide leader in sports broadcasting. When I graduated college, I had one goal—become a sports anchor at ESPN. I worked hard to get there, market after market, Hattiesburg to Biloxi, Biloxi to Nashville, Nashville to Atlanta, then eventually to ESPN.

ESPN is based in Connecticut, where I still have a home. Once, when I was still at ESPN, there was a giant snowstorm. Schools were shut down. A lot of offices were shut down, too. I thought, "I don't want to go to work." I called my friends Jo and Kim and they said, "We don't want to go to work either—let's play hooky." But I was scheduled to anchor *SportsCenter*. So I called in and said, "Um, yeah, I'm not going to be able to make it. The roads are too bad."

They said, "But Robin, you have a big SUV."

I said, "Yeah, but I'm…you know, I don't know how to drive in snow really well."

They said, "Well, what if we send somebody to pick you up?"

I said, "No, that's okay. See, I'm Southern and I don't really want to be in a car through a snowstorm."

So they gave me the day off.

My friends and I played in the snow all day. Then we went to Naples Pizza and *SportsCenter* was on. Several people turned to me and said, "Aren't you…" I just smiled and said, "Yep, but you don't see me here. You don't see me!"

When I think of my closest friends, like Jo and Kim, they are all from the eighties and nineties. I am most comfortable with people who knew me before I was on national TV every day. They are so amused when folks come up to me asking for an autograph. When someone wants to buy me a drink, my friends like to joke: "Robin can afford it, buy us a drink!"

*　*　*

That February, as I waited the two weeks for my next blood test, I tried to shake off the exhaustion that was my constant companion. No matter how much I slept, I woke up bone tired. It was winter. I wasn't feeling well and I desperately wanted a sick day. But when you're on morning TV, there is no calling in sick just because you're feeling punky and you want to sleep in. Your job is to help all the people who don't want to get out of bed start their day on a positive, well-informed, entertaining note. You don't call in because you want to spend the day in your PJs, watching movies in bed. And you certainly don't call in because you want to frolic in the snow with your friends. Can you *imagine* how many iPhone videos would show up online if I called in and then went to Central Park to play in the snow with my dog and my friends?

Every once in a while, my friends and I gather at my home in Connecticut. Those are fun times when I've got my beloved dog, KJ, with me and we all bundle up and go out for a walk. It only takes one snowball to start a fight. Someone balls one up and then it's *on*.

There's an art to throwing snowballs. You've got to make them quickly and efficiently. You've got to aim them with both speed and precision. Then you've got to run like the dickens when they start coming your way. With snowballs, you've got to be able to dish 'em and take 'em.

After I had the second set of blood work done, I waited for the all-clear call. When Dr. Oratz called, I could tell from the tone of her voice something was wrong. She said, "Robin, you need to see a specialist." Her words came hurling at me like a dirty snowball, the bad news a block of ice packed in the fresh, soft flakes of her care and concern. But I couldn't run from the voice at the other end of the phone. I couldn't dodge the news that was coming my way. I did what we do when we can't measure the threat or manage our fear. I froze.

CHAPTER 3

MD Say Whaaat?

*T*he next step, the doctors explained, would be to have a bone marrow biopsy. Let me try to explain what I understood. When you're sick, but you don't look it and you don't yet *feel* it, your body can do a good job of harboring the fugitive illness. A bone marrow biopsy is like a SWAT team sent in to search a high-rise building. If something is hiding, the procedure will find it out.

It's a painful procedure: A long needle penetrates your skin, then your flesh, then the bone and into the middle of the bone. It's from there that they take out the marrow. It's the furthest from the outside of your body that you can get to the inside of your body. But it is effective. So as

I lay on the table, I willed my mind to not focus on the discomfort, but on the outcome. When this test was over, I would know what was wrong. Maybe I had developed some kind of anemia. Maybe I had caught a bad virus, and because I'd powered through my exhaustion for the Oscars, it had turned into something I now had to address. A severe case of mono would explain both the elevated white counts and the exhaustion.

There's a story I've told before. When I was a freshman basketball player at Southeastern Louisiana University, my coach, Linda Puckett, devised a challenging drill. She instructed the team to stay in a crouched position as we slid all the way around the court. We were not to stand up until we reached a certain point. I was in the middle of the pack as we did the drill. When we were finished, Coach Puckett got right in my face and said, "Hon, you are going places in life." It turned out that I was the only one who remained in the crouched position for the entire time.

When it comes to the things that matter, like my health, I have a great ability to focus. Back in March 2012, I thought that was all this was about—something in my body was telling me it needed my attention. I was confident that if I focused on my health, went to the doctors, did what they told me, everything would soon be back to normal.

A recurrence of cancer must've been nestled in the back of my mind, but my oncologist had sent me to have tests done on my blood cells. If the nodule had been of concern, another tumor developing, then Ruth would have taken the lead. I didn't think that another round of cancer was what I was facing.

That was the end of March. After my appointment, I headed off for a much-needed weeklong vacation. Amber and I like to go to Key West during Final Four weekend. Where would you rather be when you're watching college basketball? Inside an arena or outdoors? We opt for the latter. We can position the television in our house so we can watch it from the pool. I'm being very generous when I say pool; it's about the size of a large bathtub. But it's great. Actually, it's perfect.

I treasure my vacations. I don't have to worry about 3:45 a.m. wakeup calls. No need for me to spend an hour in a makeup chair or get dressed up in the latest fashion. On vacation, if I'm not in my swimsuit, I'm in a pair of board shorts, Kai-Kai flip-flops and a ratty tank top. That's the beauty of Key West. It's very laid-back, easygoing. I've been going for so many years that I even get local discounts. The only problem is when a cruise ship is in port. The tourists, who aren't locals, come up and ask for autographs and pictures. I don't mind, but I enjoy being just an anonymous local so much more.

A group of friends and I have owned a little two-bedroom bungalow in an unassuming neighborhood for years. We have rocking chairs on the front porch and a white picket fence. Our neighbor next door, Tom, gives the best massages on the island. A few doors down, walking distance, is our favorite restaurant for dinner, the Flaming Buoy Filet Co.—you must have the spicy chocolate quesadilla for dessert. And right around the corner from our house in the heart of Old Town is the most authentic family-friendly Cuban restaurant, El Siboney. It's a hidden jewel and a local hot spot, especially for lunch. Their homemade sangria is out of this world. That's pretty much how I spend my time in Key West: eat, drink and be merry.

My favorite part about spending time in Key West is riding my bike everywhere. We have these old bikes: mine is orange, Amber's is white, but they both have sweet and cheesy floral baskets. Our bikes are so old you can hear us coming from a mile away—we just *squeak, squeak, squeak* down the road. We always take the back roads and go past the cemetery. My favorite tombstone says, "See? I told you I was sick." It's so much the spirit of Key West that even the gravestones make you smile.

But this time it was also Katie Couric week. She had agreed to sit in for me when I was on vacation. I want to make it abundantly clear that Katie and I are *good*. We like each other and have always had the utmost respect for each other. No problemo whatsoever. Got it? Our show had been fighting an intense ratings war for months, and we were just on the brink of overtaking the *Today* show, Katie's former team. Keep in mind they had an incredible 852-week winning streak going. So having Katie as a guest host made news and invited speculation. Plus our network ran endless promos touting her return to morning TV. Perhaps we could have explained it to the audience a little better, but many viewers thought I was going to be fired and replaced by Katie.

There was an upside. So many people felt sorry for me and thought that I was going to lose my job, that everywhere we went people wanted to treat us to dinner and drinks. It's such a wonderful element of the human spirit: how we cheer for the (perceived) underdog. People kept asking, "Are you worried about this?" All I could think was that my back hurt from the bone marrow aspiration and I'm waiting for this call. I thought, "The doctor will call. Like they always do and they'll give me the all clear."

It wasn't until I was back from vacation that I finally got the phone call. It had been a week and a half, going on two weeks, since my bone marrow biopsy. It was so stressful waiting for the results while contending with the postvacation blues. I wasn't poolside. I wasn't on my bike. I was back at work, still feeling under the weather and exhausted, waiting for that dang phone to ring.

I'll never forget it. I was sitting in my den, watching TV and I answered the phone. It was the specialist. The times I'd talked to him before, he'd had a joking manner, which I liked. Right away, I could tell from the tone of his voice that this was serious. I just didn't know how serious. He went on to describe in medical terms what he had discovered in the bone marrow. Pending further tests, all indications were MDS.

I said, "Slow down, slow down."

He said, "MDS."

I said, "I have MS? Multiple sclerosis?"

He said, "No, not MS. Myelodysplastic syndrome, a rare disease that we used to call pre-leukemia."

I was so confused. "I have pre-leukemia?"

He explained what myelodysplastic syndrome was and how I'd have to come in for further testing. He explained that MDS was actually an umbrella term for a group of diseases that affect the blood and bone marrow. The range of diseases ranged from "mild and easily managed" to "severe and life-threatening." He said that while MDS presented primarily in patients over the age of sixty, you could be affected at any age. He also said that one of the concerns was that depending on what kind of MDS my system showed, it might develop into a severe form of leukemia called acute myelogenous leukemia, or AML. In AML, the bone marrow revolts on the body entirely, creating clusters of cancerous cells called leukemic blasts that can build up and overtake the healthy cells in your body. "But let's not get ahead of ourselves," he explained. "What we know is that the preliminary results indicate MDS, and we must begin to act quickly to get as much information about how the disease is presenting itself in your particular case."

I just sat back on the couch. I was numb. I had no idea what this was. None. Then I went and did the very thing we always tell people not to do—and that's go on the Internet. The terms that kept coming up, again and again, were: "leukemia," "bone marrow transplant," "poor survival" and "dead."

It scared the daylights out of me. A half an hour before, I'd never even heard of MDS. I was on the computer and I couldn't even spell "myelodysplastic syndrome." I was just reading scary fact after fact about the prognosis and survivability. Maybe I was just hitting all the wrong pages, but it was not good. I remember I started shaking. I was alone and I just started crying hysterically. I couldn't believe this was happening.

CHAPTER 4

#1

I waited until the next day to share the news of my diagnosis with Amber. We met at the gym in my apartment building, worked out with our trainer, Angel, then came back upstairs to my apartment. I was glad I had waited a day; I was calmer and had time to sit with the news for a while. Like me, Amber had no idea what a bone marrow transplant or MDS was. I went over what the doctor had said and what I had read on the Internet. We were both just baffled at the idea that I could have this illness that we'd never heard of, with a treatment we couldn't picture or really understand. It was so different from the breast cancer diagnosis. We both knew exactly what that was, and we knew people who had beaten it.

I explained that the next day I had an appointment with an oncologist, and Amber cleared her schedule to come with me.

"We're stronger than this," Amber said, squeezing my hand.

"Whatever *this* is," I said.

"Whatever *this* is," she whispered back.

Then she hugged me, and I felt so grateful knowing that whatever was ahead of me, I wouldn't have to go through it alone. I pride myself on being strong for other people. It's a gift to have someone in my life that has, again and again, shown that she is more than capable of sharing any load that I have had to bear.

The next morning, it was back to work. After nearly twelve years on *GMA*, my morning routine is, as you can imagine, well honed. My first alarm clock goes off at 3:45 a.m. Yes, I said my first alarm. On my nightstand, there's a clock/radio alarm set to the latest hits. With Beyoncé or Lady Gaga blaring, I hit the snooze button. My BlackBerry alarm is set for 4:00 a.m. I purposely place it across my room so I actually have to get out of bed and turn it off. I get back in bed and turn on the TV. I spend a few minutes watching ABC's *America This Morning* to get a sense if anything has happened in the world during the few hours I was sleeping. At 4:30 a.m., I take a shower...while listening to my friends on WABC, ABC's New York station. Shortly before 5:00 a.m., I take KJ out for a quick walk so she doesn't have to cross her legs until the dog walker comes at nine. I leave the TV in the kitchen on for KJ, and I always wonder: When we mention her name on *GMA*, does she start barking up a storm? By 5:00 a.m., I am out the door.

At 5:05 every morning, I head downstairs where my ride awaits. We're fortunate that the show sends a driver to pick us up every morning. Actually, I don't think they trust us to get to work on our own so early in the morning. Dario is my driver. As soon as I climb into the car, he says, "God bless you, Miss Robin!" And I say, "To you, as well." Then we're off for the ten-minute drive to the studio, listening to gospel tunes in the car.

Back in spring 2012, *Good Morning America* was still the number two morning news show. I'm very competitive by nature. I never experienced a losing season in any sport until my senior year at Southeastern. That really stung. At the local TV markets where I worked, I often enjoyed the feeling of being number one. Especially at the station in Nashville, where we won a number of prestigious Peabody Awards and were dominant in the market. And, of course, at ESPN we had no competition.

It was different at *GMA*. We were the perennial underdog to the *Today* show. I've always been proud of the work we have done there, and I never felt as if what we did was second-rate at all. It's difficult to change people's habits in the morning. We all have our routines. When I started at *GMA*, I had close friends who still watched the other show. They had grown up watching Matt Lauer, Katie Couric, Ann Curry and Al Roker, and despite our friendship, they couldn't change their morning ritual.

After I became the third co-anchor with Charlie Gibson and Diane Sawyer, we came within forty thousand viewers of beating the *Today* show one week. It was very exciting, but that was as close as we came. When our current roster came together, things really began to change. George Stephanopoulos, a gifted political correspondent, joined the show as an anchor in 2009. ESPN alum Josh Elliott joined the show as news anchor in 2011. Sam Champion was our beloved weather anchor, and rounding out the team was Lara Spencer as our lifestyle anchor.

The five of us as a team had an undeniable chemistry, and we consistently started chipping away at the *Today* show. What you see is what you get on our show, and our affection and energy in the morning is real. We really like one another, have fun with one another and respect one another. The audience could sense that. Sam, Josh, Lara and I hung out together a lot after work. George would join us occasionally, but he has two young girls at home he wanted to spend time with.

There's a rush to playing from behind, in seeing the gap shrink week after week. We could feel the audience begin to shift and follow us more and more. We all brought something different to the table. George Stephanopoulos is the grown-up. He's very buttoned-up, but even he began to loosen up a bit without losing the essence of who he is. Sam Champion has a booming laugh but is serious and compassionate when out in the field covering storms, tornadoes, hurricanes. Josh Elliott is the tall, handsome jock, who melts when talking about his precious little daughter. Lara "I Brake For Yard Sales" Spencer is a bundle of energy who has perfected the art of covering pop news. I am often referred to as being the heart and soul of *GMA*. I'm serious when need be but not afraid to show emotion and empathy. When I'm asked why we have been so successful the last few years, my response always is the same: It's because of the team in front of and behind the camera. The audience can tell we truly like each other, and we make others feel good, too. Our goal has remained the same: to produce the best possible program each and every morning.

The morning of April 19, 2012, was like any other, except that after the show I had plans to meet Amber and have a follow-up appointment with the MDS specialist. I was nervous; I still didn't fully understand what MDS was. But at the same time, I was eager to see him again and get more information. Work can be a great distraction when you're in the early stages of diagnosis. I said a prayer before jumping out of the car and let the day come at me.

I arrived at the studio in my sweats that morning and the first people I saw were our security team: Rich, Tony, Annie and Walter. Sometimes, especially if we are having popular stars on the show, a crowd is already waiting outside at five in the morning. They get a kick out of seeing me with no makeup and bed head.

I headed right to my dressing room. My assistant, Sonny Mullen, waited for me, along with Elena and Petula. My control room producer of three years, Emily O'Donnell, came in a short time later and reviewed the segments of the show with me. Emily graduated from Emerson College in 2005, a writing major and journalism minor. She related to my health struggles, because all four of her aunts on her father's side have had mastectomies. While Team Beauty worked its magic and Emily ran down what lay ahead in that morning's show, I thumbed through six newspapers: the *Wall Street Journal*, the *New York Times*, the *Washington Post*, *USA Today*, the *New York Post* and the *Daily News*. It felt good to be at work; it took my mind off my upcoming doctor's appointment.

I don't meditate as much as I'd like to, but there's a way that the hum and the buzz of a morning TV show forces you to be in the moment and makes you feel profoundly connected to the world around you. If I had been in another line of work, I might well have found myself at 5:30 a.m. in my PJs, Googling MDS and saying, "Woe is me. Woe is me." Reading the newspaper, listening to Elena and Petula talk and getting ready to greet the show's special guests helped me connect to how much I love my life and my work. I didn't know what this diagnosis meant for my future. The truth is, tomorrow is not promised to any of us. But as I sat in my chair, I said a prayer of appreciation for all the wonderful people whom I work with, all the people who help me do what I love to do best: wish a good morning to America.

Our executive producer, Tom Cibrowski, came to my dressing room around 5:45 that morning to go over last-minute changes. Lori Stokes, morning anchor at WABC, was still on the air at that time. She has such great style. Sometimes what she's wearing helps inspire my outfit for the day. After Tom's check-in, I quickly got dressed and ate a little something. I'm not really a coffee drinker, but I did eat a boiled egg before the show (not the yolk). Then I took a banana with me to the set to nibble on during breaks.

We had a good show put together for that day. Cuba Gooding Jr. came on and talked about his inspiring new TV movie, *Firelight*. The cast of *The Avengers* came on. Superheroes in the studio! A great Nashville band, the Civil Wars, were performing, fresh off their double Grammy win for Best Country Duo and Best Folk Album. Every year I host a country music special—it's a little-known fact that I used to DJ a country music show in the early days of my career—so I was excited to see them play. One of the many things I appreciate about working at *GMA* is that no two days are the same. I've always had various interests, and being at *GMA* allows me to indulge my many passions. I'm as comfortable talking about politics as I am about sports. I feel at home everywhere, from the Country Music Association Awards to the ESPYs and everything in between. Maybe it's because as a proud military brat I grew up all over the world, in different cultures and meeting people from all walks of life.

Soon it was showtime. I popped in the main makeup room across the hall to briefly chat with Josh Elliott and Sam Champion. Always good for a laugh or two. Then I headed down the hall to check in with my girl Lara Spencer. It helps to know what we're each wearing. Want to make sure we're dressed for the same party, so to speak. George was behind his closed office door prepping for the show. Don't blame him at all; the hustle and bustle in the hall can be distracting.

A humongous elevator took me from the second-floor dressing rooms down to the set where the anchors sit when we open the show…aka "home base."

Every morning, before I walk onto the set, I blow a kiss skyward and I say, "Morning, Daddy, watch over Momma." Then I go to home base and begin my day. My father passed away in 2004, so the crew has seen me do this for almost a decade.

There have been a handful of times that the morning schedule has gotten disrupted because of breaking news or an unexpected guest, and I'm rushed out to the set and the crew starts yelling, "No, no! You've got to go back! You've got to go back!" And Angie, our stage manager, whispers to the control room, "Give Robin two seconds."

I didn't even notice at first that other people were observing me greet my father and blow him a kiss. But now they look for me to do it. So on the rare occasion when I forget, I rush backstage, look up to the heavens and say good morning to my father.

After greeting my dad, I walked onto the set with a big smile on my face. The usual controlled chaos, as we call it, was comforting.

Stagehands who had already been hard at work for hours milled about. I did cut-ins for local morning shows in Detroit, Pittsburgh and New York. It was business as usual that morning. No time to contemplate the uncertainty of my upcoming doctor's appointment. Or to reflect on all that scary stuff I read on the Internet. I was alive. I was doing what I loved. I had the privilege and honor of being welcomed into living rooms across the country. It was a good morning.

That morning, after we completed the 8:30 hellos at *GMA*, we were walking back into the studio and our senior executive producer, Tom Cibrowski, said in my earpiece, "I want to tell you first. We did it. It's official. The numbers are in and we won." I just started pumping my fist and saying, "Yes, yes, yes!" I didn't know whether to yell it out loud or wait for Tom to whisper it into the others' ears. I decided to wait and once we all knew, George, Lara, Sam, Josh and I started jumping up and down like little schoolkids.

Yes, even the reserved George Stephanopoulos.

We went back into the studio and we still had twenty minutes of the show to do. We finished the show, and then there was a big celebration in the studio. We were all hugged up. From there we headed to our main office to have a champagne toast. For one blissful moment, I wasn't thinking about my doctor's appointment later that morning. There, in that newsroom, looking at all of those faces. I felt so proud of our team. I told the entire ABC News division this was not just about the show, "If you've ever answered a phone for *GMA* or cut a piece of tape, I don't care if it was yesterday or 852 weeks ago, you're a part of this. This is just as much about you as it is about the five of us." I wanted everyone to feel a part of the victory, because they were.

I remember Jeffrey Schneider, head of PR at ABC, wanted me to do some more press. I said, "Don't get me wrong, I'm really excited. But there's something I've got to do."

I left the champagne toast at the office near Lincoln Center and picked Amber up at her Hell's Kitchen apartment.

Then we drove to my doctor's office on the Upper East Side. We really didn't say much in the car. We were both apprehensive about what the doctor might say. This was the first oncologist that I saw whose specialty was MDS.

It was such a pendulum swing of emotion. I had always imagined how I would feel once

GMA became number one. I pictured being euphoric, literally dancing in the streets. But I was just numb. It took us about twenty-five minutes to get to the doctor's office. The waiting room was full, so the receptionist kindly allowed us to wait in the doctor's office. He was running late. We waited for him in his small, cluttered office for about thirty minutes. All of that waiting. Pure agony.

Finally, he came in and slumped in the chair behind his desk. He looked tired and he opened a bottle of Diet Coke for himself, commenting about the need for caffeine. I didn't mention that I'd been up since 3:45 a.m.

Amber and I were both on the edge of our chairs directly across from him. I appreciated that he didn't talk just to me but to Amber as well, making sure that she felt a part of the conversation and process. "So myelodysplastic syndrome, what does that even mean?" he began. "Well, myelo is bone marrow. Most people don't even know what the bone marrow is other than that they might have eaten it as osso buco in an Italian restaurant. Most people don't know what the bone marrow does, so the first thing we talk about is, the bone marrow is a very important organ. You need your heart, you need your brain, you need your lungs and you need your bone marrow. Your bone marrow makes blood cells. It makes the white blood cells that fight infection, and it makes red blood cells that carry around oxygen and it makes platelets—little tiny cells that help you clot. So when we're talking about the bone marrow, we're talking about your body's ability to make the three blood cells that give you life. If your bone marrow doesn't work, you've got problems with the production of these three life-saving cell lines."

Amber and I looked at each other as if we'd just been dropped into a med school biology class and neither one of us had read the books or reviewed the notes. We were following along, but just barely.

The doctor could tell that we didn't really understand the severity of my condition. It was as if he thought, "Maybe this will get your attention." He put my stats and test results in a computer. There was a graph showing one year and two years with a dot in the middle. He turned the computer screen so Amber and I could see the dot.

I asked, "What's that?"

At first, I thought I had one to two years to do something about what I was facing.

He said, "That's your life expectancy if you don't do anything."

One to two years? That was my life expectancy? It couldn't be. Just moments before I was drinking champagne with my colleagues, celebrating a victory that had been years in the making. It was as if I were looking at my life through a kaleidoscope. One moment it was all bright confetti, the next moment it was just a sliver of light bursting through clouds of darkness.

Once it had sunk in, I kicked into warrior mode. I leaned forward and slapped my fists on his desk and said: "Okay, what do we do?"

The specialist said, "The only possible cure is a bone marrow transplant."

I remember hearing that word *cure*, and I hung on to that sliver of hope for all it was worth. There was a chance we could defeat this, game over. A chance was all I needed.

CHAPTER 5

Celebrate the Now

After the appointment, I dropped Amber off at her apartment and headed home. I needed time alone to digest the news. I'd just been told that I had less than two years to live if I didn't have a transplant. In order to have a transplant, I needed to find a near-perfect match. I had no idea what that would entail.

I was so relieved to enter the refuge that is my apartment. KJ greeted me exuberantly, and I hugged her back. Good news or bad, number one or number 101, she has nothing but love for me. I sat on the sofa next to my big picture window and looked out onto the Hudson River. One of the first things that came to mind was my dear friend, the legendary college basketball coach, Pat Summitt.

The first time I met Pat was in 1987, when I was a cub TV sports reporter down the road in Nashville. Her University of Tennessee Lady Vols had just won their first NCAA championship. It was the beginning of a history-making streak that made Pat the all-time winningest coach in NCAA basketball history, man or woman. Pat and I have been good friends ever since. In 2011, at the age of fifty-nine, Pat was diagnosed with early onset dementia linked to Alzheimer's disease. She said at the time: "There's not going to be any pity party and I'll make sure of that." She went on to coach the Lady Vols the following season and then stepped aside, and she is now head coach emeritus. The way she has faced her illness with such grace and strength is admirable. She is still teaching us all invaluable lessons.

Every time I see Pat, I wonder, "Is this the time she won't remember me?" But I know that I will never forget the many things she has taught me, including this: When you are down and you don't know how to pick yourself up, start where you are. I can hear Pat's voice saying the words in my head, "Left foot, right foot, breathe."

Left foot, right foot, breathe could describe my entire life the spring of 2012. Even after meeting with the doctor and receiving that devastating news, I didn't have much time to sit with the news of my diagnosis. I had about an hour, then I needed to change clothes to attend the wake of the mother of my longtime producer, Karen Leo. Her mother had passed away from cancer. At the viewing, Karen was so appreciative that many of us were there to support her. She knew this was a big day for our show, but we are family first, and we were there when Karen needed us. I was not the only one on an emotional roller coaster on the day that our show became number one. Karen had to orchestrate her dear mother's homegoing service. I mean, truly—we've all got something.

After the wake, I went back home to change for the big party the network was throwing to celebrate our win. Number one for the first time after 852 weeks. I was fried. I could hardly believe my day: number one, MDS, Karen's mom, GMA party. I put on some skinny jeans and my favorite jean jacket lined with Hermès silk. The GMA party was only a few buildings down from my apartment on the same street overlooking the Hudson River.

When I got downstairs, Sam, Josh and Lara were standing at the front door of my apartment building. I was so excited to see them! I thought that maybe somehow they all realized what I'd been going through and they were there to comfort me and escort me to the party down the street. *Welllll*...actually they were a little tipsy from celebrating and they were lost. We had a good laugh and walked arm in arm down the street to our rooftop party. People stopped us along the way and congratulated us.

It was a gorgeous April evening on the rooftop. I remember I just held my breath for a moment as I took in the brilliance of the early springtime sun setting over the Hudson. Our house DJ, the one and only DJ Kiss, was spinning the best dance tunes. Everyone was so incredibly happy. We finally did it. We finally broke the streak and beat the *Today* show after 852 weeks. Sam and I did the limbo...how low can you go?!

I almost told Ben Sherwood, the president of ABC News, on that rooftop what I had learned just hours ago. I almost took him aside and said, "I have MDS. If I don't find a match, I have less than two years to live." But seeing his smiling face, listening to the booming beats of one of the best dance parties I have ever been to, I couldn't do it. How could I? I was looking at him, beaming, proud—and rightly so—of all we were able to accomplish under his leadership. I couldn't dampen all that joy with my dire news.

I looked around at the team. We have such a hardworking and young staff, especially the overnight shift. They are the ones who in the wee hours are putting the final touches on the show while we sleep. Many of them had to leave the party early to get back to work, but not before we took picture after picture on that magical rooftop.

Before I left the party, I stole a few moments for myself. I walked over to the quieter end of the rooftop and just took in each and every person, the warmth and hope on all of their jubilant faces. This was a moment that they had dreamed of, too. It wasn't how I had imagined it would be, secretly sitting with my heartbreaking news, but I prayed it was for every one of them. Thank God I could say that I had truly enjoyed the journey, because if I had saved all of my joy for the destination, I would have missed it. We are all so focused on getting "there," but you have to be careful. Sometimes, I sense a lot of times, "there" ends up feeling different than you expected.

It was difficult not to let my mind wander. If I found myself on that rooftop becoming depressed, I realized that I was living in the past. If I started to become anxious, I knew it was because I was living in the future. I was truly only at peace living in the present.

It was then that I looked to the heavens and thanked the good Lord that he had allowed me to live long enough to see this special moment. I then quietly left the party early, silently chanting to myself like a little schoolkid:

> *We're number 1, yay!*
> *We're number 1, okay?*
> *What did you say? Hey!*
> *We're number 1, yay!*

CHAPTER 6

Letting People In

I couldn't sleep that night wondering how I was going to tell my friends and family about my diagnosis. I was so worried that no matter what they said, they would be thinking, "Here she goes again…" I didn't want pity. I most definitely didn't want to be a burden. What I wanted to say was, "I wish I could tell you this, deliver the news, and at the very same time take away all the worry. I'm still me. I just have a terrible diagnosis, and I wanted to let you know because you're important to me and I wanted to share it with you."

One of my persistent thoughts was "Here I am, putting them through this again." Do you know the "what now?" friend? The phone rings, you look at the number and you think, "Oh boy. What now?" I never envisioned myself being *that friend*. My friends never ever made me feel that way. But that was one of my biggest fears, both when I was diagnosed with breast cancer and then again with MDS. I didn't want to be the burdensome friend. I wanted to be the fun one. I always pride myself on being the life of the party; good for some laughs. Pollyanna Roberts. I've always been an optimistic person. Being optimistic is like a muscle that gets stronger with use. Makes it easier when the tough times arrive. You have to change the way you think in order to change the way you feel.

I called my siblings, Butch, Sally-Ann and Dorothy, and although they were devastated to hear that I was sick again, they really heard me when I said that a cure was on the table. They were also anxious to take the test to see if they might be a match. Telling Mom was much more difficult. She'd been battling her own health issues, and the last year had been hard. She had high blood pressure, arthritis and a heart condition. She'd had a knee replacement that didn't go well. It was hard to explain to her over the phone that I had this mysterious, rare illness that most people couldn't spell or really pronounce. I gave Mom the broad strokes—I had a secondary illness to the breast cancer, I was going to bring home swab kits to test Dorothy and Sally-Ann and, most important, the doctors thought that they could cure me. That was all my sweet, eighty-eight-year-old mother needed to know.

Deborah Roberts, my ABC news colleague, Gayle King from CBS, Tonya Lewis Lee (Spike Lee's wife) and Theresa Moore (a friend from my ESPN days) started what they call "Robin's lunch" when I was diagnosed with breast cancer in 2007. It was a way for them to keep an eye on me and see for themselves how I was doing. Every few months we still get together to discuss life, our families and just a smidge of the latest gossip. Just the five of us, no one else. Many have tried to invite themselves to join us over the years, but we prefer the intimacy of a small group and the history we share together. The one and only time we broke our rule and let someone else have lunch with us was my mom!

It was at one of our luncheons that I told the group about my MDS diagnosis. Tonya had just gotten emotional talking about how thankful they all were that I was doing well and had survived cancer. It was such a sweet moment that I didn't want to ruin it by telling them what I was about to face. But I knew it would be difficult for us all to get together again before I went public with the news. So I waited until the end of our lunch and quietly told them. We hugged, we cried and we knew we would always be there for one another.

Though my friends never felt that way—that I was the "what now?" friend—I cannot tell you how many hours I spent in needless worry about being a burden. Oh, gosh, that's one thing that's changed in the past year. I know—with my head and my heart—that life is too precious to fritter away so much of it with needless worry.

I remember in 2007 when I called my good friend Jo after I was diagnosed with breast cancer. She and Kim, also one of my closest friends, were very upset.

Jo was crying and I said, "It's okay, Joey."

She said, "I just can't deal with this, Robbie Rob."

She and Kim call me Robbie Rob.

I tried to calm her down and said again, "It'll be okay."

She said, "It's just too much. I was just talking with my mom and my dad. He is facing a health crisis, too, and now you."

I listened and expressed my sympathy for her dad.

Then Jo said, "This has been a really bad week for me."

And I said, "A bad week for you??? Um, yeah, Joey, things have been a little worse for me."

That made us both laugh because I knew what she meant. It was terrible to hear that your father and your best friend each got a bad diagnosis during the same week. But when I thought of that conversation, I thought, "Oh, I don't want to call Jo and share this kind of news again."

But I did. And because they are such amazing friends, Jo and Kim drove down from Maine and met me and Amber at my home in Connecticut. We sat out in the backyard that Saturday night and just spent hours talking and crying. All four of us were big crybabies. I remember Kim was just inconsolable. I was a basket case, too. They were just so angry that I was going through this again. They knew how serious it was the first time, and they just wanted to be able to take on some of it for me.

But the best part of the evening was that there were whole hours when we sat around the fire pit and didn't say a word. We were together as a group, but they knew I needed silence. That can be very hard for friends. But Jo, Kim and Amber can be with me in the quiet. Sometimes, they would just reach out and touch my hand or squeeze my shoulder. It was like once we'd cried and yelled and raged at the injustice of it all, we decided we're just going to sit here and be together. We didn't have to fill the silence with stories of what we did or what we were going to do, although we did that, too. And I think it's often very hard for close friends to understand that sometimes you want them to be there but you don't have to say anything, that their presence is as powerful as anything else.

I am a woman of deep faith, but I was angry with God. Why was I being tested again? Why would I have to put my loved ones through this again? Over the course of my struggles, many have asked me if I ever lost faith. Stopped believing. The simple answer is no. I feel it's okay to get angry with God. He can take it. Just don't stay angry. It takes courage to believe that the best is yet to come. I hold steadfast to that belief, especially when I come face-to-face with adversity.

CHAPTER 7

I Want to Live

*M*y doctors understood that my MDS was most likely caused by the chemotherapy that treated my breast cancer. MDS is a mysterious illness. For many patients, there is never a smoking gun, never an explanation of why their bone marrow had been permanently damaged. But for me, knowing how I had developed MDS was no comfort at all. Instead, it yanked me back—five years into the past—to my breast cancer diagnosis. At the time, I thought *that* was the fight of my life, and I thought it was a fight I had won.

My journey with breast cancer began in July 2007. I was simply stretching my arms when I noticed a lump in my right breast. I thought to myself: "Funny, I don't remember feeling that when I showered this morning." I had recently moved full time to New York City and hadn't found a doctor there yet. My colleague and dear friend Deborah Roberts referred me to her doctor, Albert Knapp. I scheduled an appointment with him for a general checkup, not mentioning the lump in my breast. I know, crazy, right? Perhaps if I didn't mention the lump, I thought, it didn't really exist. After all, my mom had repeatedly said: "We're lumpy people." My sisters and I had felt lumps over the years and they always turned out to be nothing. But deep down I knew this was different, because it felt different. This time the lump was very hard and didn't really move when I pushed on it.

Since it was my first visit with Dr. Knapp, he sat with me in his office before examining me. He wanted to know my family history. He has a warm, easygoing nature that put me at ease. It felt as if he had been my doctor for years. Again, I did not mention the real reason why I was there. Later, I was surprised to learn that 80 percent of people diagnosed with breast cancer have no prior family history. Eighty percent! It makes you wonder why there's so much attention paid to disclosing prior family history.

Dr. Knapp proceeded to examine me — just the

basics, a "check under the hood and kick the tires" kind of exam. He was about to leave the examining room when I finally spoke up. "Um, Dr. Knapp, just one more thing before you go—could you check out this lump in my breast?" In the news biz that's called burying the lead. That was the first thing I should have told him. He gave me a breast exam and immediately ordered a mammogram and an ultrasound. I walked a couple of blocks to the radiology center. Since it was the end of the day, I was told, if I could wait they would squeeze me in. I don't know how many times I've heard stories of others having to wait months for a routine mammogram. I'm told if you have a lump, most places around the country will make an exception and see you in a more timely fashion. I believe in being patient and persistent. That is especially true when it comes to your health.

My mammogram came back normal. Good thing Dr. Knapp also ordered the ultrasound. As the technician was performing it, Dr. Mona Darwish, the attending physician, watched the screen. She has an extensive background in breast cancer work, and her trained eye picked up a tumor that had not been detected with the mammogram. It's not unusual for that to happen. This is especially true for young women whose denser breast tissue makes it harder to detect abnormalities. I can't stress how important it is for younger women and those with a high risk for breast cancer to have ultrasounds.

Dr. Darwish told me she wanted to do a core biopsy. I just wanted to get out of there. I was tired and hungry. It had already been a long day. When I asked her if we could do it another time, she gently squeezed my hand and said, "Why don't we just take care of this right now." Truth be known, if I had gotten off the examining table, there's no telling when I would have come back. Dr. Darwish was patient and persistent. (Sound familiar?) I agreed to have the biopsy—a memorable experience, to say the least. I'm not a fan of needles, especially one being inserted into my breast. Dr. Darwish said she would get the results back as soon as she could.

After GMA the following morning, I flew to Atlanta for an assignment. As the plane pulled up to the gate, I turned on my BlackBerry and cell phone. There was an e-mail from my then assistant, Ayana, saying that Dr. Knapp's office had called, and I needed to answer my cell phone because he would be trying to reach me. Just as I finished reading Ayana's message, my phone rang. It was Dr. Knapp. He asked if there was any way I could come to his office. I told him I was on the road and to please just give me the news now. He didn't want to but I insisted. I was still in my seat on the plane when he gave me the test results. "Robin, it's cancer."

I know he said more than that, but to me it sounded like the adults talking in a *Peanuts* cartoon. "Wawppp, wawppp, wawppp…CANCER… wawppp, wawppp, wawppp." I do recall agreeing to have a breast MRI the next day in New York and to meet with a breast surgeon.

There is no way to prepare yourself to hear the words: *You have cancer*. Trust me, it's less than ideal to be sitting on a plane when you hear it. After all, in the movies when you learn you have cancer you're seated in the doctor's office holding a loved one's hand. I was all by myself, surrounded by strangers, about to get off a plane in Atlanta. When I boarded in New York I was just Robin. Now I was Robin with breast cancer. My eyes started to fill with tears, and I put on sunglasses so no one would notice.

A driver was waiting to take me to Pine Mountain, Georgia. I wanted to call Amber. We'd been dating less than two years at that point. I also wanted to call my family and friends to let them know I had cancer. But I didn't want the driver to know what was going on, because I wasn't ready for the public to learn about my diagnosis. I'd only had minutes to digest it myself. The driver could not have been nicer, but he was also a bit inquisitive, and I knew he'd be listening in on my conversation. So I played a little guessing game with my loved ones. "Remember how I told you I was going to have that thing checked out?" I asked, in a quivering voice. "What do you think I found out?" I guess my tone was a dead giveaway. They knew. They'd been praying for the best, but were prepared for the worst. And here it was. The Big C.

Revealing my diagnosis to Amber and my family was difficult. I remember in particular telling Sally-Ann. She was just back in her flood-damaged home that had taken nearly two years to rebuild following Hurricane Katrina. I called Sally-Ann and she sounded so happy. She was in her car at the drive-thru of the newly rebuilt Popeye's near her neighborhood in New Orleans. (We both like two pieces of white meat—spicy—with french fries.) When I told Sally-Ann I had bad news she got out of line and parked her car. Then I took a deep breath and I told my oldest sister that I had been diagnosed with breast cancer. Willie, her college sweetheart and husband of twenty-five years, had died of colon cancer the day before Thanksgiving in 2002. I could hear the fear in her voice that she could lose me, too.

What is so remarkable about that day is that in the midst of being scared and shaking with my personal crisis, I could become so uplifted and inspired by bearing witness to someone else's tragedy. As my mom always said, everybody's got something. I was in Pine Mountain to interview Michael and Jeri Bishop, whose only son, Jamie, had been killed a few months earlier in the horrific shootings that took place at Virginia Tech in 2007. Jamie had been a beloved teacher there, and his parents were still numb with grief. Nevertheless, they had agreed to talk to me for a story that would air the first day the students returned to campus in Blacksburg.

The Bishops are such lovely people. They welcomed me into their home and fed me delicious cherries. Their warmth touched me, and it was all I could do not to collapse into their arms and cry, "I have cancer." But I pulled myself together. They had lost their son in one of the most tragic ways imaginable. I was there to comfort them.

The Bishops spoke so eloquently and movingly about Jamie. When I asked them what they wanted the students returning to know, Jeri said, "I want them to know that they are in the right place at the right time." Her comment was in reference to President George W. Bush's words during a memorial service that the thirty-two people killed were in the wrong place at the wrong time. The Bishops felt that despite the tragedy, their incredible son had been where he was supposed to be. He was a passionate teacher making a difference in countless lives.

I hugged the Bishops good-bye and got back in the car to return to the airport. I was desperate for some privacy. All I wanted was to get home. But wouldn't you know it, my flight was delayed, and it was almost 11 p.m. before I walked through my front door. I crumbled like an accordion on my couch and had a good long cry. Something I had wanted to do ever since I heard Dr. Knapp utter those words almost twelve hours earlier.

The next day I had a breast MRI, and Amber went with me to meet my surgeon, Lauren Cassell. She's the absolute best: a little dynamo in designer dresses and killer high heels, a force of nature, adored by all her patients. Dr. Cassell clearly explained the situation to me. My tumor appeared to be a little more than two centimeters. During surgery she would also check my lymph nodes. I barely have a scar thanks to her brilliant work. More important, she expertly removed my tumor and got clean margins the first time. She spends countless hours reviewing X-rays and images of the breast. She's gifted in knowing how much beyond the tumor to remove. Cancerous tumors are tricky, because it's not just removing the tumor but also any minute particles it may leave behind. Many patients have to go back a second or third time because the surgeon didn't get enough. Not the case with Lauren Cassell.

I endured many months of chemotherapy and radiation. I remember when my hair started to fall out from the chemo. My beloved mother was staying with me. She wanted to be with her baby girl when I began treatment. Two weeks after my first dose of chemo my hair started coming out in clumps. Momma was in my kitchen cooking her world-famous collard greens. I went to her bawling my eyes out, holding chunks of my hair. She sweetly comforted me with one arm, while stirring her collards with the other. I don't think she wanted me to get too close to her pot of delicious greens. I cherish that memory.

Amber, my dear siblings and friends were there for me every step of the way. Diane Sawyer was a constant source of comfort. We always have each other's backs. In fact, to celebrate my last chemo treatment, Diane snuck in some Popeye's chicken for me—she has a knack for knowing exactly what you want. Diane also knew my mind was always racing and so I had a hard time sleeping. She would send me a message late at night and tell me: "You can get some rest, I'll take it from here, I'm on watch now."

My emotions were all over the map. I was scared, angry, confused and even embarrassed. Yes, I said "embarrassed." How could I have cancer? I prided myself on being health conscious and athletic. Would people think I had done something wrong? Did I think I had done something wrong? A million questions raced through my bewildered mind, and none of them had answers.

Later answers did come, and the most lasting one came from my mother, who urged me to use my diagnosis to raise awareness about the importance of mammograms and early detection.

"Make your mess your message," Momma liked to say. And I did.

The video diary that I made of my hairstylist, Petula, shaving my head after chemo started causing my hair to fall out in clumps touched millions of viewers. I had worn a wig on GMA, because I didn't want my baldness to distract from the stories I was covering. *People* magazine was about to publish a story about my battle with cancer. The article would include never-before-seen pictures of me bald. I didn't want GMA viewers to think I had been keeping something from them, that I was ashamed of my bald head. Instead I felt that my baldness and all it represented could become an important part of the story—another way of reaching out to others who had faced cancer. Do you know that some women actually refuse to be treated for fear of losing their hair? In the words of my friend India Arie: "Hey, I am not my hair. I am not this skin. I am a soul that lives within." I wanted to make a statement that I wasn't ashamed to have cancer or be bald. I was absolutely stunned by the reaction to my video diary. The outpouring of support was overwhelming.

Not long after my video diary, I ran into a woman at Bitz-n-Pieces; it's a wig store in New

York. It's really much more than that. The talented people who work there are like little angels. Many clients are there looking for answers at difficult times in their lives. This particular woman and I were bringing our wigs in for tuneups. She said I had given her the strength to talk to her friends and her colleagues about her illness. I was thrilled for her, because I knew she was now opening herself up to a source of great comfort. She said she had hidden her illness from them for fear that they would treat her differently. But her friends had seen that I was still able to work, and that gave her the courage to speak openly.

Midway through my treatments, I was at the White House to do an interview with President Bush's press secretary, Tony Snow. He had recently revealed he was facing cancer for a second time. While there I was told that the First Lady, Laura Bush, wanted to see me in the private residence for tea. Mrs. Bush has a family history of breast cancer. She personally invited me to accompany her on a portion of an international breast cancer initiative with the Susan G. Komen Foundation, and I couldn't pass up this opportunity. My doctors cleared me to travel—although getting my mom's blessing was far more difficult. Remember, I was in the middle of chemo treatments. I spent time with Mrs. Bush in Abu Dhabi and Dubai, in the UAE and in Riyadh, Saudi Arabia. I met some incredible women on the trip. Breast cancer is the number one killer of women in the UAE. Many succumb because the stigma surrounding the disease in that part of the world prevents them from seeking early detection.

Cancer forced me out of my comfort zone. But the reality is that in life, there are no true comfort zones. Life comes at us in ways that we can't predict or control. My breast cancer battle taught me that, more than almost any other challenge I had faced to date. By the time I was cancer free, I was confident that I'd gotten the lessons and I'd done the work that had been my spiritual assignment. Cancer was nothing more than a chapter in my life's story. It would never *be* my life's story.

At the same time, I made a very personal decision. I decided, and I let my closest friends know, that if I got cancer a second time, I would not seek treatment. I would roll the dice and live as long as I could, on my own terms.

I'd just had a grueling chemo treatment, the type of chemo that was nicknamed "the Red Devil" because of its color. I wanted to crush the syringe with my bare hands. I felt the worst I had ever felt at that point. During that treatment, I was literally on my knees, looking up at the heavens and whispering, "Oh God, no more. No more. Not again. *No mas.*"

I honestly thought I wouldn't put myself through this ever again. No more poison coursing through my veins. No more tubes. No more needles. I thought, "I'll take the time I have left and I will travel the world." Maybe I'd finally get my pilot's license. But no more barbaric treatments that tortured my body with only a vague promise to prolong my life. What kind of life would that be?

But this is the thing. Everything changed when I was diagnosed with MDS. The doctors said that a transplant would not be treatment, but a cure. I knew that there was a cure on the table. Even though it meant more chemo, even though I knew that my immune system would be destroyed and then rebuilt again, cell by cell, I had only one thought: "I want to live."

CHAPTER 8

Me & Diane

When Charlie Gibson retired from GMA, there had never before been an all-female anchor team in morning television. From the beginning Diane and I dubbed ourselves Thelma and Louise. We didn't particularly want to go over the edge together, but every morning was a wild ride. Now she always says to me, "Remind me, are you Thelma?" And I say, "No, honey, you're Thelma; you always have top billing. I'm Louise, you're Thelma."

We still send e-mails back and forth: *Hey Thelma, hey Louise.* Because when you think of Thelma and Louise, they were gutsy women and what we were doing was seen that way: making history as the first all-female national morning anchor team. Many questioned whether or not it would work to have two women as co-anchors of the show, never been done before. Our producers felt we were both good at our jobs, we'd already been working together, so why wouldn't we continue that way even without Charlie?

It's a funny thing about Diane. We can walk into a room together and people come right up to me and treat me like a long-lost relative.

"Hey, Robin!"

"Robin, what's up?"

"Yo, Robin, looking good."

By contrast, people talk around Diane, whispering about her in the third person:

"That's Diane Sawyer."

"Hey, isn't that Diane Sawyer?"

"Wow, it's Diane Sawyer."

But the thing is that you *could* treat Diane like she's your long-lost cousin. She may seem like this gorgeous, intimidating, smart-as-hell, cool glass of water, but at the heart of it, she's a warm, Southern-born woman who is, above all, absolutely and categorically comfortable in her own skin.

Only someone who is so comfortable in her own skin could be so giving and so kind. From the moment we started working together, to the moment that we bonded as sister friends, Diane has been the epitome of generosity. When the chips are down and life is at its worst, when you think you have *no* options, there's Diane.

Shortly after my MDS diagnosis, I ran into Diane at a luncheon honoring her husband and the cast of *Death of a Salesman*. We both needed to sneak out because we had to get back to work.

We were leaving and I just stopped her and said, "I need to tell you something."

She said, "Okay."

I said, "I'm ill again. I don't have time to get into it, but we need to talk."

I hadn't even made it back to the office before she e-mailed me and said, "I need more details, let's talk now."

So we had a long conversation. And she simply said, "I'm on it." Within days, she knew more about MDS than I did. She called doctors all across the country while coordinating with Rich Besser, who is our chief medical editor. Rich, Diane and I were like this little stealth team, undercover, doing the research, weighing the options. Rich and Diane weren't giving my name when they talked to doctors; they were just gathering vital information. Eventually I added Tom

Cibrowski to our tight circle of confidence. Tom is my executive producer, but also a dear friend. Plus, I felt somebody at work needed to know if I started to call in sick frequently.

Diane Sawyer should have been a doctor. Her ability to process, catalogue and interpret the most complicated medical information is nothing short of stunning. Usually when someone is in crisis, I'm the person who can coolly sift through information and make decisions about the best line of action, but from the moment that I whispered my news into her ear, Diane took charge, and I was so grateful. She is not a colleague. She is not an air-kiss associate. She is my friend and my lifeline. She was one of the first people I saw in our family's yard after Daddy died. She not only got herself to the Gulf Coast but she managed to rustle up food from one of our favorite restaurants, Mary Mahoney's. She wanted to be sure we had gumbo waiting for us when we came back from the funeral home. That's just Diane. She will be someone I know and love until I draw my last breath.

CHAPTER 9

Finding My Match

After my father died in 2004, a wonderful writer named Missy Buchanan sent me one of her books to share with Momma. The book was called *Living with Purpose in a Worn-Out Body*, and the title went directly to the heart of what I saw in my mother's elder years. Mom had just celebrated her eightieth birthday, and the health issues were piling up. Yet she was still a force to be reckoned with in the community, still fighting the good fight. She was known statewide for her work with the governor's office, but she also took on passion projects closer to home, such as helping the Boys and Girls Club build a beautiful recreation center in the Pass after Katrina. (Momma believed in the power of afterschool programs; no idle hands on her watch!) She lived with purpose even as she faced serious health challenges. I sent her Missy's book right away.

I didn't know for several months that Momma had not only read *Living with Purpose*, but she found Missy's number and called her.

"How did you know what I was thinking when you wrote that book?" Momma asked Missy.

And with that, a special friendship began. Several years later, Missy offered to help Momma write the incredible story of her life from living in poverty in Akron, Ohio, to receiving a $200 scholarship to Howard University, where she had lunch with Eleanor Roosevelt; from being stationed abroad in locales as far-flung as Japan and Turkey to becoming the first black president of the Officers' Wives Club in Mississippi.

Missy traveled from her home in Texas to the Pass, and the two women spent happy days together eating gumbo and telling stories. By then Mom was in her late eighties, and she wasn't always up for the company. Missy would stay at a nearby hotel and wait for Mom's call. Missy is the rare soul that understands, truly understands, older adults: their fears, struggles and hopes. My mother could not have found a better collaborator, and I am so proud of her book.

Now it was April 20, 2012, the day of Mom's big book party. It was a beautiful sunny day in the Pass. Friends and family had traveled near and far to celebrate Mom. Upper Room Books were the hosts, and the venue was Oak Crest Mansion, an elegant and beautiful Southern home from the 1920s that miraculously survived Hurricane Katrina. Set on twelve bucolic acres, the mansion features a chapel, a gazebo and a great room where they serve traditional afternoon tea by the fireplace. More than 250 guests turned up for Mom's book party, and it looked more like a wedding when we entered the banquet hall, full of white linen round tables and big bouquets of hydrangea.

It's a funny thing how much being on national TV is like being a military brat. When you're on TV in every town in America, you don't really have a home base. But that's why my home in Mississippi is so important to me, because it gives me my home base. When I walk through that door I smell an aroma that could only be home. I sit in Momma's chair, and see that rickety old TV, and it's grounding, it's nurturing. If I only stayed in New York City and went to all the premieres that I'm invited to, and all the trappings of being where I am...Well, that's never going to happen. I can't even finish that sentence, because it would just never happen. It doesn't speak to me. It's not who I am or who I will ever be.

I remember Mom beaming as my big sister Dorothy sang the title of Mom's book: "This is *My Story*, this is *My Song*, praising my Savior all the day long." Our cousin Steven accompanied Dorothy on the piano. There wasn't a dry eye in the house.

No one at that reception could have imagined the pain we were experiencing as a family. After the book signing we returned home, and I took out swab kits for my sisters. My best shot to beat MDS was a bone marrow transplant. Doctors told me it was my only option for a possible cure. I desperately needed a genetic match.

I have two sisters and one brother. Butch is the oldest, and while he wanted to be considered a candidate to save his little sister's life, his age and his own health issues ruled him out. Sally-Ann is the next oldest. She's a television anchor in New Orleans. They love her there and she loves them right back. Dorothy is the next oldest. She's an artist and an administrator and probably the most creative person I know.

Dorothy and Sally-Ann were eager to swab the

insides of their cheeks. But before we began, Sally-Ann's longtime prayer partner and sister-in-law, Phyllis, led us in prayer. I certainly was in need of a miracle. I didn't tell them that there was only a three-in-ten chance that either would be a match. A lifetime in sports has taught me that the beauty of life is that odds are meant to be defied. Miracles happen every day.

I was remarkably calm as my sisters took the test to see if one of them might be a match. Sure, I went through a range of emotions, anger, fear, etc. But Mom always taught me we have choices. Never more so than after Dad died, when she said, "You can have sad sorrow or happy sorrow." I choose to be happy even in difficult times. Uplifting thoughts and actions. Nowhere is it written that we shouldn't be happy. We don't get extra bonus points for drudgingly going through life.

In the weeks that it took to get the results, I prayed every day for a miracle. Diane Sawyer was a wonderful resource, doing the legwork of investigating what the best next steps for me would be when—"not 'if,'" she would say—I found my match. Every time I talked to Diane on the phone, I could hear her flipping through pages of her notes. If the match is such and such, this would be your best hospital. Depending on the type of donor you have, and what kind of match it is, this would be your best bet.

The plan was for my nieces to take the test next, if it turned out that neither Dorothy nor Sally-Ann were a match. I remember asking my mother if my dad had any children we were never told about. I said: "Mom, I promise not to get mad, in fact I'm giving you this onetime pass to come clean: Does Daddy have any other children?" Momma was horrified, she said, "Oh, mercy, no!"

I pride myself on the fact that I never played the race card. But if I could not find a match within my family, it seemed like a race card could be played on me. The National Marrow Donor Program has more than eight million Americans in its database. A Caucasian person who doesn't find a match in their family has about a 50 percent chance of finding one in the database. For African-Americans, that number could be as low as 7 percent. African-Americans tend to have a more racially mixed genetic makeup than their white counterparts—think about the range of skin tones that exist between a Michelle Obama and a Halle Berry, a Serena Williams and a Beyoncé, or an Alicia Keys and a

Jennifer Hudson. The same diversity that makes our culture so rich also makes finding a precise genetic match more challenging.

There are so many stories about people, especially people of color, who wait a year or more to find a match. Even when huge campaigns are mounted and thousands of people register, a match isn't always found. A genetic match is the most literal definition of a needle in a haystack. Every time I thought of the doctor's chart and that dot that was placed right between a year and two years, I knew how dire my situation was. I didn't have a year to wait for a match. I needed a match and I needed one *now*.

And yet, the whole time I was waiting for results, there was work. Every morning up at 3:45. On the air by 7:00. *Good Morning America.* Later, when my coworkers found out the secret I'd been keeping, they would wonder how I did it. How did I show up every day and not just fall to pieces under the sadness and the fear? How did I keep it together? How did I not crack and say, "Hey y'all, back up. I'm sick"?

When I had those "Woe is me" moments, the "me against the world" moments, I would think of Momma. Everybody's got something. Momma would always say, "Why is my something any worse or more significant than anyone else's?" It's not. It's just not.

I bet if we all threw our problems in a huge pile and saw everyone else's, we'd grab ours back. Don't compare your life to others'. You have no idea what their journey is all about. That's why I always give people the benefit of the doubt; it's one of my rules to live by. There may be a reason why someone is having a bad day; there's often something that we can't see. She is not necessarily a bad person, just someone facing a bad situation.

We all have doubts and fears. The thing about fear is that it only needs the tiniest space, the size of an eye of a needle, to get through and wreak havoc. Maddening, but true. So when I was struggling and in doubt, I would simply take the next small step. I would stop and think: "No, life is not tied with a beautiful bow all the time, but it's still a gift. I'm going to tear away the wrapping like a little kid at Christmas."

In the church of my childhood, they said, "First the faith, then the works." I held strong to my faith, and then I got what I'd been praying for: a match. The day I got the news, about three weeks after my sisters had each swabbed their cheeks, was like one of those old television commercials where Ed McMahon pulls up in front of your house to let you know that you have just won the sweepstakes. I couldn't wait to share the news with my family.

First, I called Dorothy to let her know she was not a match. She was disappointed but told me later she never thought she'd be the match. Mom needed her more than I did. Dorothy was the sibling who lived closest to Mom and always took her to her many doctor appointments. She'd pick up Mom on the way to church. It was devastating to Mom when doctors told her she could no longer drive. She felt her independence had been taken from her. It's one of those difficult times for an aging parent. Mom always looked forward to hitting the road. I still miss how she would say when she pulled into our driveway, "Home again, home again, riggity jig jig."

When I got the test results back, I gave Sally-Ann a call. You'd think I would have led with, "YOU'RE A MATCH!" But we had a nonchalant conversation for a few minutes, then I casually said, "Oh, by the way, you're a match." I think I'm just getting my hearing back, that was how loudly she shouted for joy. But I know how much my big sister hates needles and hospitals. I needed a miracle, but I also needed to give her a graceful out. "Do you want to do this?" I asked softly. Sally-Ann was uncharacteristically silent for a moment and I braved myself for her response, whatever it might be. "I don't *want* to do this, baby sister," she said. "I was *born* to do this."

CHAPTER 10

A Meeting with the President

The week before Mother's Day, I met my first transplant specialist. Mom was resting at my apartment, and Dorothy and Amber came with me to the doctor's office. Looking back, I can see how, little by little, Dorothy had begun to shift into the Momma role. At the time, though, I just thought that Mom was aging but would be around for a good long time to come. She'd had numerous health scares before, but she'd always bounced back.

Dorothy later said that at that appointment I looked like a little kid sitting in the dentist's chair for the first time. I didn't mean to pout, but I could feel my bottom lip trembling and the tears welling up in my eyes. I was so frightened.

That first doctor's visit was a chilling introduction to the world of bone marrow transplants. This particular doctor was all doom and gloom. She spent so much time telling me about the high mortality rate of having a bone marrow transplant that I half-expected her to end the appointment by handing me a shovel and telling me to go ahead and start digging my own grave. One thing that I understood very clearly from her words was that with the transplant, timing was everything. You don't want to wait too long to do the transplant, but you also have to make sure that you time it so that you are ready—mind, body and soul—to take the risk of the procedure. Do you remember that dot on the graph that the first oncologist had shown me? The "if I do nothing, I have between one and two years to live" dot? If the transplant did not go well, if I contracted a serious virus after completely wiping out my immune system, then I could die within weeks or even days after the procedure.

How could this be? How could this possibly be the truth of my situation? Amber and I clutched hands and held on to each other for dear life, as if the ground beneath us was shaking with seismic force. We had waited for hours, *hours*, to meet with this doctor, and by the time she had finished with her litany, I felt more confused and more full of despair than I did when I arrived.

When I stepped out of the office and turned on the phone, it almost blew up in my hand with all of the messages. The office had been trying to reach me, and my assistant, Sonny, had been doing her best to protect me. Something big was going on. Ben Sherwood, the president of ABC News, had been trying to reach me. Jeffrey Schneider, the head of PR, was calling, too. Sonny was one of the few people whom I let into my confidence, out of absolute necessity. It's hard to keep a secret when you work for one of the country's top news networks. But I didn't want to discuss my situation with anyone at work until I had a clear understanding of my diagnosis and a clear plan for treatment.

I call Sonny my baby-faced assassin. She's from Pennsylvania and graduated from Fordham University in 2006 with a BA in communications and media studies. After graduation, she did volunteer work with the Jesuit Volunteer Corps and spent time in the Gulf Region helping people get back on their feet after Hurricane Katrina.

After I was diagnosed with breast cancer,

Sonny was in our studio audience holding up a sign: HEY, ROBIN, I JUST VOLUNTEERED FOR A YEAR IN THE GULF AND NOW I NEED A JOB. I was impressed with her boldness and creativity in finding employment, so I told her: "Send me your résumé and I'll see what I can do."

You know how many times I've told a young person that and they don't follow up? Sonny sent me her résumé the next day. My office was so overwhelmed with correspondence following my breast cancer diagnosis that we hired Sonny part-time to help out. She was a rock star. Nothing was too big or too small for her to tackle. A short time later, my assistant, Ayana, got a wonderful opportunity at CNN, and Sonny was promoted to my full-time assistant.

Sonny is smart and indefatigable. How she managed to convince Ben Sherwood, the president of ABC News, that she had no idea how to reach me for hours on end, without getting either of us fired, is what makes her so good at her job. Still she was relieved when our senior executive producer, Tom Cibrowski, came to her desk and said, "Robin's at the hospital, isn't she?" It was more of a statement than a question. Tom knew that I wouldn't be unreachable unless the situation was dire. Sonny nodded yes. It was such a relief to have someone higher on the food chain to take the heat for me being missing in action.

The first call I returned was Ben's. He told me the White House had called and wanted me to interview President Barack Obama the next day. Same-sex marriage was a hot-button issue that week because of recent statements by Vice President Joe Biden and others in the administration. The interview was a huge get for our team. I told Ben that of course I would do it, and I was excited to be asked. It's always a privilege to speak with the president, especially one-on-one at the White House. I was still shaken up from my appointment, and so I told Ben that I was dealing with a personal matter and would have to get back to him to discuss the details. He later told me that he thought that was strange: "The president wants to talk to you and you'll get back to me?"

But I needed just a few minutes to let myself process the fear and frustration I felt with that appointment. I had learned from my first battle with cancer that doctors who spout dire statistics don't work for me. I have no doubt that this doctor is a good physician—she came highly recommended. And perhaps there are some patients who find her style refreshing, even reassuring in some way.

But it doesn't work for me. I talked myself through the experience. I called Diane, who urged me to find another doctor. I could hear her on the phone, flipping through her notebook, Dr. So-and-So at this hospital says XYZ. Dr. So-and-So says such and such. I called Ben back. I spent most of the night not thinking about my need for a bone marrow transplant but huddled with my producers, going over topics and questions for my interview with the president.

The next morning, after *GMA*, Tom, my producer Emily and I headed to the airport for our flight to Washington, D.C. When we got there, our shuttle flight had been canceled. We hustled over to another terminal and were able to get on a later flight that would get us to the White House just in time. A car service picked us up at the airport, and we were off to see the president. Then a few blocks from the White House, we were rear-ended. The driver, of course, wanted to wait for the police to file a report, but now there wasn't the fifteen-minute window we had left for me to stop at the hotel and change. We had to improvise. I told everyone—the driver, Tom and Emily—to please hop out of the car so I could change into my power suit in the backseat. Yes, I lead such a glamorous life. But you can't be late for the president of the United States. He's kind of a busy man, running the nation.

We made it to the White House with only seconds to spare. Every time I cross that hallowed threshold, I pinch myself. In my first book, I described seven rules to live by, and one of them was never play the race card, the gender card or any other card. It makes me laugh when people think that because I'm black I somehow have a special relationship with the Obamas. The Bush family was the first presidential family to welcome me, again and again, into the White House. I attended my first State Dinner during the tenure of George W. Queen Elizabeth of Britain was the honored guest, and as I made my way down the receiving line, President Bush—no secret that he was an ESPN fan—called me out, "Hey, SportsCenter!" I remember thinking, "I'm in line to meet the Queen of England, and the president of the United States has just recognized me from a job I haven't had in years. How cool is that?"

Amazing things happen when you let your passion be your purpose. My father's passion for flying led him from pretending a broomstick was the joystick of a plane in the basement of his New Jersey home in the years of segregation to a distinguished career as a pilot for the hallowed Tuskegee Airmen. My mother's passion for education led to a distinguished career in public service that began after her sixtieth birthday, after she'd raised four children and seen them all through college. My passion for sports: the little girl who moved to Mississippi at the age of nine—just me and my RC—but who was always game to see how high she could jump, how fast she could run, what feat her body could accomplish next, led me to the White House for dinner with the Queen. Where else do miracles like this happen to everyday people? One of the things that I think people know is that despite our troubles and our missteps, I am bullish on America. This is my country, the land that I love.

Once we were on the ground, reporters in the White House press corps began to tweet that I had arrived for my exclusive interview. There was much speculation that the president would reverse his position on same-sex marriage. But we had no way to know for sure if that would be the case.

At 1:30 p.m. sharp, President Obama walked into the room, and our team all rose to greet him. I'd interviewed him several times, the first being in 2007, when he first announced he was running for office. He always remembers that I was one of the few national journalists to request interviews with him. At one point, he was so far behind Hillary Clinton in the polls that many reporters discounted him. I never did. I never count out anyone.

I began the interview by asking the president straight out, "So, Mr. President, are you still opposed to same-sex marriage?"

He said, "At a certain point I've just concluded that for me, personally, it is important for me to go ahead and affirm that I think same-sex couples should be able to get married." The president of the United States had just officially endorsed marriage equality. It was historic, and my interview made headlines all around the world.

One of the things that touched me most was how the president spoke about how his views had evolved, where so many of us learn and grow: at the dinner table. He said, "You know, Malia and Sasha, they've got friends whose parents are same-sex couples. And I—you know, there have been times where Michelle and I have been sitting around the dinner table. And we've been talking…about their friends and their parents. And Malia and Sasha would— It wouldn't dawn on them that somehow their friends' parents would be treated differently. It doesn't make sense to them. And frankly, that's the kind of thing that prompts—a change of perspective. You know, not wanting to somehow explain to your child why somebody should be treated differently, when it comes to the eyes of the law."

Many fellow journalists wondered why President Obama selected me for that interview. I can't remember another time a reporter was scrutinized like I was. The person asking the questions is not important; the answers are what people care about. You know what my biggest concern was when I was sitting across from the president of the United States? It was when Emily held up a large note card that read: LIPSTICK ON TEETH. I'm not joking. In fact, she framed the card and has it hanging in her office.

There was so much ahead of me in my health journey, but I'll always remember that spring 2012 as being the kind of roller-coaster ride where I ricocheted between screams of joy and cries of fear. I was diagnosed with MDS on the very same day that *Good Morning America* became the number one morning show for the first time in 852 weeks. I met with Dr. Doom and Gloom on the very same day the president of the United States invited me to the White House for an announcement that made history. I've always been a person who is focused and present. It's part of my athlete DNA. You'll never score, literally or metaphorically, if you're mentally making your to-do list while you're supposed to be lining up to take your shot. But that spring, when the highs were so high and the lows were so low, I learned even more the importance of being in the moment. As I sat across from the president, I tried to let myself feel all the goodness and the grace of my position, how lucky I am to do what I do for a living and how much my hard work in the field has paid off. When we reached number one, I tried to let the sweetness of the moment sink in. For over a decade, I had gotten up at 3:45 a.m., headed to the studio and given our beloved viewers and our talented team—both in front of the camera and behind the scenes—everything I had, and it had paid off. We were number one. As much as I could, I let myself feel it.

* * *

I remember getting a call from one of my *GMA* senior producers, Kris Sebastian, just after my interview with the president. She said: "Do you have any idea how big you are right now? How big this story is?" I was so much in the moment when I was doing the story. I was the one sitting there across from the president of the United States when he uttered those historic words. But once it was over, all I wanted to do was get home to Momma.

Dorothy had already taken a lot of time off from work and had gone back to Mississippi. Once I got home, I would have to manage caring for Mom, for the rest of her visit to New York, by myself. I know that a lot of you have done this juggle: managing your own health issues while at the same time managing the care of an elderly parent.

When I walked into my apartment after getting home from D.C., Mom was scooting around my apartment in her power chair. I was mentally and physically exhausted from the day's events. I told Mom that I needed a moment just to catch my breath. I went into my bedroom to change into my sweats and then I heard a terrifying crash. I went running to Mom's room and was so relieved to see that Momma was not hurt. The damage, as I quickly surveyed the room, was minimal. The end table was overturned, and the glass lamp that once sat on it was shattered into a gazillion pieces all over the floor. The cord of Mom's power chair got tangled with the leg of the end table. Mom was leaning down in her chair, trying to pick up pieces of glass.

"It's okay, Momma," I whispered. "I'll clean it up."

I softly implored her to go in the living room while I picked up the slivers and fragments.

What I saw in the living room breaks my heart to this day. Mom was slumped in her chair like a scolded child. Her head hanging down, she said, "I'm so sorry, honey. I can't do anything right. I'm destroying your beautiful home, I should just leave." All I could do was hug and tell her how much I loved her. I wasn't mad—how could I be? But she didn't seem to believe me.

My mind flashed back to parallel moments in my childhood. My mom had so many beautiful things that she had collected during my father's travels with the Air Force. As the wife of an enlisted officer, we never had a lot of money, but she scrimped and saved and bought mementos that made our home come alive. You can't do much to military housing except change the paint. But Mom made each of the many cookie-cutter homes we lived in special. I was a rambunctious kid, full of energy, always happy to toss around anything that bounced. How many times had I broken something in my mother's house? How many times had I cried harder than she would have ever yelled? How many times had she held me and told me that things don't matter, people do? Now it was me, holding her, wiping away her tears and whispering assurances. But Mom wasn't a child. She was an elderly woman doing her best to grow old with dignity.

The next day, Mom was scheduled to discuss her book on ABC's *The View*. In the last years of her life, Mom seemed to be on her own roller-coaster ride, rolling from fragility to fierceness and back again. The morning of her TV appearance, she was back in fine form. My Team Beauty—the Glam Squad, Elena and Petula—worked their magic on Mom. Diandre, my trusty stylist, dressed her in a stunning copper-colored St. John outfit bought special for the occasion. It was wonderful to be able to give Momma the royal treatment. After the Glam Squad was done getting Mom ready for the show, she looked in the mirror and jokingly said, "Can I help it?" Meaning, "Can I help it that I look this good?" And she did look good.

During the interview, she was so funny and so generous with her life lessons that she had the audience and the ladies of *The View* eating out of her hand. I was particularly moved by a moment Mom and Whoopi Goldberg shared on the set after the cameras stopped rolling. Apparently Mom's mannerisms and wise words resonated with Whoopi and made her think of her own mother. I'll never forget Whoopi kneeling in front of Mom, tears in her eyes as they spoke. Whoopi had lost her mother just two years be-

fore. I thanked God in heaven that I still had
mine.

CHAPTER 11

Tea & Sympathy

That June, Lara Spencer and I traveled together to London for the Queen's Jubilee. I still hadn't told her about my diagnosis. Sam was the only co-anchor who knew. Back in late April he figured out on his own that something just wasn't right with me, and I confided in him. I appreciated how he kept the news to himself. Everything changes when you tell someone you're sick. I just wanted to be treated like Robin.

I went off to London with some very good news. When the tests first came in about Sally-Ann being my match, the first indications were that she was a 3-for-3 match. By the time additional tests had been completed, it showed that Sally-Ann was a 10-for-10. She could not have been a better match for me if we had been born identical twins. While so much of my journey with MDS was puzzling and seemed so unfair, I knew that news like this was more than a gift; it was a big, flashing neon sign from God reminding me to let myself be led by faith and not by fear.

Lara and I always have a great time working together. She left us in 2003 to host *The Insider*, but she returned in 2011 and I was so glad. We have a similar zest for life, and neither one of us take ourselves too seriously. We are both nuts about sports, especially tennis. Lara was also a sports reporter at one time, and she attended Penn State on an athletic scholarship for springboard and platform diving. A huge bonus is that we have the same size shoe, so we share! I knew it would be my last work assignment abroad for some time, so I really let myself enjoy every moment, from a champagne toast with Lara on the plane to getting dressed up in a fascinator hat for the Jubilee. We stayed with our crew at the Metropolitan Hotel in the heart of London. The hotel restaurant off the lobby turns into a raging nightclub in the evenings. We didn't have to venture far to enjoy ourselves after work. We were in London for only a few days, but we made every moment count.

✳ ✳ ✳

I always enjoy visiting London. The first time I went, I was about seven years old. We happened to arrive on the Fourth of July. I remember asking my parents: Why are there no fireworks here? Ooops! The entire family was together: Mom, Dad, Butch, Sally-Ann and Dorothy. We stayed at a quaint bed-and-breakfast. Mom enjoyed having afternoon tea: milk, not cream, and lemon was a no-no. It was accompanied by a three-tier tray of delicious finger sandwiches, scones with yummy cream and jam, sweet pastries and cakes.

Some of my favorite family photos were taken at Hyde Park. One is of me squished between my two big sisters. Sally-Ann was in a full-on teenage rebellious stage. She had a big white headband and a poncho she made by ripping a hole in our mosaic tablecloth. Dorothy struck a model pose with one hand in her pocket and her big white purse slung over one shoulder. I, in pigtails and knee-high socks, stood frozen at attention with both hands by my side. Another photo is of me and my handsome big brother, who is wearing a snappy corduroy blazer. It was a treat to have him on vacation with us. He was in college at Rutgers at the time. We are twelve years apart in age, so I was going into the first grade when he headed off to college. I treasure the picture of Butch and me sitting at the edge of a fountain in Hyde Park, feeding the pigeons.

My Grandma Sally actually traveled to England in 1953. Her son, my uncle William, was in the military and stationed there. Aunt Bessie was about to have a baby, and Grandma Sally wanted to be there. Grandma had never ventured far from Akron, Ohio. She was terrified of flying (Butch isn't a big fan of flying, either), so Grandma boarded the *Queen Mary* and set sail for England. She arrived just in time for Queen Elizabeth's coronation, and she joined the throngs outside Buckingham Palace. She brought back to Akron little coronation trinkets and keepsakes. She proudly displayed them in her home on Lucy Street, next to the latest issue of *Jet* magazine.

How could she ever have imagined that decades later her granddaughter would have dinner with the Queen of England at the White House? I told you about the Bushes inviting me to my first State Dinner…*"Hey, SportsCenter!"* was how President Bush always greeted me. Well, earlier that day I interviewed Mrs. Bush for a segment on *GMA*. After the interview I told her about my grandma attending the Queen's coronation and my mother's hope that I could share that story with Queen Elizabeth. Sure, Mom, no problem, I'll just chat up the Queen. When I was going down the receiving line to greet the Bushes along with Queen Elizabeth and Prince Philip, I froze. I was walking away when Mrs. Bush said: "Your Majesty, this is the young woman I was telling you about. Her grandmother was in London at the time of your coronation." I can't even remember the Queen's response. But I do remember Mrs. Bush's thoughtfulness and my mom's excitement when I called her later that night.

Another fond memory I have of London is when my folks joined me at Wimbledon one year. They both enjoyed traveling, and I often invited them to come along with me on assignments. We stayed at the Langham Hilton. It has a glass elevator with the stairs winding around it. Mom and Dad would get in the elevator, and their baby girl would take the stairs and race them to our floor. I can still see them laughing in the elevator as I bounded up the stairs two at a time.

You have no idea what it was like to see my folks, in their Sunday best, sitting in the crowd at Wimbledon. I had always dreamed of them being there to see me play on Centre Court. Being in the press box for ESPN was a close second. I had a microphone in my hand instead of a tennis racket, but it was every bit as sweet. London will always hold a prominent place in my heart.

* * *

When I returned from London, I decided the time had come to tell George, Josh and Lara about my diagnosis. I spoke to George first. George is a true gentleman. He reminds me a lot of my father. Reserved, quiet and devoted to family. Like my dad, George is quick to laugh. He has to be, since he is married to the hilarious, not to mention gorgeous, Ali Wentworth. Since George is somewhat of an introvert, I thought it best to tell him on the phone. I didn't want to make him uncomfortable with such personal news.

"I'm just in awe of how you've handled this," George said. "All this time, coming to work, doing your job, never showing a sign that something was wrong. I love you and I know you are going to beat this. You'll hit it with all the courage and grace you've shown your whole life."

A few days later I received an e-mail from George. He'd had more time to absorb what I told him. It was one of the most thoughtful e-mails I have ever received. He shared scripture with me. That comes easier to him than you may think, because his father is a Greek Orthodox priest and his sister is a nun. I felt closer to George than I ever had at that point. It was at that moment I realized just how much we do have in common.

I told Josh and Lara together. Josh and Lara are extremely talented and pure energy. Full of life like two big, affectionate golden retrievers. I love it when we hang out after the show, as we often do. It was most difficult to tell them because they were so emotional—we just kept hugging each other and crying. I could sense they were truly scared for me, and I knew they were also wondering what was going to happen with the show. As I had looked to Charlie and Diane for guidance, Josh and Lara now looked to me.

Everyone wanted to know what I needed, and I told them, "What I need, more than anything, is normalcy." When you're facing a health crisis, you crave normalcy. So much in your life is not normal anymore. You feel reluctant to tell anybody, because you don't want to be treated differently.

When Nora Ephron died of leukemia, I could tell that some people she knew were upset that she hadn't shared her diagnosis. What I know is this: Each of our journeys is different and personal. There's not a one-size-fits-all when it comes to this or any other type of life-threatening illness or challenge. You've got to do what is best for you.

I understand why Nora chose to be so private about her illness. Because you just want to be you, she just wanted to be Nora. She just wanted people to say, "Hey, let's go to dinner. Let's do this or that." When you tell people you're sick, your friendship changes. As much as your friends don't want it to and they try not to change, they can't help it.

What I wanted most of all was for friends to be normal. Don't treat me like I'm on the *Titanic*. *"Don't you say your good-byes, Rose."*

When I address a group of people and talk about my story and they're asking me questions—especially when it's a cancer-related forum—I will say to the audience at some point, "There are people sitting next to you that you might not even know that they've gone through this or are going through that, and they don't want you to know, and that's their right." And I can look out at the audience and see the people who have kept their battles private almost exhale. They've been wondering, "Am I a bad person for not telling people? For not sharing this?" I take that pressure and guilt off of them and say, "No, that's your decision. That's your choice, as this has been my decision."

Recently, my friend and colleague Amy Robach agreed to do a mammogram, on air, as part of a "GMA Goes Pink" campaign to kick off Breast Cancer Awareness Month. The idea was for Amy, who'd never had a mammogram, to demystify it for women who might be nervous. As Amy explained, "I'm forty, and the truth is

I'd been putting off getting a mammogram for a year. Between flying all over the world for work, running around with my kids to school, ballet and gymnastics, like so many women, I kept pushing it off." Amy was nervous about the producers asking her to do her first mammogram on air and she came to see me. She knew that I was a believer in "make your mess your message." But she was apprehensive about having cameras film such a private moment. Remembering the thousands of women who went in for mammograms after I revealed my breast cancer diagnosis on air, I urged her to do the segment. "If one life is saved because of early detection, it's worth it," I told Amy.

She was so nervous that morning, but she bravely did her first mammogram on air. I remember that she had this gigantic smile on her face when the segment was over. "It hurt so much less than I thought!" she said. "It was like nothing." Then a few weeks later, there was a diagnosis: Amy had breast cancer. She later told me, "Robin, your words kept echoing inside of me: If I got the mammogram on air, and it saved one life, then it would be all worth it. It never occurred to me that life would be mine."

CHAPTER 12

Knox-Vegas

*A*s many times as I've been to Knoxville, or Knox-Vegas as I like to call it, this particular trip in June was special. I was to be inducted into the Women's Basketball Hall of Fame. Despite her health woes, Mom wanted to be there. So I arranged for a private plane to first pick up my brother and his family in Houston, then stop in the Pass for Mom, Dorothy, her daughter Lauren and Sally-Ann's daughter, Judith. With Butch was his daughter, Bianca; his son, Lawrence; and Lawrence's very pregnant wife, Kelli. She was carrying twins! My niece Lauren looks like my sister Dorothy's twin. She is studying to be a nurse and is currently a doctor's assistant. Judith is the first doctor in the family...a proud graduate from my parents' alma mater, Howard.

Anyone who has followed my journey knows that I have been blessed with an incredible family. There have been times when I've felt as if I almost need to hide that light under a bushel—because I was born with the jackpot: successful, community-minded, high-achieving parents who let us know how much they loved us every single day and siblings who hold me up, help me grow and make me laugh. It has been this way for almost half a century and now the loving and learning and living goes on with a whole new generation. I treasure nieces and nephews and, even though I can't believe my brother and sisters are old enough to be grandparents, there are now grandkids and great-grandkids in the mix, too.

I know that I have cleared incredible hurdles in my career and with my health because of this family and because of this hard-earned love. I used to try to play it down, but not anymore. I am not going to apologize for the idyllic childhood and the wonderful siblings and the Christian home I grew up in. I know how blessed I am and I am thankful, but I also know it's not that way for everyone. I was talking to a young woman recently who was going through her something and she said, "I don't have sisters to watch my back like you do. I didn't have the kind of mother you did." And I said to her what I've begun saying to people across the country, "Then why not let the legacy of love and support start with you?" The Robertses of Pass Christian, Mississippi, didn't spring up from a well of familial perfection. My parents worked hard to create a certain environment for us and then there was a responsibility for my siblings and me to hold up the traditions, to mend the fences when we wanted to tell each other off and keep on stepping, to keep the love going for one another and for the generations to come.

When I suggested to this young woman that she could be the one to turn the tide, the one to begin a circle of love and support with family and friends (I believe family doesn't need to be just blood relatives), you should have seen her face. We live in a society where we believe we can change anything: our bodies, our bank accounts, our careers, our hometowns. We are mobile and proactive, and we are big dreamers. It's the American way. But when it comes to matters of home and hearth, we too often believe that the hand we were dealt is the only one we've got. It's not. People need to take more ownership and say, no I haven't been loved. No, I don't get along with my siblings and it has never been this way in my family, but you know what, *starting now* it is. It's going to be different. Why not be the one to start the kind of family you've always wanted to be part of?

I'm blessed that I am able to do special things for my family, such as arrange a private jet when my mother's health was failing...I never take it for granted, and they fight me every step of the way. They don't want me to feel like they expect me to do anything extravagant for them. To the contrary, when Mom arrived at the airport, she slipped me a twenty-dollar bill. She does it every visit. She calls it "greasing my palm." So sweet.

A number of old friends were in Knoxville for the ceremony, and I was grateful to be able to tell them about my treatment face-to-face. A group from my alma mater, Southeastern Louisiana University, made the trip from Hammond to support my entry into the Hall of Fame. They were touched that I told them personally before the rest of the world found out.

I got a chance in Knoxville to share the news with

ESPN executive John Walsh and his wife, Ellen. I love them, and they were also very close to my mom. Val Ackerman, onetime president of the WNBA, I remember pulling her aside and telling her in the lobby. I remember telling Pat Summitt about my diagnosis. I wondered, how am I going to do this? Here she is, dealing with all of her health challenges. But I told her, and her embrace was more than a hug—it was as if she was physically gifting me with a wellspring of strength and courage that would be with me for months to come.

I wanted to tell my friends, as many as I could in person, because I'd learned a few things since my breast cancer diagnosis. This is how naïve I was in 2007. I thought I was just telling *GMA* viewers because they are like family. They invite us into their homes every morning for breakfast. I told everybody who is close to me, so now I'm going to tell everyone else. I didn't realize back then that for a morning show anchor to share a major medical diagnosis on TV was a media moment that would be picked up by digital, radio, print and TV outlets all over the world. When I sat in that chair and shared my news with the *GMA* family, I didn't think, not for a second, that it would mushroom the way it did. This time around, it was important for me to get to as many relatives and friends as I could. Being in Knoxville for my entry into the Hall of Fame was a great balance to the bad news that I had to share. The celebration of my athleticism was a reminder that "I've got the physical chops to deal with this."

I knew that when I returned from Knoxville, I would go public with my diagnosis. It was time. I was going to begin pre-treatment for the transplant, which would entail having a PICC line put in my arm. PICC stands for "peripherally inserted central catheter." It's a small tube that's inserted into a peripheral vein, usually in the upper arm. The line would enable my doctors to have prolonged and safer access to my veins. Since the line would stay in my arm, it would be hard to hide. It has to be bandaged to prevent infection; it has to have a sleeve cover.

The PICC line would facilitate the pre-treatment for the transplant, which would be supervised by my oncologist. It was going to be a daunting series of daily chemotherapy sessions to wipe out my entire immune system so it could be built back from scratch with new life from Sally-Ann's stem cells.

The night before the induction ceremony, a reception was held for all the honorees and our family and friends. I had the pleasure of sharing an intimate evening with the other inductees: Olympians and National Champions Dawn Staley, Nikki McCray and Pamela McGee. Dawn was recently inducted into the Naismith Basketball Hall of Fame in Springfield, Massachusetts. While at ESPN I covered her college games at Virginia and Nikki's at the University of Tennessee. Pamela is closer to my age. She, her twin sister, Paula, Cynthia Cooper and the legendary Cheryl Miller won back-to-back national titles at USC.

Six-foot-five Inge Nissen was one of the first Europeans to come to the US to play at one of the first powerhouses in the women's game, Old Dominion. She also happens to have a wicked sense of humor. She had us all cracking up at the dinner. Also honored was Nancy Fahey, head coach at Washington University and the only coach in NCAA Division III history to win five national championships. She had a fun bunch of friends and players with her in Knoxville. You could hear them comin' from a mile away…good times!

Mom caught a chill, so Butch ran back to the hotel nearby to get her a blanket. All he could find was a bedspread, so he wrapped that around Mom. It was quite a sight to see Mom in her wheelchair, draped in the hotel bedspread. But I was so happy she was there. An informal

Q-and-A session, moderated beautifully by Debbie Antonelli, the esteemed basketball analyst, closed the evening. As always, Momma got in the last word. She addressed the room and said that she was thankful that she was well enough to make the trip. She said that at her lowest moment, she remembered something she had once heard: A prisoner was behind bars and had a decision to make. He could either look down at the dirt in his cell or look up, outside his window, and see the stars. Mom said, "I decided a long time ago, when I was hurting, not to look down, but rather to look up at the stars. Sitting in the audience tonight, as I look at my daughter and all of the inductees who share the stage, I am surrounded by stars." That was Mom. She defied so many odds from her humble beginnings to become one of the most eloquent women I have ever been blessed to know.

It's funny how you can so quickly connect the dots when you're looking back. My mom suffered a stroke a few weeks later. This was her last trip, even though we didn't know it at the time. She sat next to me at the induction ceremony, and Amber was on the other side. There were little signs that Mom wasn't doing well. She was kind of quiet, especially for her.

When they called my name, my six-foot-nine nephew, Lawrence, escorted me up to the stage so I could accept my award. He played college basketball at Baylor and Mississippi State. For a few years he was in the NBA with the Memphis Grizzlies, and he is still playing professionally overseas. After I accepted my award, I saw Pat sitting to the side of the stage. I said, "You're going to have to come over and say hello to Momma." Sure enough, Pat came over, bent down and hugged Momma. Seeing them together like that meant so much to me. I don't know of two braver women.

CHAPTER 13

Breaking the News

After returning from Knoxville, back home in New York, I didn't sleep much. Monday, June 11, was the day I would share the announcement of my illness with *GMA* viewers. That was because it was also the day I was to begin pre-treatment for my transplant. I kept going over in my head what I planned to say, and I couldn't stop wondering how it would be received. The next morning, I huddled with Diane and Rich Besser in the loading dock before I returned to the studio to tell the world that I was once again facing a life-threatening illness. As I said earlier, for the longest time, the three of us considered ourselves a stealth team, contacting in secret doctors and hospitals across the country, looking for the best possible care.

Anne Sweeney, the president of Disney/ABC Television Group, made the trip from Los Angeles to join us in the studio that morning. She and Disney chairman and CEO Bob Iger had already assured me several times that I would have whatever I needed to fight this. Every time I speak with Bob, I remember when Mom had met him at a wedding in the 1980s. His assistant at the time, Karen, was getting married to Mom's best friend's son, Andy. I think I was a teenager before I realized "Aunt" Wanda really wasn't my aunt. She and Mom were more like sisters growing up together in Akron. Bob wasn't the CEO of Disney then; he was a high-ranking executive with Disney/ABC and was based in LA. Mom got his business card and told him about her very talented daughter working in Nashville. I'm sure she told him he should hire me, and a few years later, there I was.

It didn't matter to Bob or Anne how long I would be on medical leave. Though I had literally screamed out loud when doctors first told me it would be approximately six months. The most important thing to Bob and Anne was that I return to good health. Again, such grace, and for that I am so grateful. I can't tell you how many horror stories I've heard from others about losing their jobs while out on medical leave. Come on, here you are, fighting for your life—and you have to worry about your job? The constant threat of joblessness that so many patients face infuriates me beyond belief. Thanks to Bob, Anne and Ben, I knew my anchor chair would be waiting for me.

But it was much more than that. The way they rallied around me was not only a comfort to me but to Amber and my family as well. To my siblings, I'll always be their baby sister, living the farthest from home, in New York City. With Dad gone and Mom so sick, they worried about me even more. Seeing the genuine concern from my colleagues and especially my bosses put them at ease. When I sat down on the couch with our team: Josh to my right, George to my left and Lara and Sam next to George, I noticed that the stage managers had Velcro-ed a box of Kleenex to the couch. "Never a good sign," I joked. Then I took a deep breath, and with nothing on the teleprompter I spoke from the heart:

We've often said that you, our viewers, are our family. As family, we want you to hear things from us. As many of you know, five years ago, I beat breast cancer. You, your love, and your prayers, helped me win that fight, and that's something I'll never forget.

Sometimes the treatment for cancer can lead to other serious medical issues. That's what I'm facing right now. It's something that's called MDS: myelodysplastic syndrome . . . It's a rare blood disorder that affects the bone marrow. Dr. Richard Besser has been holding my hand through this and he'll have a lot more information about MDS on our website.

The reason I'm sharing this with everybody now is because later today, I begin what's known as pre-treatment. It's a PICC line in my arm and I didn't want you to be concerned if you saw a bandage tomorrow. It's going to be there to draw blood that has to be monitored regularly and also to administer drugs . . . for a period of time. All to prepare me for a bone marrow transplant.

You have heard me say I'm abundantly blessed. In fact, in Good Housekeeping, *in an article written before this diagnosis, I said, "I'm freaking blessed." The reason I say I am blessed is because my big sister is a virtually perfect match. She's there with Diane and Anne Sweeney.*

Up until that point in the announcement I had managed to hold it together, but as I shared the miracle of Sally-Ann being my match, I could feel the tears welling up and my voice begin to catch. "She is going to be my donor," I said.

Sally-Ann pointed heavenward and whispered, "Thank you."

I took her cue and joyfully said, "Yes! Thank you, Lord!"

Then I continued sharing what I knew and what I believed about the path ahead:

The doctors tell me this is going to be a tremendous help in me beating this. Bottom line: I am going to beat this. My doctors say it and my faith says it to me.

George, Lara and Sam all joined in assuring me that I was not alone in this battle and I recalled something that my former colleague and dear friend Chris Cuomo had shared with me. He said, "Focus on the fight, not the fright." That is why I was so touched when Josh said, "I know I speak for everybody at home, but especially those of us on the couch. This is why you have a team. So we can be here for you. We want you to know. This is our fight, not your fight." I was so moved. I stopped holding back the tears and reached for the Kleenex.

I know how lucky I was to have colleagues who are such close friends and to have friends who are like family. I was about to begin, literally, the battle of my life. Again. But I also felt, wholly and completely, freaking blessed.

After I made the announcement, I was numb. Our studio crew seemed to be in shock. I retreated to my dressing room with Sally-Ann. Amber was waiting for me there with other close friends. Friends who were there to comfort Amber as much as me. Not much was said nor needed to be said. Everyone in that room had known for a few months what I was facing. My cell phone wasn't the only one buzzing constantly; so were theirs. So many people were reaching out it was overwhelming. This was the very reason I waited to go public. Already life was different, changing rapidly.

Sally-Ann and I locked eyes. Her life was different now, too. She's beloved in New Orleans, where she has been on the air since the 1970s. In the Big Easy, I'm Sally-Ann's baby sista. She's a vital part of the community, having launched a mentoring program called Each One Save One. But now Sally-Ann was known far beyond the South, all across the country. I knew Sally-Ann was exhausted, so I told her to get some rest at my apartment before we headed to the hospital to begin pre-treatment chemo.

* * *

I dropped her off at home then stopped by our GMA office with Dr. Rich Besser. I knew the staff would have a lot of questions, and I knew that as ABC's chief medical health editor, Rich would have answers. I wanted to ease our team's concerns. This was new territory for all of us. How long would I be in the hospital? How long before I could come back to work? Would they be allowed to visit me, hug me?

It was standing room only in our office. We have TV monitors everywhere, and it was odd to see my announcement being played over and over on various networks. Thankfully, someone grabbed the remote and turned off all the TVs. I began by saying I knew many of them had recently battled their own health issues. Sandra and Thea, both producers, had faced their own challenges, and I called them out. I wanted them to know how their bravery inspired me. Another producer, Gary, had just had a death in the family. He had recently returned to work, and his eyes were so sad. I let the team know that he was still grieving and in need of their good wishes, too. I wanted them to know that this moment wasn't just about me. Everybody's got something. I wanted them to know I saw their somethings, too.

I showed the team pictures from our party on the rooftop, that beautiful Thursday night in April, after we bested the *Today* show and became the number one morning show in America. "This was the same day I was diagnosed," I explained. "But it didn't stop me from going to the party, dancing, doing the limbo with Sam." I held up a photo. "Look at all of your smiling faces. There's no reason not to continue smiling in my absence. I am confident that our team will continue to flourish, and I'll be cheering you on from the sidelines."

I didn't realize that this was Will Reeve's first day as a *GMA* intern. Will is the son of Christopher and Dana Reeve, and I had known him as a child. So much about this past year involved things coming full circle.

I first met Will's mother in the 1990s. Dana Reeve had a daytime talk show with Deborah Roberts. I would fill in for Deb, and I remember seeing pictures of Will. He was the cutest little boy, and he would come to the studio. Dana and I would spend time talking after the show and often ran into each other at charity events.

I remember thinking, "Wow, here she is juggling her husband's illness, being very active in the fund-raising and the research." She believed with all of her heart that Christopher Reeve was going to walk again. He, too, was convinced he was going to walk again, and although it didn't come true for him, it moved mountains for the spinal cord injury patients who benefit from his legacy.

I'll never forget the first time I met Christopher Reeve. Even though he was in a chair, he had a larger-than-life presence. He was Superman in that chair. It was inspiring to see the joy with which Dana juggled the various roles in her life: caregiver of Chris, Will's mom, media personality. She was also an actress and a cabaret singer. She was talented in so many ways.

We knew that Chris's future was uncertain. But it was a shock when Dana, a nonsmoker, was diagnosed with lung cancer and died less than two years later. It was such a tragedy. I remember looking at Will, an orphan at thirteen, and thinking that he seemed so tiny to be facing such a monumental loss. I remember seeing the news coverage of Will at his mother's memorial, with his older siblings. His hands were in his pockets and his head was down and I thought, "Oh, my gosh. Is he going to be okay?"

I always have such an affinity for the interns we have at *GMA*. They often reach out to me through my assistant, Sonny. So I have a lot of one-on-one meetings with the interns in my office. I also host a lunch for the interns every year, and I truly believe that I get as much as I give to them. The college students who come to work with us every summer are so creative and so energetic. I love the sparkle of infinite possibilities in their eyes. They are such bright lights, I know I'm going to be working for at least one of my former interns someday.

So I pay attention to the new faces on the studio floor. The moment I saw Will Reeve I thought, "Wow, he's an Adonis. He's such a wonderful combination of both his parents." He is just this handsome, charismatic young man. He turned out okay. Better than okay. His parents did such a miraculous job with the limited time they had with him here on earth. Meeting him, you would not think he had any hardship in his life. Back at school that fall, Will wrote a paper about my announcement and the fact that it fell on his first day of work at GMA.

My right wrist began the summer of 2012 bare and untanned, but then I was rummaging around my room and stumbled upon an old Livestrong bracelet I had taken off after my mom died of lung cancer six years earlier and figured that it was good a time as any to put it back on. So, I began my internship at ABC's Good Morning America *on June 11th with a Livestrong bracelet, an empty briefcase and not a clue what to expect.*

I walked into the 66th Street headquarters at 9:30 a.m. that morning expecting some kind of welcoming committee or at least a place to put my stuff, but the girl who greeted me at the elevator seemed anxious and preoccupied and told me to sit in the office chair in the corner until everyone arrived.

Nobody came to talk to me, so I pulled out my phone and looked up the news, just in case anybody needed me to report a story or make a lunch reservation. It was the first thing that popped up. Breaking News. Robin Roberts, GMA co-anchor, has been diagnosed with myelodysplastic syndrome.

I absorbed what I was reading and looked up and into the newsroom, where it finally made sense. Robin had tearfully announced her diagnosis on air that morning after keeping it secret for a few months while she sorted out her new life. I looked back down at my phone to do some research on MDS, in case anybody needed me to report on it. Suddenly, everyone who has ever appeared on ABC Television hurried into the newsroom and congregated by a TV mounted on the wall. Someone cued up that morning's show and played Robin's announcement. Faces darkened and BlackBerrys appeared, and then she walked in and the phones went back into pockets and the faces tried to smile.

Robin, flanked by her cohosts and Dr. Richard Besser, stood at the front of the room underneath the televised version of herself and walked everyone through her disease and her plan. She was stoic, passionate and strong, but most everyone else lost the battle and cried. She, however, insisted that she would not. She was a fighter, supported by God and

her family and friends and statistical advan-
tages.

I got to talk with Robin when she had (in-
creasingly rare) free time, and we spoke about
how we had met years ago when she was
friends with my mom, and she told me how
she admired my mom for her strength and re-
siliency, and that she looked up to me, of all
people, for those same qualities. I told her that
I got by on luck and the love of family and
friends, and that she deserved my admiration
far more than I deserved hers. She said that
that's how we all get by.

A few days before she left to prepare for her
transplant and subsequent quarantine, Robin
handed out these multicolored bracelets. She
said the colors represent springtime and re-
growth. Wear them if you want, she said, so
you don't forget about me completely while
I'm gone. At least remember the prayer. It's
called the Prayer for Protection.

I shed a lot of tears reading Will's paper. He
embodies resilience, strength and courage.

After addressing the staff, I went to my private
office to catch my breath. Sonny, my rock, quietly stood at the door, gently telling my col-

leagues not to come in right now. I needed a moment to myself. I didn't want to check my e-mails or voice mail. I just wanted to be still. I closed my eyes and took deep, long breaths. Time seemed to stop. When I opened my eyes, Sonny was still standing guard. Thank you, Sonny.

CHAPTER 14

Assembling My Team

*W*hen Sally-Ann and I got to the treatment room later that day, we turned on the TV. It happened to be on CNN and at that very moment, they were doing a story on what I had disclosed that morning. The anchor, Alina Cho, was sensitively and thoughtfully discussing my situation. Then she began to interview Dr. Gail Roboz, the director of the leukemia program at New York–Presbyterian Hospital. Even though I wasn't her patient, Dr. Roboz explained my condition better than anyone had at that point. There was something special about her that resonated and comforted me.

The nurse preparing me for chemo spoke highly of Dr. Roboz. Although she was at a different hospital, the nurse was very familiar with her work. Sensing my interest, she asked me if I wanted Dr. Roboz's phone number. I think my response was: "Uh, yeah!" It was at that moment that I realized good doctors and nurses want only what's best for the patient.

How many medical segments had I done on GMA? You hope that it helps people. You hear from the viewers that they were sitting at the breakfast table or ironing a shirt for work and they heard something on TV that saved their lives. Then it happened to me. Television, the medium in which I work and have dedicated my life to, helped me find a great doctor when I needed her most.

I called Dr. Roboz from the car on my way home. I thanked her for her professionalism in discussing my case. She knew I was seeing another doctor at another hospital and simply said I could consult with her any time. "I'd be happy to help in any capacity," she said. She was obviously knowledgeable, but also upbeat and humorous. She was realistic about the odds, but she also made me believe that I could beat this.

Sally-Ann could tell how much better I felt after talking with Gail. I knew I wanted to switch doctors, but how? It was a real dilemma, because

I'd just started my pre-treatment consisting of five consecutive days of chemo. As the nurses explained to me, this was a different kind of chemotherapy from the treatment I'd received before. It was as if my body was a pasture and this chemo targeted just the weeds. It wouldn't affect the grass.

I needed two doctors to lead the team for my care. One would be an oncologist, someone who knew MDS inside and out and would guide me through the chemo and pre-treatment regimen that would prepare my body for the transplant. The second doctor would be a transplant specialist, someone who would supervise the care of both me and my donor, Sally-Ann, then lead me through the transplant and the critical period afterward when my body needed to rest, heal and, hopefully, accept Sally-Ann's cells.

Instinctively, I knew I wanted Gail to take over as my oncologist, but I had already started my pre-transplant treatment at one hospital; could I possibly switch midtreatment? I know this sounds silly to say, but I didn't want to hurt anyone's feelings. Maybe it's the Southerner in me. Always trying my best to be polite and considerate of others' feelings. Would it be rude to go with another doctor? Will people think I'm being a diva? That I don't trust them? That I don't believe in them?

Diane and Rich had already talked to numerous physicians across the country on my behalf. They found two doctors they were hoping I'd switch to but wanted it to be my decision. When I mentioned Gail Roboz to both of them they could barely contain their excitement. She had been their top choice, too! Rich made the initial call to my current doctor to explain my decision. The doctor could not have been more professional. He totally understood and just wanted me to be comfortable, and that was the only thing that mattered. I would complete my week of pre-treatment with him and then continue with Gail. No hard feelings.

Gail's mother and father are both renowned doctors, and they can do the hula, too (I found that out when we happened to be vacationing in Hawaii at the same time). They are very cute. She didn't tell them I was a patient, and she knew they watched *GMA*. So before Gail appeared with me on *GMA* she gave them a call. They said, "You weren't going to tell us?" As doctors, both of them are very discreet, but Gail valued my privacy.

One of the things that Gail helped me get clear

about was that although the chemo from my breast cancer treatment caused my MDS, there was no looking back and no reason to regret the choices I had made. There was no way that I would've or should've risked dying of breast cancer for a tiny risk that five years down the road I might develop a secondary disease that I couldn't even spell. Gail said, "You treat the disease you have as aggressively as possible. And, by the way, if you ever read the package insert that comes with Tylenol, I'm not sure you'd ever take one again." Her point being there are risks with everything.

Changing transplant specialists would be a little tricky. There are a number of excellent hospitals across the country specializing in stem cell transplants. I heard a lot about Fred Hutchinson Cancer Research Center in Seattle, M. D. Anderson Cancer Center in Houston and Boston's Dana-Farber Cancer Institute. Rich accompanied me to Dana-Farber for a visit. My dear friend Jel was in town and went with us, too. I was extremely impressed with Dr. Robert Soiffer and the nursing staff. I talked with other doctors, too, and I was impressed with how complimentary they were of one another. The stem cell transplant world is a tight, caring community.

They are willing to share information with one another.

I was told repeatedly, "All things being equal, choose a place closest to home." After being released from the hospital following the transplant I would still be required to stay close by for a few months. Was I willing to relocate to Seattle, Houston or Boston? Thankfully one of the best hospitals in the entire world was right across town: Memorial Sloan-Kettering Cancer Center. Problem was I had already seen a transplant specialist there. Remember the doctor with the dire outlook? But Rich and Diane were very high on Dr. Sergio Giralt, the chief adult bone marrow transplant specialist at MSKCC. He trained and worked for many years at M. D. Anderson, which is known for its cutting-edge clinical trials. I could have the best of both worlds with Sergio.

We decided to meet off campus to discuss the possibility of switching to him. We had a glass of iced tea at a sandwich shop near MSKCC. He wasn't exactly warm and fuzzy at first, but there was something about him. Unlike the previous doctor, who was so negative, Dr. Giralt said, "It's not going to be easy, and I don't know all of the facts about your case, but you're young and you're strong, and I believe that we can beat this."

He was so upbeat and so positive and so *we're going to do this*. He wanted to be part of a team. Some doctors can be egocentric and they want to be God. They're like Alec Baldwin in the movie *Malice*, in which he played a surgeon. "I don't have a God complex," he said. "I am God." Dr. Giralt was just the opposite, very humble. He told me that he would be happy to be on my team, but I—as the patient—was the team captain. His humility and spirituality really meant a lot to me.

Again, Diane and Rich proved essential in helping me switch doctors. I was hesitant. I thought, "These are the ones I picked, I can't change my mind now." Rich and Diane both said, "Uh, yeah, you can." Dr. Giralt told me to take my time and think about it. It was an important decision. I was still a few months away from my body even being ready for the transplant.

It turns out that transplant is such a cutting-edge field that doctors are less proprietary about patients and information. Dr. Giralt was very familiar with Gail and had no problem at all working with a doctor from a different hospital. I felt like I was ordering à la carte off the menu: transplant specialist from Memorial Sloan-Kettering, oncologist from New York–Presbyterian/

Weill Cornell. Fortunately, both were covered in my medical plan.

I thought about it for a few days, talked it over with Amber and my family and decided: Why wouldn't I want the head of transplants at MSKCC? Once again, Rich made the initial call to my current transplant specialist and it went okay. Just okay. So I wasn't exactly surprised when this doctor called me. Let's just leave it at this: We had an awkward exchange, which confirmed to me that I had made the right decision to go with Sergio.

I was having to deal with all of this as many TV news organizations and magazines were dissecting my decision to go public. Like I had a choice? Sure, I could have just disappeared from national TV for six months after being in people's homes every morning for more than a decade. Come on. There's an intimacy to morning television. Viewers are inviting you to the breakfast table and into their bedrooms. They feel like you're a part of their families, and we feel the same way about them. What a privilege, and for that, I thank my lucky stars all the time.

The next day, I sat in my dressing room and had my hair done. Or as I like to say, "getting my hair did." For some reason, Josh Elliott, our news anchor, gets a big kick out of this weekly ritual. One time he tweeted a photo of the two of us with my hair wrapped under a plastic cap. His followers thought it was a hoot. I loved it when a few black women joked with Josh, reminding him that: *You don't mess with a sister on Hair Did Day!*

Hair Did Day was always a good time for Sam Champion and me to grab some alone time, and I looked forward to when it was just the two of us, talking and catching up. The reaction to my announcement was so immediate: Every hour of the day, there were hundreds of e-mails, Facebook messages and tweets. It was as if a flash mob of viewers and *GMA* fans assembled out of nowhere and were singing and dancing their hearts out, letting me know that they had my back. Sam encouraged me to take it all in. He said: "The love you give all the time is rushing back to you." He was so right. The love that I felt from what quickly became known as #TeamRobin gave me a strength that I'd never felt before. I want you, the readers and *GMA* viewers, to know that when I needed it most, you gave me courage and filled my tremling heart.

CHAPTER 15

Eyes on the Prize

You might think that when you are preparing for something as big as a bone marrow transplant that time might slow down so you can sit with the enormity of all that has been placed on your plate and all that looms ahead. But here's the thing about fighting for your life: You have to move like lightning.

It helped that as a college basketball player, I racked up career highs of more than a thousand points and a thousand rebounds. My teammate Bugs joked that she missed shots on purpose so I could grab the rebound. I prided myself on being a complete player, doing my best to excel on offense and defense. I'm comfortable with a lot of things coming at me at once, and while my athletic background did not prevent me from being diagnosed with cancer or MDS, it did give me the skills to fight whatever challenges I've had to face.

I worked hard as an athlete, and that gave me faith in my ability to handle any situation on the court, no matter how big or strong my opponent was. When fear knocks, let faith answer the door. Just imagine that for a moment. Fear knocks on your door, and when it opens faith is standing there. Trust me, fear will go looking for another door to knock on.

What I appreciated about my team of doctors is that we were all "eyes on the prize." Is a cure on the table? Yes, it is. What do we need to do to get there? Well, we need to quickly and efficiently line up a donor; and we were so incredibly lucky and blessed to have sister Sally: a sibling donor who—thank the Lord—was not only wonderfully healthy but also willing. There is not a second of the day when I take Sally-Ann's consent in this process for granted. She was in no way under any obligation to say yes. And if she had said no, for whatever reason, you wouldn't have been reading about it in a book. There would have been no television footage of me saying, "Sister Sally was a perfect match, but she was too afraid of the process to go through with it." I would've respected her choice and her privacy. I would have then done what many have to do: pray they can find a donor on the registry.

Believe me, in the time that I've spent on the battlefields of bone marrow transplant, I've heard of many men and women whose siblings and family members either wouldn't get tested or wouldn't go through with the process when it was discovered they were a match. Happens every day. Sally-Ann gave the transplant community a huge gift by being the public face on the donor side, by saying, "I will step up to the plate, I will see what my stem cells can do and I will testify to how relatively painless donating life-giving stem cells can be." It has been my choice to make my mess my message. The same doesn't necessarily extend to my family who I hold so dear. I am just blessed that my sister wanted to do this, and as a broadcast journalist herself, she knew the good it could do by letting the television cameras and press follow *her* journey, too. Her incredible TV station in New Orleans, WWL-TV, rallied around her. They gave her the time off of work to be there for me and with me. Her station did stories on the need for bone marrow donors and held bone marrow drives. My sister has unselfishly given to her beloved community. And when we needed that community the most, they came through for the Roberts family and countless others.

Once we found my match, the next thing the doctors said we needed to do was to put our finger in the dam and prevent my bone marrow from misbehaving or malfunctioning even more prior to the time that my body was ready to go forward with the transplant. That was why they initiated pre-treatment in June 2012, just weeks after my diagnosis.

I went into warrior mode. I knew a long medical leave was looming, so I wanted to work as much as possible while I still could. It also helped me emotionally to keep as normal a schedule as possible. That meant rise and shine at 3:45 a.m., to the studio by 5:00 a.m. After my signature drum roll we were off and running for two hours of *GMA*. I went to my normal after-show meetings munching on Greek yogurt sprinkled with almonds and cinnamon, then headed off to the hospital for a few hours of chemo. The first few days were okay, but by midweek the chemo began to take its toll. It began to get a little harder to eat, and I would begin to get weary. Fridays couldn't get here fast enough. I spent the weekends in bed recuperating. Yes, long days but also happy days, because I wasn't just living with the diagnosis; I was fighting. I had a game plan. I had hope. One of my rules to live by is: Focus on the solution, not the problem. And that was exactly what I was doing.

The amazing thing is that once I started to wear PICC covers on the show, people started sending fashionable ones to me. Who knew that these very medically necessary items came in jewel tones, leopard print and lace? I started wearing covers that color coordinated with my short-sleeved dresses, and the audience response was off the charts: Every day we got e-mails, tweets and Facebook messages from patients who also had PICC lines, family members, nurses, doctors and just regular viewers. Having the pre-treatment for the bone marrow transplant was no walk in the park, but the hundreds of PICC covers I was sent and the thousands of messages I received brightened my days.

Donna Svennevik/ABC

I don't know the name of the first viewer who sent me a designer PICC cover, they seemed to show up by the dozens—almost simultane- ously—but I want to thank all of you who saw that line in my arm and sensed that this would be a gift that I would appreciate. Because I did. Those covers made me feel like a warrior, armed for battle. I remember the moment when we chose a leopard-print PICC cover to match my camel and black sleeveless dress. I looked in the mirror and thought, *"Roar!"* Those covers made me feel so strong. And even more, they gave thousands and thousands of patients out there an image that wasn't of a weak person floundering in a hospital gown and hoping for a miracle in a sea of bad news. I know, because my team and I read every e-mail and every letter; those PICC covers made many a transplant patient feel like he or she was a warrior, too.

I wanted to be as strong as I could before the transplant. My doctors encouraged me to remain active. I'm not much of a runner, as I prefer to get my cardio done on a reclined bike, and I've enjoyed doing Pilates for several years now. There's a great studio within walking distance of my apartment. Joie runs the place, and as soon as I walk through the door and see her smiling face I am at peace. Joie and I have a lot in common. She's close to her siblings (one named Sally) and had to deal with aging parents as I did. I treasure our conversations about life. My instructors are young, vibrant and patient. I especially like working out on the reformer. The slow movement of the machine, the isolation of each muscle, reminded me that even when we are ill our bodies are incredible machines. When I leave the studio and Joie says, "See you next week," we both reply in unison, "Good Lord willing and the creek don't rise."

Sally-Ann injected herself for five days with a drug to induce the production of stem cells. She stresses that she had no side effects and adds, "I am terribly afraid of needles, but it wasn't a problem." I was there with Sally-Ann every step of the way. Some days I couldn't stop crying. I'm used to being the giver, and it was very hard but very enlightening for me to understand what it's like to be on the receiving end.

I kept asking Sally-Ann if she was scared. She said she didn't feel any fear. She always trusts that everything is going to work out as it should. Every afternoon, before we got out of the car at the treatment center, she started singing a hymn, "We need Thee. Oh, we need Thee."

* * *

Sometimes I hear a hymn and I think, "Oh, that's a sweet song." Other times, I hear a hymn and then days or weeks later, it comes back to me—like a piece of musical comfort playing in my head. On July 13, 2012—Friday the thirteenth—Mom suffered a stroke at home. She had been on the phone talking with a friend. She was in bed and suddenly the room began to spin, her vision became distorted and she knew something was wrong. She had just gotten a new cell phone and was unfamiliar with how to use it. Phone records show she tried to dial Dorothy shortly before midnight but was unsuccessful. Mom told us she then decided to just lay there and let God take her home. She wouldn't fight it. She woke up about 3 a.m. and was still here, so she decided to try calling Dorothy one more time. In complete darkness, completely disoriented, she was able to dial Dorothy's number. God wasn't ready to take her just yet. Dorothy called 911 and got to the house about the time the ambulance arrived. It was all of a sudden much more than a song: *We need Thee. Oh, we need Thee.*

Amber and I were on Fire Island that weekend. I wanted to get some rest before beginning another week of pre-treatment on Monday. Cell service out there can be very spotty. I finally checked my messages late Saturday afternoon. There was a message from Sally-Ann saying I should call Dorothy, because Mom was in the hospital. Sally-Ann didn't make it sound urgent; Mom had been hospitalized a lot that year. A couple of months earlier at her book party she had joked that after so many years of taking her medicine, she decided to stop, because apparently it wasn't working.

I called Dorothy and she told me Mom had had a stroke. What?! I wanted to get off the island and fly right home to Mississippi, but Dorothy told me to wait. Mom had transient ischemic attacks, or TIAs, before; these are temporary mini strokes. But the doctors weren't sure if this was the same thing. It seemed worse this time. Her vision was impaired, she couldn't swallow and she had difficulty speaking.

Sunday morning, Mom was doing better, and she told my sisters and brother to get out of her hospital room and go to our church. I was incredibly relieved. It appeared Mom was going to rally yet again. My siblings insisted it was important for me to have my week of treatment and wait until the weekend to go home and see Mom.

* * *

That month, Ben Sherwood held a company-wide bone marrow drive. Many of my colleagues showed up and got their cheeks swabbed. More than two hundred ABC staffers joined the registry. Another five hundred joined online. Within weeks, a few received calls that they were possible matches. I was so proud of my amazing team, and I said a silent prayer for every patient waiting to receive the news that I had gotten the day the phone rang and I learned that Sally-Ann was my match.

While Sally-Ann was taking trips to New York, preparing for her cells to be harvested, Dorothy was back home caring for Mother. After my week of treatment, I traveled to Mississippi every weekend to be with Mom. Again and again, Dorothy, Sally-Ann and I marveled at how upside down our world would have been if Dorothy, who lives just minutes away from Mom—as opposed to Sally-Ann, who lives in another state—had been my match.

Oh, my goodness, the chaos that would have ensued. Anyone who has ever cared for an aging parent knows the complexity of the arrangements. Mom's health was failing, but she was still the boss. And let's be clear, she was not an easy boss. She wanted to go home after being released from the hospital, but we as a family had thought, "Well, she needs to go to a rehab facility." Earlier in the year, she had been to a wonderful nursing center that had a rehab unit, and we thought that after the stroke the nursing center would be the best place for her to return. She had such terrific results there before and loved the residents and staff. But this time, Mom wanted no part of that. This time she wanted to go directly home from the hospital.

It was helpful that we had discussions about this when Mom was healthier. I know it's not easy to have end-of-life conversations with our parents. Momma had a way of finding the humor in it. She always thought she would pass away before my father. One day she asked me and my sisters to come by the house. She then instructed us to point out the pieces of furniture and family heirlooms we wanted when she died. When we asked her why in the world she was asking us to do this now, she replied: "I know your father. He can't be alone. When I die he'll be remarried within a year, and I don't want her [his new wife] to get anything."

Momma's humor was also on display when Dorothy was selected to be the one to make decisions for her if she was incapacitated. Dorothy took that responsibility seriously and began to ask Momma questions. Did she want to be put on life support? No. What about CPR? Momma exclaimed: "Oh, mercy, give me a chance!"

On one particular day, Dorothy went to see her in the hospital, and knowing that there would definitely be some bullets aimed at the messenger, my sweet sister sent a social worker in there to tell Mom that the nursing center was what the siblings had decided: We didn't want her to reside there permanently, just to continue her rehab until she was strong enough to go home. We asked the social worker to explain to our mother that she had stopped making progress in the hospital rehab and they were going to discharge her. A lot of people don't know that a hospital won't just keep you if they feel you are ready to do rehab outside of the hospital. But Mom saw right through the social worker, and she ordered her to send Dorothy in.

Dorothy called me later and said the only word she could use to describe the look on Mother's face was "Whoa!"

She looked at Dorothy and said, "I want to go home."

Dorothy was so rattled by the tone and force of her voice: "Oh, my goodness. Mom, do you mean your earthly home or do you mean your heavenly home?"

Mom would often say stuff like, "I want to go home," meaning heaven.

But Mother clarified herself; she said, "I want to go to my house in the Pass."

Dorothy tried to reason with her, "Well, Mom, you know, the doctors really feel like you need to have more care, and I just don't know how that'll work."

As hard as it was for me to be dealing with pre-treatment and the stress of caring for an aging parent long-distance, Dorothy was on the front lines.

Mom said, "You can do it. You can get people to help you."

So it was decided. My siblings and I had met and planned, spoken to doctors and looked at the medical facts. But at the end of the day, Lucimarian Roberts was the mother, and it was her life. We could not put her in the facility against her will.

By the time Dorothy called me that evening, she was very upset and very emotional, because she knew what it meant. She was going to have to take time off from work to get Mother situated. She was going to have to find and manage home health-care aides. Fortunately, in recent years Mom had been using a wonderful service called Home Instead. Henrietta was Mom's primary caregiver from Home Instead. She would run errands with Mom, take her to doctor appointments and do light housework. But Mom's condition now was more than Henrietta could manage. We also needed hospice care.

Once again, Dorothy's life was not going to be her own. Imagine if on top of all that, she was having to fly to New York to do preharvesting treatments for me? As a child, in church, I had heard again and again that God does not give us more than we can bear. Watching Dorothy be not only a daughter to our mother, but also her health-care manager and her eyes, ears and hands as each of those things failed, I knew that there was a reason that Sally-Ann was my match.

CHAPTER 16

Venice

I've always enjoyed attending the V Wine Celebration in Napa. It's a major fund-raiser for the
V Foundation for Cancer Research, founded by
legendary basketball coach Jim Valvano and
ESPN. Jim Valvano was the first to receive the
Arthur Ashe Award at the ESPYs, and he died
just eight weeks after receiving the award in
1993. As a cancer patient, Jim witnessed how
slowly scientific breakthroughs made their way to
the bedsides of patients. As a coach, he knew the
power of investing in young, brilliant talent. The
V Foundation has raised more than $100 million
in the two decades since Jim's death, and that
money has gone directly to early-career physicians and scientists at the leading cancer centers
all around the country.

The wine event is a lively gala and auction that is held at one of Napa's finest wineries and is the foundation's major fund-raiser. As such, it holds a special place in my heart. I so wanted to be there, as in years past, but I just wasn't up to traveling cross-country. Since I couldn't be there in person I sent a video. I talked about what it meant for me to receive the same honor as Jim at the ESPYs. That night in 1993, in establishing the V Foundation for Cancer Research, Jim said: "We need your help. I need your help. We need money for research. It may not save my life. It may save my children's. It may save someone you love." In the video I then said, "I couldn't imagine twenty years after Jimmy V's speech that mine would be one of the lives saved. Because of everyone who responded to his challenge, because of all the donations, research and support." Thinking of Jim, I went on to say: "Now I need your help for MDS research." That night they raised $1.2 million in my honor strictly for two grants for MDS research. Talk about make your mess your message.

It was around this time that my friend Jo came up with the idea of the Prayer for Protection bracelet. It was simply a friend saying, "We've got to do something. What can we do?" It was simply

Jo going, "What can I do? I want Robin to know that we love her, and that we're thinking of her." She came up with the idea of putting "Light, Love, Power, Presence," the key words from the Prayer for Protection, on a bracelet, knowing that these words are so important to me. The prayer my mom had taught me as a small child.

She chose the bright springtime colors of MDS, colors that signify the rebirth that my transplant would bring, and sent it to me. It was a total and wonderful surprise. Passing it around among a few friends, and it's our little thing. I gave it to my colleagues on the set, and then many watching said, "I want one!" We were like, "Oh, my goodness!" and we teamed up with Be the Match, the bone marrow registry. A simple gesture of love that Jo designed has sold over four hundred thousand bracelets, with every last cent going to Be the Match. So much good from a friend just saying, "What can I do?"

For many months I had plans to help my friend Kim celebrate her fiftieth birthday in Italy. Tuscany, to be exact. The trip was scheduled for mid-August. When I was diagnosed that spring, my doctors asked if I had anything pressing coming up. I told them I had my heart set on going to Italy in August. Kim was there for my fiftieth, and I wanted to be there for hers. It also gave me a goal. If I could be well enough to travel to Italy, then I'd know I had the strength to endure a transplant. At first Gail was a little more onboard with the plan than Sergio. Both of my doctors agreed to do their best to schedule my treatment so I would be in peak condition for the transplant, and for Italy. They couldn't make any guarantees. It's not exactly something you can time to the precise moment. They asked me to trust them, and I did. I promised them that if the time came and they felt it would do more harm than good to travel, I would listen to them. Trust is a two-way street.

I struggled with going ahead with my plans or spending that time with Mom in the hospital. One day it looked as if she would be discharged, and the next day it would be anyone's guess. As I said, Mom was still the boss. She would often kick us out of her hospital room; she was fiercely independent, not wanting to be a burden. As if she ever could be. In the end, my doctors and my siblings felt that with just weeks to go before transplant that it would be a psychological boost for me to get away. What I was about to face was as much mental as it was physical.

Amber and I flew to Florence and, along with a group of Kim's nearest and dearest, stayed in an old farmhouse in Tuscany. Rome was just a few hours away by car, so one day Amber and I decided to visit the Vatican. My longtime friend Gayle King told me about a wonderful tour guide, Angelo. He was able to get us special access to the Vatican. We spent time in the Pope's private chapel, where he prays before meeting the masses. I kneeled at the altar and said a prayer. Not for myself but for all the people who had been praying for me and for my mother. I felt plenty of prayers were already being said for me. It was a calming moment that I would later reflect back on, posttransplant, when I was in isolation.

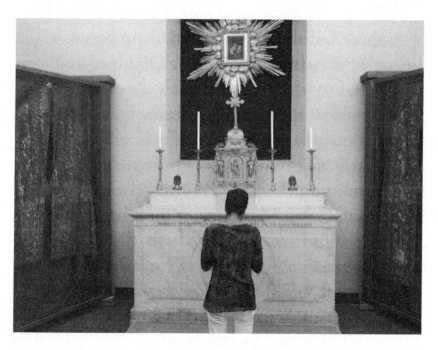

I also enjoyed traveling to Venice. I had never been there before. What a spectacular and special city. Walking out of the train station and seeing the canals, the gondolas, wow! We took a water taxi to a neighboring island, Burano. It's called the colored island of lace. You should see the bright-colored houses, balconies with multicolored flowers. Side streets are filled with elderly women embroidering the most delicate lace. Such a tranquil, calm setting. Angelo was able to get us a lunch reservation at Trattoria al Gatto Nero. It was the most delicious Italian meal I have ever eaten. The wine was flowing, and the pasta, the fresh local fish and the dessert were perfect. Everyone in the group was wearing the bracelets that Jo had designed. I close my eyes and I'm there again. Serenity now.

It meant so much for me to be there for Kim. Fiftieth-birthday celebrations have become such a rite of passage. Sure, sand is draining from the hourglass, but at fifty you're still young enough to try new things.

When I was diagnosed with an aggressive form of breast cancer at the age of forty-six, I wasn't sure I'd see my fiftieth. Grateful that I did get there, at first I planned this big, elaborate party. I knew I wanted to celebrate on an island. I decided on Vieques, an island-municipality of Puerto Rico. A brand-new hotel was opening just in time for my birthday. Amber's good friend Jason is a noted event planner. (He escorted her to the Oscars while I was working.) We met, and he had a big board full of details and how people were going to fly in and how I was going to have all these fancy presents waiting for them. It just kept mushrooming. The guest list was out of control. Finally I said, "I'm sorry, this is a lovely idea, but it's not me. I just want my family and closest friends, all I really want is a candlelight dinner on the beach. I don't need to do this—who am I trying to impress with this party?" That's the great thing about turning fifty. You start to truly tap into your authentic self.

So instead we found a place in Turks and Caicos, a villa that had all these different rooms and different bungalows. It was like a small compound. And with me were just the people who I wanted there most. We had so much fun. Just being together. Shortly after returning from the trip I was going to dance on *GMA* with Maks Chmerkovskiy from *Dancing with the Stars*. I had been rehearsing with his brother Val for weeks back in New York at their SoHo studio. Before I left on the trip, Val made me a video of our routine so I could continue to learn all the steps. My dance floor in Turks was the sandy beach. One two, cha cha cha.

Amber remembered my saying that all I wanted for my fiftieth was to have dinner on the beach. That was the main thing. Well, it was the day of my birthday celebration. We were all walking on the beach from our villa to the hotel restaurant for lunch. On the beach I saw some workers laying down what seemed to be a dance floor on the beach. It was an overcast day, and we were all bummed about the weather. I remember asking everyone: What do you think that dance floor is for? My friend Julie quickly replied: "Oh, it's probably for a wedding."

We went off to lunch, and when it was time for my party it began to rain. The hotel staff members came in golf carts and they took us up to a different villa, and it was beautiful. Colorful balloons and birthday banners. I was wondering why Amber looked so sad, and I said, "What's wrong? This is gorgeous. Thank you, honey, this is wonderful." She said, "No, that dance floor on the beach...that was for *you*. We were having a party on the beach, but it rained." How sweet was that? She remembered that was all that I wanted—to have dinner and dance with my friends on the beach.

It was great to be out on the beautiful water during our trip. Amber, Lois Ann, Cathy, Scarlett, Linda, Julie, Crystal, Carol, Beth, Bert and I chartered a boat one afternoon. Jel gets seasick, so Jo and Kim stayed on shore with her and went shopping. We had been sailing for a while enjoying rum drinks the crew provided. Bert noticed we were kind of circling, not venturing far from the harbor. Crystal, one of Amber's closest friends, knows a lot about boats. She knew something was up, too. Crystal went up to the captain and he admitted they really didn't have a license!

I guess he thought, "Let's get them liquored up on cheap local rum and they'll never know the difference." I have to say, we were happy campers. Jel, Jo and Kim were waiting for us on the dock when we returned. They said we were quite a sight. I'm sure we were.

My favorite part of the trip to Turks and Caicos was our breakfast together every morning. Just sitting around, talking, laughing, planning our day. My dear friends are scattered all around the country, from Maine to California. Our time together is precious. We don't buy each other fancy gifts. We prefer to simply be together and make memories.

Celebrating Kim's fiftieth in Italy was such a powerful reminder of my own fiftieth birthday in Turks and Caicos. I was so happy that I was able to time my pre-transplant treatment in a way that enabled me to be with my friend on her special day. At the same time, there was a kind of emotional wall that I hit toward the end of my trip to Italy. The entire summer I'd gone through pre-treatment, kept my spirits up and my body moving, because I wanted to go to Italy with my friends. Now that I'd reached that goal, it was time to go back and start the MDS battle in earnest. There was the bone marrow transplant waiting for me and all the recovery that entailed: six months off of the air, while Sally-Ann's cells would—best-case scenario—find their way into the bone marrow and start making healthy red blood cells, white blood cells and platelets.

I remember reading an excerpt from Pat Summitt's book in *People* magazine that was the very definition of the right words at the right time: "I'm interested to see where a combination of faith and science will take me.... With or without this diagnosis, I was going to experience diminishment. We all do. I know God doesn't take things away to be cruel.... He takes things away to lighten us. He takes things away so we can fly."

I thought of Pat Summitt's words as I flew back from Italy and prepared myself to face all that lay ahead. I reminded myself that my load was being lightened. Fly, Robin, Fly.

Mom

*W*hile I was returning from Italy, Dorothy got a call that Mom was in a semi-coma. The oxygen wasn't releasing from her body so she went into what they call a carbon monoxide coma. Dorothy was so scared, because in the last conversation she'd had with Mom, Mom was still afraid that we were going to place her in the nursing center. Dorothy stood at her bedside at the hospital, telling her over and over again, "Mom, we're gonna take you home. We're gonna take you home. You said you didn't want to be here and we're gonna take you home."

When Mom finally regained consciousness, she was in a state of delirium. The doctors later told us that this was because Mom was hallucinating. Dorothy spent the entire night in Mom's hospital room, and Mom did not sleep at all. Dorothy begged the hospital attendants to give Mother something to help her sleep. Once she'd had some rest, they released her, and Dorothy took her home.

They say when it rains, it pours. On the Gulf Coast, as we know all too well, sometimes when it rains, it storms. Dorothy and her daughters, Jessica and Lauren, were running back and forth to the house, caring for Mom, when Hurricane Isaac rolled up to the Coast.

I could hear the strain in Dorothy's voice. She had taken a leave from work to care for Mom, and she was at home with our mother from seven in the morning until seven at night. At 7 p.m., a hospice nurse would arrive, and Dorothy would get some sleep. Mom came home with a feeding tube and a whole array of medicines that needed to be administered, and symptoms that needed to be monitored. Dorothy had a little notebook that she carried around with questions she had for Mom's doctors and all of their responses and instructions. I could look at that little notebook and see how tightly she clenched it; in between the names of medicines I'd never heard of, medical symptoms that none of us could pronounce, there was all this worry and fear and love that was scribbled onto every page.

I kept telling Dorothy, "You've got to get more help. You've got to get more help." And I know that she was concerned about the cost. Anyone who has cared for an aging parent knows how costly it can be. Medicare only pays so much, and when you want to stay in your own home, as Momma did, all of that attendant care? That's on you—and the family. Mom has always been fiercely independent. Never asking or wanting her children to provide for her. Dorothy knew I had the resources to chip in more, but she was resistant to me paying more than what she saw as my fair share. But when your mother is so ill and there is one sibling who is doing the majority of the on-the-ground legwork, it's not about splitting the bill. I thanked the good Lord in heaven when Dorothy finally let me hire some more care and ease, even a little, the burden she had so generously and lovingly taken on.

On August 28, 2012, I was with Sally-Ann and her husband, Ron, at Memorial Sloan-Kettering as she prepared to donate her stem cells. At the same time Hurricane Isaac was preparing to make landfall on the Gulf Coast. Dorothy and her girls were with Mom and they had already, wisely, had a generator set up at the house in case they lost power.

Sally-Ann was in a hospital bed, watching her New Orleans TV station on her laptop. Anyone who's ever been to New Orleans knows that my sister is the Oprah of her market, and the love that the good people of N'awlins have for my big sister is rivaled only by the love she feels for them. Sally-Ann is always watching her local station, even when she's far away from home. For her, it's like keeping track of her people; the whole city is her extended family.

I watched in awe as the apheresis machine recycled blood from her body, removing the stem cells into a pouch with my name on it. I remember just staring at the bag, knowing how many in my situation would give anything to see a bag of lifesaving stem cells with their name on it. It took two days for Sally-Ann to have her cells harvested, and this was day two. All I could do was cry. Sally-Ann insisted she wasn't in any pain, and she didn't appear to be, but I was still a basket case witnessing such a selfless act.

My dear friends Lois Ann and Cathy had traveled from the West Coast to spend time with me before my upcoming transplant. Although Lois Ann lives on the West Coast, she is a true Southern belle. She was a sorority girl at the University of Alabama. Roll Tide! A mutual friend introduced us in the early 1990s. We've been thick as thieves ever since.

Lois Ann and Cathy wanted to be in the *GMA* audience for my last show, which was supposed to be that Friday. Wednesday night we went to dinner at one of my favorite neighborhood restaurants, Loi, which had delicious Greek dishes. We talked about the wonderful vacations we had taken together and the ones we would take in the future. Before dessert, everyone went to the restroom, so I decided to check my messages.

Dorothy had left me a voice mail that Mom wanted to talk to me. I was so excited, because Mom's stroke had made it difficult for her to speak. My excitement was short-lived when I returned Dorothy's call. Hurricane Isaac made it impossible for the hospice nurses to make it to the house. Dorothy knew Mom had suddenly taken a turn for the worse, and over the phone described Mom's condition to the nurse. The nurse said to Dorothy: "If there's anything you want to say to your mom you should do it tonight." I couldn't believe what I was hearing. I immediately told Dorothy that Sally-Ann and I would get home as soon as we could.

When I returned to my apartment, Sally-Ann was sitting at the window, having her quiet time. Ever since my sister was a little girl, you could find her upstairs in her room, sitting in a rocking chair, sometimes doing a crossword puzzle, sometimes not. The crossword puzzle was a legacy from Dad. He loved them; my brother Butch does, too. But the sitting and the rocking, that's all Sally-Ann. And I could see that she wasn't absorbing the full force of Dorothy's news, she was so still, so silent, just staring out the window. I said, "Oh, Sally-Ann, I'm sorry to do this to you, but, do you understand what our sister is saying? Our mother is on her journey home."

Back home in the Pass, Dorothy had reached out to a tight circle of friends with the news that the end might be near. The thing about living in a small town, news travels fast. While the Sisters Three, as we call ourselves, and Butch were trying to absorb the news, care for Mom, figure out what we wanted and needed to say to her, the phone was ringing off the hook. Mom had sooooo many people who felt they were like family. She touched their lives, and they wanted to know how she was doing, could they come see her, what could they do for her in the time that was left. It was all too much to bear. The doctors said Mother was transitioning, which sounds so peaceful. But it felt like chaos all around.

When the hospice people got to the house, they asked Dorothy, "Have you eaten since morning?" She wasn't sure. Then they asked, "Have you showered?" And my niece was so tickled that in the midst of it all, Dorothy was offended. She asked, "Do I stink or something?" But realizing that it had been a while since her last shower, the hospice workers took over and Dorothy got showered.

The next morning they got Mom cleaned up, gave her her medicine and fed her. It actually seemed like she was doing okay. There was a moment when we all thought, "She's going to do what she always does. She's going to rally."

Momma was still having trouble communicating, but she managed to let my niece Lauren know that she wanted to go out to the sunroom. Lauren's fiancé, Brian, picked her up, put her in the wheelchair and they took her out. The rain was still coming down but it was, everyone remembers, oddly peaceful. Mom looked at pictures and, in particular, paused at a picture of Harneitha.

Harneitha was Mom's best friend, and she perished in Katrina. Harneitha and her husband,

Dr. Maxey, decided to ride out the storm in their home in Long Beach. Dr. Maxey had health issues that made it difficult to evacuate. One of their sons stayed with them in the house. Tragically, the Maxeys were literally swept from their home in the raging floodwaters. Miraculously, their son survived. Mom managed to ask Lauren to tell her the date. It was August 29, the day that Katrina hit. It was also the day her dear friends died. My mother might have rallied, but I think by pulling out Harneitha's picture, by reminding us of the date, she wanted to send a message: Gather near, children, the clock is ticking.

The night before, on my frantic walk home from the restaurant, I called my executive producer, Tom Cibrowski. I told him about my conversation with Dorothy. I needed my last show to be the next day, Thursday, instead of Friday, as we had originally planned. I explained to Tom that I could do one more show, but then I needed to fly back home to Mississippi right after. I knew that the producers had a lot planned for my final show, but I needed to get home. Tom was totally understanding and sympathetic.

Early the next morning as I was preparing to leave for my final show, Sally-Ann said: "Are you sure we should try and go? The airports are still closed because of the storm; it could be dangerous. Mom always rallies."

I looked her square in the eyes and said, "Sister, dear, I'm going home. If you want to hitch a ride, fine. If not, I'll go by myself."

Honestly, I don't remember much about my final *GMA*. I do recall saying at the beginning of the show that tomorrow was supposed to be my last day but things had changed and I needed to get home to Mississippi. I didn't go into any more detail, because Mom became very private after suffering her stroke in July. She didn't want anyone outside of the family and close friends to know of her declining condition. Such a proud woman, my mom. During the show we had a story about my journey to that point. Revealing my diagnosis in June, all the doctor appointments and showing Sally-Ann's stem cells being collected. Leading into the piece I shared one of my favorite quotes: "Life provides losses and heartbreak for all of us—but the greatest tragedy is to have the experience and miss the meaning." I was determined not to miss the meaning of what I was experiencing and to share it in the hope of helping others.

My sister joined me in the studio after the piece aired. Many were just as concerned and curious about Sally-Ann...was she in any pain? Remember, she had just gone through two days of having her stem cells harvested. Sally-Ann smiled brightly, as she always does. Her daughter, Judith, would later tell her: "So many people, Mom, wonder what their purpose is in life, and now you know your purpose. Your purpose is to give bone marrow to your sister Robin. Every cell in your body is about the business of giving your sister new life. How beautiful is that?"

Martina McBride was also part of my final show before medical leave. I've gotten to know Martina and her husband, John, over the years. I had the pleasure of being in her music video for her hit song "I'm Gonna Love You Through It." It's a beautiful song about family and friends being there for a loved one going through cancer. Martina was on tour but made a detour to be with us that morning in New York and sing that inspirational song. What a dear friend. It was the first time I saw Sally-Ann break down in tears. Martina was singing "I'm gonna love you through it" and Sally-Ann just lost it. Then everyone in the studio started crying, too. I joked, "You guys have to stop crying, you're supposed to be comforting me!" But I meant it when I hugged Sally-Ann and said, "Come here, sister, it's gonna be okay. I'm gonna love you through it, too."

Many colleagues were in the studio that morning holding #TEAMROBIN signs. We all should be so blessed to feel the love that I did that morning. Humbling. My last words were: "To my GMA family, my family there at home, I love you and I'll see you soon." I then defiantly pumped my fist. While I believed I'd be back in the mix, deep down inside I just didn't know. When the cameras stopped rolling, I stood and told everyone in the studio how much I loved them. How proud I was of them. To keep on keepin' on in my absence.

My thoughts were never far from Momma. Before we could fly home that Thursday, Sally-Ann had to be checked out by Dr. Giralt. He examined her, she was fine, and he also went over options with us. Dr. Giralt was aware we were going home to be with Mom, and I didn't know how long I would be there. Sally-Ann's freshly harvested stem cells had to be implanted within a certain time frame. It was Thursday, and I was scheduled to be admitted into the hospital on Monday. Dr. Giralt understood my only concern was Momma. My transplant would have to wait.

He also gave Sally-Ann a gift. She was consumed with worry about her stem cells. Would my body accept them? Would she be to blame if it didn't? Dr. Giralt assured my sister: "You have done everything we have asked of you. If the transplant is not successful, you need to know it's not your fault." His caring, thoughtful words were another confirmation I had made the right choice in switching to him.

We got word that the airport down home had just reopened, so we headed to the plane. In the car I sent Dorothy a message that we were on our way! She sent a text that Mom was resting comfortably and also said: "Our dear mother is on her journey home." I showed Sally-Ann the text, and she just stared out the window in disbelief. We were in constant prayer that we would make it home in time.

It seemed as if the flight to Gulfport took forever. A driver met us at the airport and had to maneuver around downed power lines and trees. Streets were flooded, forcing us to turn around several times. It was an eerie reminder of when I flew home to find my family after Hurricane Katrina.

When we arrived home late that afternoon, Momma did not take her eyes off of me. The stroke made it difficult for her to speak but she was communicating with me through her compassionate eyes. Her voice, when she could summon it, was softer than a whisper. It was as if she waited to make sure that we would be okay. She waited to see that Sally-Ann was okay after having millions of her stem cells harvested. And she waited to know that I had what I needed, that her baby girl was going to be all right.

The house was full of activity. Dorothy; her daughters, Jessica and Lauren; Lauren's young son, Ryan; Sally-Ann; Ron and hospice nurses. Sweet, spiritual music was playing softly in Mom's room on her boom box. Mom's doctor made a house call and examined her. He said he had no idea how long Mom had. She recognized him and even joked with him. She was receiving nutrition through a feeding tube since the stroke left her unable to swallow.

After the doctor's visit we all gathered in the living room, where for decades we had celebrated Christmases together as a family. Mom's spirits were always lifted when she heard laughter in our home. She came to understand that having a sense of humor offset the challenges of growing old. She told Missy, her confidante and cowriter: "I often think that humor may be God's gift to those of us in late life, a salve for challenging moments."

At this moment it was challenging to find anything to laugh about. I was scheduled to be admitted into the hospital back in New York in four days. But how could I leave Momma? And if I went back to New York and began the transplant process, I would not be able to travel back home if she passed away. Knowing that was unbearable. My sisters insisted Mom would not want me to jeopardize my health by delaying my transplant. I thought of Sally-Ann's stem cells in the freezer waiting for me. We decided we would take it one day at a time.

Everyone was exhausted. Sally-Ann, still wearing a bandage from her procedure, had been away from her home in New Orleans for a week. Dorothy had not left Mom's side since she brought her home from the rehab center more than two weeks ago. Butch, who spent a lot of time with Momma in the hospital, is a schoolteacher in Houston. He was going to drive to the Pass after school on Friday. So Sally-Ann and Ron decided to go on to New Orleans, which is only about an hour from Mom's house. And Dorothy and her girls would go home, too, to Long Beach, only twenty minutes from Mom. I would stay with Mom, and we would all gather again in the morning.

I was emotionally and physically spent. The house seemed so quiet, except for the music coming from Mom's room. Eating was out of the question; my appetite was nonexistent. Whenever I came home Mom would always have my favorite dinner waiting for me. When I was younger it was her fall-off-the-bone barbecue spare ribs and potato salad. But lately it was Mom's pork chops, cabbage and fried corn bread. She always added sliced tomatoes and cucumbers with Italian dressing. I think the cast-iron pot she cooked the cabbage in is older than I am. Before we would even finish dinner she would already ask me what I wanted for breakfast. Her fried apples were simple and delicious: a little butter, cinnamon and nutmeg and a lot of love. Unfortunately, I did not inherit Mom's knack for cooking. The best thing I can make is...a dinner reservation.

That evening I went into Mom's room. The gospel music was still playing softly. The night attendant, Jeanette, had just fed Mom, and she was resting comfortably. Jeanette told me that Mom usually became very coherent in the middle of the night and they would talk. I told her if that happened tonight to please wake me if I was sleeping. I kissed Mom on her cheek and

My parents at a
formal military
event. I remember
anxiously waiting
for them at home
to hear all about
their night.

ROBIN ROBERTS
PERSONAL COLLECTION

My daddy could
always make me smile.

ROBIN ROBERTS PERSONAL
COLLECTION

Who knew this
little six-year-old
would grow up
to be a lifetime
member of the Girl
Scouts?

ROBIN ROBERTS
PERSONAL COLLECTION

Such a treat when Mom and Dad came to visit me in New York. Loved our dinners together. ROBIN ROBERTS PERSONAL COLLECTION

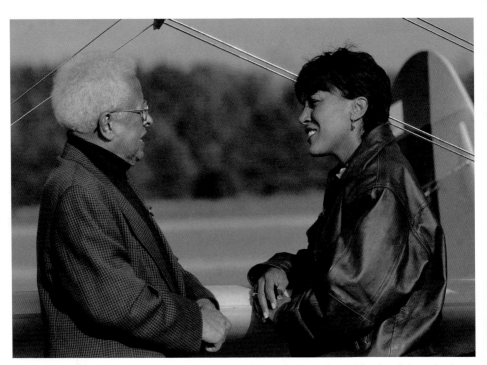

With my dad in Tuskegee, Alabama, before I flew a plane like he did with the Tuskegee Airmen, November 2003. JAMIE MARTIN/ABC

Momma had a great time on the set of *The View*, May 2012.

DIANDRE TRISTAN

Special to have Mom's oldest friend, Mrs. Middleton, at Momma's homegoing, Pass Christian, Mississippi, September 2012.

ROBIN ROBERTS PERSONAL COLLECTION

My siblings and I are proud to attend events honoring our father and his fellow Tuskegee Airmen, D'Iberville, Mississippi, November 2013.

ROBIN ROBERTS PERSONAL COLLECTION

On the *GMA* set in 2005 with fellow co-anchors Charlie Gibson and Diane Sawyer. What a privilege to learn from the best.   IDA MAE ASTUTE/ABC

Dancing always lifts my spirits. Getting my groove on with Lara Spencer and Tom Cibrowski.

IDA MAE ASTUTE/ABC

April 19, 2012: Sam, Josh, Lara, George and me celebrating *GMA* becoming #1. Later this same day I received my MDS diagnosis.

Celebrating with Sam at the *GMA* rooftop victory party, April 19, 2012.

Diane and Sally-Ann after I made my MDS diagnosis public on *GMA*, June 11, 2012. IDA MAE ASTUTE/ABC

With friends and colleagues in my apartment at the rager I threw the night before I was admitted into the hospital, September 9, 2012.

So happy when I was finally able to eat again several days after the transplant. Soup's on! ROBIN ROBERTS PERSONAL COLLECTION

My sisters got a big kick out of seeing my dear friends Deborah Roberts and Gayle King. ROBIN ROBERTS PERSONAL COLLECTION

Brightened my day when Sam and Josh came to visit me. I still wear the froggy slippers at home.

ROBIN ROBERTS PERSONAL COLLECTION

Jo and Kim made several trips from Maine to see me in the hospital.

ROBIN ROBERTS PERSONAL COLLECTION

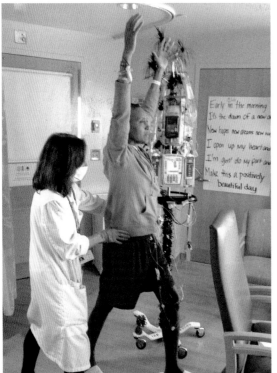

When I could, I did yoga in the hospital.

NAMASTE. ROBIN ROBERTS PERSONAL COLLECTION

Saying good-bye and thank you to the nurses and staff at MSKCC before heading home after thirty days. There is no *I* in *TEAM*. COURTESY MSKCC

This was all I could think about when I was in the hospital for a month. Home sweet home, October 9, 2013.

ROBIN ROBERTS PERSONAL COLLECTION

Hearing Mandisa sing "Stronger" on *GMA* brought Dorothy to tears.

HEIDI GUTMAN/ABC

Michael Strahan feeding me birthday cake on the one-year anniversary of my transplant, September 20, 2013. IDA MAE ASTUTE/ABC

My trusty assistant, Sonny Mullen, at my one-year "birthday" party, September 20, 2013. IDA MAE ASTUTE/ABC

September 20, 2013: pointing skyward like sister Sally. Thank you, Lord!
IDA MAE ASTUTE/ABC

Visiting Pat Summitt at her home in Knoxville, Tennessee. Her dogs are never far from her side. JON LEMAY/ABC

One of the highlights of returning to *GMA*, singing the song I co-wrote with India Arie. It certainly was "A Beautiful Day." IDA MAE ASTUTE/ABC

Amber and I headed to my fiftieth birthday celebration in Turks and Caicos, November 2010. LOIS ANN PORTER

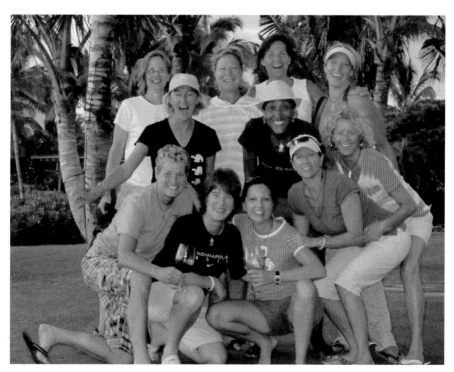

Maui, August 2013, with the friends who loved me through it: (front row) Beth, Carol, Linda, Scarlett; (second row) Cathy, me, Jo; (last row) Julie, Kim, Lois Ann, Amber. CAROL STIFF

Amber with her beloved Frances just days before she went to doggy heaven, November 2013.

Couldn't take my eyes off of KJ when she finally returned home on my one hundredth day from transplant, December 29, 2012.

Thankful to be back at the Oscars in 2013 wearing a Marc Bouwer gown. RICK ROWELL/ABC

With King James backstage at the ESPYs after being presented the Arthur Ashe Award, Los Angeles, California, July 2013.
SCOTT CLARKE/ESPN

Sally-Ann and I are always humbled when organizations honor us, Los Angeles, California, October 2013.
ROBIN ROBERTS PERSONAL COLLECTION

What a thrill to take to the sky in a P-51 like Daddy, Los Angeles, California, July 2013. ROBIN ROBERTS PERSONAL COLLECTION

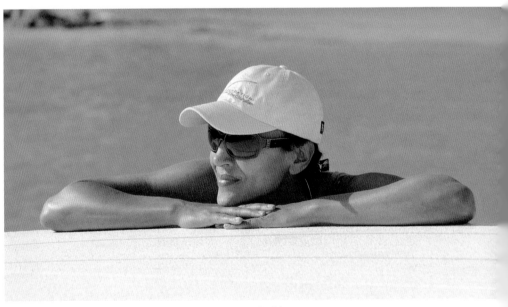

I'm always at peace when I'm surrounded by water. LOIS ANN PORTER

was about to leave the room when Jeanette asked me if I wanted to sit and stay for a while. We sat on Mom's chaise lounge in the corner of the room. It was usually covered with books, mail and clothes, but Jeanette was using it to nap while Mom rested a few feet away. I was thankful that Jeanette decided to turn off the music. It was becoming a bit much, and I think we all welcomed the break, even Mom.

Jeanette started to tell me how much she was learning from my mom. What? Mom could barely communicate—how was she inspiring this young woman? Jeanette said Mom talked to her about her life, and listening to Mom's stories was uplifting. Mom never referred to someone as being a stranger; she said "strangers" were people she just hadn't met yet. People were drawn to Momma: black, white, young, old and everything in between. Folks were drawn to Mom's humility, wisdom and spirituality. She loved to talk, but she was also a good listener. She taught us that everyone's story has significance. I carry that invaluable lesson with me every day.

I was surprised when Jeanette told me one of her last conversations with Mom was about how she raised her children. She questioned whether or not she was there for us enough. Granted,

Mom didn't have homemade cookies waiting for us when we got home from school, but I can never remember her not being there when we needed her. Off and on she was a schoolteacher and had held other jobs to help make ends meet. But, for the most part, she put her dreams on hold until I, the youngest, went to college. It was only then, and with my dad's blessing and encouragement, that Mom accomplished lofty goals outside the home.

She never made it her goal to be the first woman of anything, but she certainly was. Mom served on numerous boards of directors; she was the first woman to chair the Mississippi State Board of Education, the first woman to serve as president of the Mississippi Coast Coliseum Commission and was one of the chairs of the New Orleans Branch of the Federal Reserve Bank of Atlanta. Both she and Dad were also very active in leadership positions for the Presbyterian Church (USA) on a national level. Mom served on the church's Self-Development of People committee and literally traveled the world, visiting such far-flung countries as Egypt and Guatemala to see how lives were being changed because of the church's participation.

Sitting a short distance from Mom, I told

Jeanette that my mother had no need to worry. She was an amazing and caring mother. That I was proud of her and blessed to be her daughter. When people ask me what is the secret of my success I tell them: "Being the daughter of Lucimarian and Lawrence Roberts." Just as I finished saying that, my mom coughed. We jumped up and rushed the few steps to her bedside. She turned her head and took her last breath. I was kneeling next to Mom's bed, holding her hand and looked up at Jeanette, who checked her pulse. She nodded her head. Momma was gone. Absent from the body, present with the Lord.

CHAPTER 18

A Lake House

I couldn't believe that Momma was gone. I also couldn't believe that I would be the one to call and tell my siblings. I had always dreaded receiving "the call" from one of them.

I was too numb to phone Dorothy, so Jeanette did. It seemed as if it took my big sister only a few minutes to come rushing back into the house with her girls. Sally-Ann didn't answer her cell phone, so I called her husband, Ron. He handed Sally-Ann his phone, and she wailed when I told her Momma had just passed away. Then I called Butch. He's so much like Dad, the strong, silent type, rarely showing emotion. It was one of the few times I've heard my big brother cry.

When Mom was living, police officers in the

Pass would stop by every so often, just to check on her. Bless them for that! The night she passed, we called the funeral home and they sent not a hearse but what looked like a minivan. They backed into the driveway and they came inside and began preparing to take my mother.

There was a knock at the door and my nieces said, "That's a police officer's knock."

I was a little surprised, and it was an unexpectedly light moment in the darkest of nights, because I asked them, "Excuse me, how do you know what a police officer's knock sounds like?" And everybody laughed. We all needed to laugh.

I opened the door and, lo and behold, it was an officer. He saw the minivan and was concerned that Mom was being robbed. He said, "Is everything okay with your mother? I'm just checking things out."

I felt so bad, I said, "Our mother just died, and that's the funeral home."

You should have seen the look on his face, he kept apologizing. "I'm so sorry," he said over and over again. "I'm so so sorry."

And I got a glimpse about how the next few days were going to go. Because as much as I wanted to close the door on the world, this was not a private loss. We had lost our mother, our matriarch, but Pass Christian had lost Lucimarian Roberts. Everyone in town wanted to share their grief over losing our mother. Ours wasn't a private loss.

The officer came in and sat down for a second. He told me that his wife had breast cancer, and he'd seen me and Sally-Ann on the show that morning. We start talking, and I was crying and hugging him, wishing his wife well, and through it all, I knew that the thing that connected us was Mom.

We appreciated how the patrol officers kept an eye on Mom, because sometimes people found out where she lived and came by the house. Once a couple came by and knocked on the door and they said, "We're just visiting from Florida and we're really big fans of your daughter." Mom said, "Come on in."

I remember being horrified when she told me the story later on. But the fact is that Momma was a good judge of character. She and that couple became friends. It was cute that *they* also later scolded her for letting them in her house. They kept in touch for years and years. Momma believed in the goodness of people and she believed in the prayer of protection, that wherever she was, God was, too.

Mom had a way of taking people under her wing and making you feel special when you were talking to her. Your story mattered. And whenever she thought I was getting a little too full of myself, she'd remind me: "Robin, your story is no more important than anybody else's story. When you strut, you stumble." Meaning: When you think that you're all that and a bag of chips, you're gonna fall flat on your face. Thank you, Momma, for that invaluable lesson.

We were overwhelmed with the outpouring of love for our mother. President and Michelle Obama sent a beautiful flower arrangement to our house. It was the first time I had seen Mom's grandchildren smile in days. It was a proud moment for them. The president of the United States. They asked if they could take pictures of the flowers and Instagram them to their friends.

It was painful to make the final arrangements for Mom. The owners of the Bradford-O'Keefe Funeral Home were incredibly kind and gentle. Our families have known each other for decades, and they also handled my father's homegoing service. Mom had always said she wanted to be laid to rest in a simple pine box. We were discussing what to put on her tombstone. I had been quiet up to that point, just numb. Mom and Dad were both gone. I was left with such an empty feeling. Grandma Sally had passed when Mom was in her seventies, and I remember Mom saying she now felt like an orphan. I thought that was strange. But now I knew exactly what Mom meant. There was a lot of chatter about what words to use on Mom's tombstone. I whispered it should simply read: A CHILD OF GOD. Everyone agreed.

Dad's homegoing in 2004 was held in a large church at Keesler Air Force Base. Mom did not want that. So we decided to honor her wishes and have her service at our church in Bay Saint Louis, Old Town Presbyterian. It has about ten wooden pews on each side of the church. Knowing there would be limited seating, we decided to make Mom's viewing open to the public.

Bradford-O'Keefe was, in a word, magnificent. They thought of everything. Knowing there would be an overflow crowd, they were able to anticipate situations before they happened. Lines wrapped around the funeral home. It seemed that everyone who Mom had touched wanted to pay their final respects. Too many names to mention, including my fellow *GMA* co-anchors, ESPN colleagues, friends from near and far. At one point a large group of older black women wearing beautiful corsages decided to make their own line to Mom's casket. They were members of the National Council of Negro Women. Mom had been a part of the group for years. It got so chaotic at one point that the funeral director had to whistle loudly to regain order. I could just imagine Momma saying: "Oh, mercy!"

Mrs. Middleton was one of Mom's oldest friends, and when she heard of Mom's passing, she asked her great-granddaughter to drive her from Chicago to be at Mom's funeral. Mom and she met each other in college at Howard. Mom talked about it in her book, so this is not telling stories out of school. There was a rough patch in my parents' marriage, and Momma wanted to leave Daddy after I was born. She was fed up with being an enlisted officer's wife, and Mrs. Middleton was the *perfect* friend. Instead of insisting that Mom stay and work things out, Mrs. Middleton said, "Okay, leave him then. So what are you gonna do? How are you going to live? Do you assume you'll get custody, or will you sue him if he challenges you?" By the time Mrs. Middleton was done, Mom was like, "Um, yeah, I don't want to go through all that." You could say Mrs. Middleton saved the marriage. She gave

Mom time to realize she did still love Daddy and had faith that her postpartum blues would pass.

Another story Momma liked to tell was about how once she and Daddy went to visit the Middletons when Momma was pregnant with me. Daddy and Mrs. Middleton were laughing at Momma, because she was a little older and was surprised that she could get pregnant. I think Momma was thirty-seven at the time. Both she and Mrs. Middleton had children around the same age, and Mrs. Middleton sort of indicated that Momma should've quit while she was ahead. Well, it turns out right after that visit, Mrs. Middleton got pregnant. "I think she got pregnant that same night," Momma would say, adding, "Don't mess with karma, Cannie Middleton." Nine months later, Mrs. Middleton also had a baby girl.

So this is the same woman whose great-granddaughter called the night before Mom's homegoing. Because Mom wanted a small service in our tiny church, we were going through a seating chart and it was very difficult, thinking how are we going to squeeze all these people in.

Sally-Ann was starting to stress out and I was so excited when Mrs. Middleton's great-granddaughter called and told us that she was going to be there. But Sally-Ann said, "I'm sorry. There's no room." And I just blew up and said, *"That's Mrs. Middleton! We will find room for Mrs. Middleton at Momma's funeral!"*

Right away, Sally-Ann said, "Yes, yes, of course, you're right."

September 5, 2012: Momma's homegoing. We all gathered at the Pass house. Dorothy's oldest daughter, Jessica, was great at organizing, so she assigned us to certain cars to ride in to the church. Our longtime friend and pastor, Reverend Robert Jemerson, made the trip from San Antonio to deliver Mom's eulogy, as he had done at Dad's service. My parents and Reverend Jemerson started a special church service in the 1970s at Keesler Air Force Base. It was called Soul Service. Before Mom's service, Reverend Jemerson told me about a recent conversation he'd had with her. He'd visited Mom in the Pass the weekend before her passing. He said she was quite clear and coherent. Mom told Reverend Jemerson: "You know, Robin is coming to see me this week. I'm going to wait for her and then I'm going home." Reverend Jemerson knew exactly what she meant...home as in heaven.

I was so touched that Charlie Gibson was there. He also traveled to Mississippi for Dad's service in 2004. Diane Sawyer and George Stephanopoulos had flown in from Charlotte, North Carolina, that morning. They were there for the Democratic National Convention and would have to return right after the service. Before entering the church I just happened to look down at my BlackBerry. There was a message from Oprah. She was expressing her sympathy and then said something I needed to hear at that very moment. She talked about when Maya Angelou was mourning the death of her mother. A short time after that Dr. Angelou was asked by President Clinton to compose a poem to read at his inauguration in 1993. Dr. Angelou had no doubt that it was her mother's heavenly intervention. Oprah went on to tell me that now my mother would do the same for me.

This is what I said at Mom's service:

If you are sitting in someone's lap right now, you have Momma to thank for that. Despite her vast accomplishments she was a humble woman. She said: "Butch, Sally-Ann, Dorothy, Robin…I want a small private homegoing. She's probably saying, "NOW my children decide to listen to me?"

As I look out on this beautiful mosaic of dif-

ferent faces...I know we have Mom to thank for that, too. She had an authentic way of connecting with people from all walks of life. Rich, poor, black, white, it didn't matter. She made you feel special.

She was sweet, had a wonderful sense of humor and was feisty to the very end. When she was recently in the hospital and couldn't reach her call button, what did Mom do? She used her cell phone to call 911 for help. They asked for her address. Mom was confused and she gave them the one in the Pass.

Our neighbors were puzzled when an ambulance showed up at the house, knowing Mom was still in the hospital.

At Daddy's homegoing I said he was a good officer. When we were stationed in a new place, he would go ahead of us to scout out everything, and we would follow. Mom has followed him to heaven. He went first to check things out. Mom told me recently: "I hope your Daddy didn't get a place in the mountains. I've always wanted a lake house." I pray Mom finally does. She and Dad are probably co-chairing committees in heaven as they did here.

I know Mom was concerned about my up-

coming bone marrow transplant. She wanted to be there but knew she wasn't physically able. She also knew I would constantly be worried about her, because once I went into the hospital and isolation I wouldn't be able to get to her if she needed me. Mom found a way to take away that worry and to be with me every step of the way on my upcoming journey. My siblings tell me it was her final gift to me. She was there when I took my first breath, and what a privilege to be holding her sweet hand when she took her last breath. Thank you, Momma. I love you.

We ended the service the same way we did at Dad's. By singing: "When we all get to heaven, what a day of rejoicing that will be." Amen.

CHAPTER 19

Roshanda

*M*omma died on Thursday, August 30. Her homegoing celebration was the following Wednesday, September 5. By the time I returned home on Thursday, September 6, I was exhausted. But I was also aware that on some level, I had to put my grieving on hold. My doctors had explained to me that the transplant battle was as much a mental battle as a physical one. There was no way that I could begin to process the full force of losing my beloved mother and be strong enough, focused enough, to go through the transplant process as well. My siblings insisted that in her passing Momma had given me an incredible gift. Dorothy said, "Mom is where she is so she can do even more for you."

As we began to ready for my transplant, there was yet another loss to endure. I had to say good-bye to my Jack Russell terrier, KJ, who had been my constant companion, my baby, for more than fifteen years. It was necessary that my home be completely sterile when I returned from the hospital after my transplant. Sergio thought it best that KJ not be there during my post-transplant recovery. It would be too easy for her to track in germs from her walks.

From the Memorial Sloan-Kettering advisement for allogeneic transplant patients:

Animals can carry diseases. They may put you at greater risk while your immune system recovers....It is best that you do not have close physical contact.

Friends in the city offered to take KJ, but I knew it would be too tempting for me to want to see her. Jo and Kim live in Maine, where KJ would have plenty of space to roam. KJ adores Jo and Kim and is always happy to see them. They have huge Great Danes that are so gentle and loving.

We called it Camp KJ and tried to make light of the situation, but the day I handed KJ over to

Jo and Kim was indescribably sad. I let her sleep with me in my bed the night before she left. All I could do was cry and hug her.

From the Memorial Sloan-Kettering advisement for allogeneic transplant patients:

Do not allow pets in your bed.

I'm normally one to follow the rules, but not this time. Amber and I found a midway point to hand over KJ so Jo and Kim wouldn't have to drive all the way from Maine. We met by the water in Portsmouth, New Hampshire, for an early dinner. I didn't have much of an appetite, knowing that KJ was waiting in the car.

It took me a while to actually hand over KJ in the parking lot. I kept checking and double-checking her sleepaway kit, making sure she had all her favorite toys and her bed. It was like Jo and Kim were taking temporary custody of my four-legged, furry child. People recognized me in the parking lot and wanted autographs and pictures. Many had been following my journey and knew my transplant was near. They were so encouraging and uplifting but I was a mess. I kept saying, "I'm so sorry, KJ." But as we drove off, I knew she was going to be well taken care of.

I didn't have to worry about her, and I could concentrate solely on getting well—and getting her
back. Sergio told me that at one hundred days,
I could have her home with me. That became a
big goal. Anyone who has loved a pet like I love
KJ understands. They love you unconditionally
and ask for so little in return.

* * *

After we dropped KJ off, I realized that the last
time I would have seen most of my friends and
colleagues was at Momma's funeral. It was Sunday, September 9, and the following day I would

check into the hospital for ten days of chemo, followed by my transplant and then isolation. I decided on the spur of the moment to have a party.

Amber and I threw the party together quickly, and the apartment began to fill up. Josh Elliott and George Stephanopoulos were there. Josh, remembering how much I loved walking down to the corner store as a kid, brought me a six-pack of RC Cola. That six-pack is still sitting on my kitchen counter; every time I see it, I smile. What a gift it is to have friends who really know you. What a gift you give someone when you listen with your whole head and your whole heart. That story of me and my RC could have gone in one ear and out another. But Josh was, and is, so fully present when we spend time together. If you're reading this book and wondering, "What can I do for someone I know who's going through his or her something?" Know that your gesture doesn't have to be grand. Be present. Listen.

My transplant specialist, Dr. Sergio Giralt, urges his patients to Keep It Boring. He means that everything should just tick along without anything interesting happening. In the world of transplants, interesting is rarely good. But that night at my apartment, looking out onto the

Hudson River, with New Jersey and my fond memories of my father's family—my Jersey relatives, I call them—twinkling in the distance, we absolutely did not keep it boring. We caused a ruckus. It was a *rager*. People were doing shots and telling jokes, dancing and crawling all over the couch, you would've thought it was a frat party, not a party in the home of a distinguished (wink!) television journalist.

It got so late that I had to start kicking people out. "This is great," I kept saying. "But I am going into the hospital tomorrow. I should probably try to get a couple of hours of sleep." Josh was one of the last to go. I swear he is like a teenage boy. He is a bottomless pit. After the caterers left, I found Josh in my kitchen, rummaging through the fridge, looking for leftovers. Hilarious.

Throwing that party was the best way to head off to the hospital. I know there are some people who would save the celebration for the other end, when the transplant is over and the numbers are up. I always believe better days are coming, but I'm not going to wait to embrace the perfectly imperfect moment that is now. That night of our party I felt it so strongly in my bones: "I'm still here and I want to live. I want to show the people who love me that this is a chapter I'm about to go through; it is not the end of the book." Was it going to be any better if I had spent that night in the apartment crying alone or with Amber? That party gave me strength before embarking on ten consecutive days of chemo: It reminded me that despite the devastating loss of my mother, I was still alive and I had so many people who wanted me to live.

* * *

I was going to shave my hair completely before I went into the hospital. Then I decided to have the party, and I knew George would bring his two young daughters. And I thought, "You know, I don't need to be completely bald with these young girls here." And even though they're really cool girls, Elliott and Harper, I wanted to spare them a little. So I asked Petula to just cut it short, kind of like a buzz cut. I called it my Halle Berry.

When I checked into the hospital, Petula came to cut my hair all off because it still wasn't short enough. Dr. Giralt said, "You don't want to wake up with clumps of hair falling out." And there was going to be a time when my platelets would be so low that they couldn't shave it, for risk of infection. So Petula came to the hospital and I said, "Really, we've got to stop meeting like this."

Having my hair shaved again was such a difficult moment for me. It felt so unfair to have to go down this road again. I had agreed to let ABC tape various moments of my journey for a future *20/20* special, but I also was firm that I wouldn't decide until well after the transplant what I wanted to share on air.

The special has since aired, and for all the moments of vulnerability, there's only one moment that makes me flinch—seeing myself having my hair shaved—because I can see on the screen how angry I was. I'm not that kind of person. I'm never that harsh. But when I was speaking, it was as if I were speaking to the disease and I kept saying, "I'm in control. I'm in control. I will decide when my hair comes off. Not you."

I might not have liked how I looked at that moment or the venom in my voice, but what I was feeling was real. I am not Saint Robin. I have good days and bad days. Triumphant moments and moments that make me weep like a baby who just wants to be held by her momma. Petula shaving my hair before I endured chemo, again, was one of those weeping moments. Just pure vulnerability.

I know I'm not alone in how punishing it felt to lose my hair. There are studies that show that many women find losing their hair more painful than losing a breast. It's not all vanity. Hair is how we express ourselves. Our hair frames us. I was drawn to the song India Arie wrote for Melissa Etheridge after she had chemo and would appear on stage with a bald head. And I used that as my anthem:

I am not my hair / I am not this skin / I am a soul that lives within.

And I'm like, that's right, that's who I am. The inspiration she provided me on my breast cancer journey led to me getting in touch with India Arie for a *GMA* segment on alternate careers for the show. We all took tests and I was assessed as having strong potential as a stand-up comedian. I love to joke around, and one of my catchphrases, as *GMA* viewers know, is the Dr. Evil/Austin Powers quote, "Magma!" The tests also said that I had the potential to be a good songwriter. I decided to try the latter, and India Arie helped me write a song, "A Beautiful Day":

Wake up in the morning
And get out of bed
Start making a mental list in my head
Of all of the things that I am grateful for

Early in the morning
It's the dawn of a new day
New hopes new dreams new ways
I open up my eyes and
I open up my mind and
I wonder how life will surprise me today
Early in the morning
It's the dawn of a new day
New hopes new dreams new ways

I open up my heart and
I'm gon' do my part and
Make this a positively beautiful day

There was only one moment when I threw my weight around. I had a room picked out, but I was admitted into the hospital later than expected (because of Mom's funeral), so they gave me a different room. But I needed that window. I knew how my spirit would have crumpled without a view. I know that it's not always possible in a hospital, given cost issues and insurance drama. But as patients, we often put up with what we don't want because we don't want to be a bother. I'm telling you as someone who has faced a life-threatening illness, not once, but twice: Be a bother. Or better yet, find a family member or a friend who's good at that stuff, and let her or him be a bother on your behalf. Remember, there are no bonus points for being mild and meek when you're fighting for your life.

I think I was still feeling the party spirit because I remember, early in the chemo pre-treatment, setting up a contraband drawer in my room. I asked my friends to sneak in a Gray's Papaya hot dog. Boy did I pay the price for that hot dog. But half the fun was sneaking it in and half the fun was how good it tasted.

It was so soon after my mother's funeral, yet I had to shift my focus entirely to ten days of punishing chemotherapy that would prepare my body for the transplant that, the good Lord willing, would save my life.

Amber did a brilliant job of rallying my friends to keep my spirits and energy up. As she tells it:

The most helpful for Robin (and myself) was to have, set in place, before checking into the hospital a rotating calendar of family and friends to come in and visit. We sent out an e-mail with the dates of the transplant and had them pick and choose their weekends. Surprisingly it all came together quite easy. This gave Robin something to look forward to while giving family and friends the sense of truly helping out.

Along with their smiling faces, gifts would appear that would brighten Robin's day. My best girlfriend Crystal and I set out to buy decorations for her hospital room and IV pole. Let's just say Studio 54 had nothing on us. Complete with swirling mylar streamers her room was transformed into a thirty-day disco party. Julie brought Robin a perfectly fitted pink baseball cap that would come in handy once her hair was gone. Scarlett and Linda brought the two big panoramic posters of Maui and Greece. Those truly became posters of inspiration. Joey and Kim brought sugar-free gum and hard candy. Those were life-savers once the mouth sores set in. Lois Ann and Cathy provided the Demi Moore GI Jane poster that we hung beside her bed for those "we need to kick booty" moments. That came right when we switched rooms. It almost felt like a new room, new poster, new attitude.

Sally-Ann and Dorothy would bring all the gifts that came their way from home up to Robin. That was very sweet. To have a taste of the South, something familiar.

We knew that after the transplant, I was going to have to be in isolation for an undetermined amount of time, so my friends wanted me to find the four walls that confined me to be in-spiring. They placed two blankets given to me by GMA viewers on my bed to comfort me. One was a New Orleans Saints blanket. The other was handmade with my name embroidered on it with hearts. In the hearts were inspirational words such as *courage, strength, faith*. My friends even decorated my IV pole with disco balls. After lots of harebrained suggestions, we christened the pole with the name Roshanda, the disco name for Robin.

Amber was building her massage therapy business and clientele when I was diagnosed with MDS. She didn't hesitate to put everything on hold. We realized how fortunate we were, because many people in similar situations do not have that option. Amber knew I needed around-the-clock care, especially when I was released from the hospital. I know my sisters took great comfort in knowing that I wasn't alone. Amber and I have been a loving couple for almost ten years now, but we choose not to live together. Maybe that's why we've lasted almost a decade! Shortly before my MDS diagnosis, Amber had moved into a new apartment closer to mine. Taking care of me meant she didn't even have time to fully unpack all her boxes. She remembers how hard *her* friends worked to clear the decks so she could be there for me:

Since I was her primary caregiver, I needed to have friends take care of my beloved dog,

Frances. This was extremely helpful. I could not be around Frances, because I was in such close contact with Robin. So having my two friends Stephen and Crystal look after her meant the world to me. Crystal had Frances for a month during transplant until she had to travel. Then Stephen took her for another two months after we left the hospital. AMAZING FRIENDS!!!!!

Amber was at the hospital every day, and she never failed to make me laugh with her bright, sunny spirit. My dear sisters sung hymns, and we reminisced about all the adventures we'd shared. But there is one moment that I shared with my friend Scarlett that was so essential to my journey.

Scarlett and I met through mutual friends in the 1980s. She lives in Phoenix now, and Apple Springs, Texas, is her hometown. She loves country music and burns CDs for me. Scarlett keeps me up on all the latest country hits.

Visiting hours were over for the day, and Amber left the room with our friend Linda. Scarlett stayed behind and sat by me on the bed. I remember whispering to her, "Scarlett, am I going to die?"

She was the one friend that I could share that

moment with. Amber and my sisters were a constant presence. I didn't want to overwhelm them with the fear that the question posed. But Scarlett was leaving town and moreover, she is my deep friend.

She's only five feet five inches tall and looks like you could knock her over with a feather, but there is no such thing as the weight of the world when Scarlett is around. She is an old soul, and I've never seen a problem too big for her to handle. This time was no different.

So I asked my dear friend, "Am I going to die?" And she sat on the edge of the bed, stroking my head. I think she murmured something like, "Oh, sweetie, why would you even think that?" But it wasn't what she said, it was the way she held her space. She really reasoned with me and reassured me. She didn't become overly emotional and she didn't start crying—I knew she wouldn't. I don't know how she was when she left the room but I knew that in front of me, she lent me the strength that I didn't have at that time. I've often said when fear knocks, let faith answer the door. Sometimes when fear knocks, faith shows itself through a friend who stands by the door, squeezes your hand and answers it with you.

CHAPTER 20

The Rabbit

*T*he picture of GI Jane that my friends hung in the room proved to be especially fitting, because those ten days of chemo were my own personal Hell Week. The chemo breaks you down before the transplant can build you back up with new life.

Nausea, vomiting and diarrhea are common during the preparative treatment. My doctors did a great job controlling those side effects with medication. But the anti-emetics, the drugs that prevent vomiting, can have harsh side effects including muscle tightness, uncontrolled eye movement, constipation and shakiness. These are more unnerving than dangerous.

High-dose chemotherapy goes after cancer

cells, which are rapidly dividing. But it turns out that the cells that line your mouth, your throat, your gut, your hair and your skin are rapid dividers, too. So these are typically temporarily damaged by the preparatory regimen. Countless times a day, a nurse came in to make sure I brushed my teeth and gums with a soft sponge and then I rinsed with a saline solution to help prevent mouth infections.

I can't tell you how glad I was that Amber and I had that party. It carried me through some of my most challenging days. There were moments when I would just chuckle and the nurses would say, "You're thinking about that party." And I was. It was like, "Wow, you should have seen Josh."

The ten days of high-dose chemo before the transplant were its own kind of marathon. There were two goals of the conditioning regimen. The first was to destroy the diseased cells; the second was to suppress my immune system so that Sally-Ann's blood stem cells could engraft, or attach, to my own and start producing healthy blood cells.

The first day of my conditioning regimen, my thoughts were with Mom. She always said she never got much rest in the hospital. So true. Someone was in my room every couple of hours, poking me or taking my vitals. My blood pressure was low, so they had me on increased fluids. Chemo started at 6 a.m. It's a good thing I'm a morning person.

I got up at my usual 4 a.m. and e-mailed my friends, "You should see the contraption they have me hooked up to. Now the fun really begins. Bring it on!"

In the conditioning regimen, they count down the days like NASA engineers preparing a rocket ship for launch. Today isn't day two of high dose chemo, it's day −8. Meaning 8 more days of chemo then transplant time. I was now receiving chemo every six hours—6 a.m., noon, 6 p.m., midnight.

Day −8, also known as September 12, 2012, was a beautiful fall day. I remember sitting in my room and looking out onto the city. New York is a riot of color in the fall.

Life changes so fast.

Just a few weeks before, 6 a.m. would find me on the set of the show, joking around with Sam and Josh, interviewing guests.

Just a short time ago, I had been in Italy, waking up in a beautiful old villa, enjoying a glass of red wine under the Tuscan sun.

When I woke up the next day, God sent me a

present. One Julie Elizabeth Lennon. We both hail from the great state of Mississippi. Can't remember a time when Julie has not been in my life. She's a lawyer and lives in Dallas now. When you're about to undergo such a delicate procedure and you have to put your affairs in order, I can't tell you what a comfort it is to have a best friend as your lawyer. Her visits really lifted my spirits. She showed me old vacation photos of us in Bermuda. There was one pic of me in a white sports bra and canary-yellow shorts. What can I say? Left on my own, I've never really been a fashionista.

Day –7 brought a restless, sleepless night. The constant chemo was no joke. Thank God that Day –6 brought the end of the busulfan treatment, the chemo that had to be administered every six hours. But I started two new chemotherapies. I remember melphalan, because while taking it I had to eat ice almost nonstop. You tolerate the drug better if your mouth stays very cold throughout the treatment. I e-mailed my friends, "Ice, ice baby. Sing it with me ... Ice, ice baby."

I began calling transplant day "Go Sally, Go" Day.

Day –5 was hard. No dancing. No visitors. No food. I tried so hard not to be a Debbie Downer, but I also want to keep it real. Five days of chemo were beginning to catch up with me.

I knew that part of my chemo blues was from my mourning for my mother. It had not even been two weeks since her funeral. Reading e-mails and seeing photos that my friends sent helped to lift my spirits and gave me the strength to tell Debbie Downer to take a hike. I knew that I needed to be both mentally and physically pre-pared, because the last chemo before my trans-plant would be the toughest of them all.

The next day, I began forty-eight hours of a two-day chemo treatment called the Rabbit. The doctors explained that there was a high chance of fever, chills, mouth sores, nausea, the works. The Rabbit is a chemo designed to wipe out anything the other chemos missed. Your skin lit-erally jumps during the treatment. You feel the chemo racing around your body like a rabbit, digging up potholes, looking under anything where my damaged cells might be hiding. It was a rare moment when Amber and another loved one weren't in my room. Amber had been con-stantly by my bedside, and I implored her to go home and get some rest. There alone, I be-came a little delirious. I was in so much pain. I was so scared. I felt myself slipping away. Then

I heard someone calling my name over and over…*Robin! Robin!*

I opened my eyes and saw Jenny, one of my compassionate nurses. She was sitting on my bed, shaking me. All I could see was her wide-opened eyes above her mask. To this day, I'm convinced it wasn't Jenny's voice, but rather my mom's voice, not calling me to where she is now, but calling me back to my body, to that gloomy hospital room, telling me that I could do it, that I was meant to live and fight another day.

CHAPTER 21

Keep It Boring

September 20 was Transplant Day. I had nothing left at that point. My body was as weak as I'd ever known it. But I was surrounded by loved ones to witness this miraculous moment. Amber, my sisters, Team Beauty, Sonny, Emily, Karen. Dorothy and Sally-Ann serenaded me with the words of Diana Ross's classic love song "Ain't No Mountain High Enough," assuring me that "nothing can keep me, keep me from you."

The theme of the day was new beginnings and my loved ones set up a playlist to honor the moment. In addition to "Ain't No Mountain High Enough," we played: Stevie Wonder's "Happy

Birthday," India Arie's "A Beautiful Day," Mandisa's "Good Morning" and a favorite hymn, "Blessed Assurance."

Amber and my sisters decorated the room with balloons that symbolized that I was being literally reborn: HAPPY BIRTHDAY, HAPPY 1ST BIRTHDAY and ANGRY BIRDS. (I *love* to play Angry Birds.) They completed the décor with Roshanda-themed disco decorations: disco balls and sparkling streamers.

When Dr. Giralt entered the room, it was as lively as the discos that had inspired my IV pole's name. He smiled and said, "I can feel all the love in here."

Diane Sawyer and Sam Champion were also in the room. Sometimes people look at the photos and say, "You had colleagues there." There were no colleagues in that room, okay? Anybody who was in that room, they were family and friends.

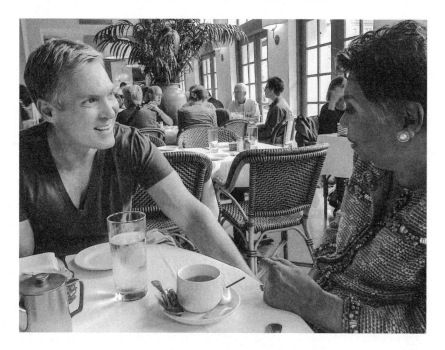

One of my favorite pictures is of my mother and Sam. He was having a crazy week and he didn't really have time for lunch. But he heard that Mother was in town, and he said, "I'll make time." After lunch, he came over to hug Momma and he said, "I needed that. Boy, did I need that." Mom had such a way of making people feel that no matter what they were going through, all was right in the world. She believed today was a gift and tomorrow represented infinite possibilities. She never preached or pontificated, but she made her point and you'd walk away feeling good, more than anything. "Oh, mercy":

Momma liked to say that as she threw her arms around you. As miraculous a moment as it was, it was tough going through my transplant without my mother. Tough knowing that just days before, I'd held her hand as she took her last breath. Whether you're two or fifty-two, when you are sick, you want your momma. I know I did.

At the moment I was reborn, I thought about Dr. Giralt's saying, "Keep It Boring"—and that's exactly what we did:

Pastor A. R. Bernard of Christian Cultural Center in Brooklyn blessed the syringe.

Dr. Giralt inserted it into the port of my chest.

Millions of Sally-Ann's cells flooded my bloodstream.

Go Sally, go!

I didn't hear anybody else. I didn't see anybody else. I remember seeing tears in Dr. Giralt's eyes, and I can see that his mouth is moving underneath his mask. He is praying, a prayer that his wife and mother-in-law taught him: Let God do His work and it will work.

* * *

When I was about four years old, my family went on a spiritual retreat to Lake George in upstate

New York. Even though I was so little, I can remember the majesty of the lake and the Adirondack Mountains. During the day, my sisters, brother and I went to children's workshops while our parents attended seminars. At night, we all gathered around a campfire. Momma sang in the retreat choir, and that summer she learned a new hymn: "How Great Thou Art." That hymn became my dad's favorite.

On the morning we were due to head home, my parents couldn't find me. The family searched for me frantically. Momma always said it seemed like an eternity before they found me, sitting at the far end of the pier. I was sitting very close to the edge, swinging my legs back and forth like a pendulum clock. I had been told not to go to the lake without an adult, but I remember thinking I had to see it one more time before we left. My father remembered approaching me carefully, not wanting to scare me and cause me to fall into the cold, deep water. My family finally exhaled when I was safe in his arms and his embrace.

Getting ready for my transplant, surviving some of the most excruciating pain I have ever known, I willed myself to remember that while my father is no longer with us, as they say in the

South, every good-bye ain't gone. When I need him most, I can feel his strength, his love, his protection. I try to remind myself that I may be sitting at the end of this long pier all by myself, but I haven't fallen into the cold water. Everybody I know, everything I love, is just waiting for me to take a walk that at times I can only take alone.

* * *

After the transplant, the room I was in became an isolation zone. As a transplant patient, you learn more about germs than you ever, ever wanted to know. And this is the thing: Bacteria, viruses and fungi live in and around us on everything. It's in the air we breathe and on the food we eat, on every hand we shake and the cheeks we kiss. The pre-transplant regimen not only destroyed the cancerous cells in my body, it also wrecked my immune system. So the first two to four weeks after the transplant were critical. My body needed time for Sally-Ann's cells to engraft and for my own body to start refilling its store of white blood cells.

From the Memorial Sloan-Kettering advisement on allogeneic transplant patients:

You will be placed on protective isolation precautions to protect you from germs....A card telling visitors about the type of isolation will be placed on the door to your room. The door to your room must remain closed. All staff and visitors who go into your room must wear a mask, wash their hands and put on gloves. The mask and gloves will be in a box near the sink.

The thing I remember most about the weeks after the transplant was that everyone who came in to see me was wearing a mask. I didn't have to wear one, but they did. Day after day, week after week, all I saw of the people that I loved was the little rectangle of their face—eyes and forehead—that the mask did not cover. Everyone who touched me was wearing gloves, and I grew to miss that, too, the feel of holding Amber's hand, the touch of my sisters' and friends' lips on my cheeks. Sometimes when I knew that they were on the way, I would stand at the door and peek out of the window of my room, to watch Amber, my sisters and my friends before they got scrubbed clean, before they donned their masks and gloves. It was a little treat in a long day to catch a glimpse of them this way—faces uncovered, eyes, noses, lips, cheeks—unmasked and unhidden.

What I didn't know was what an effort it took for Amber and my loved ones to hide their emotions: their fear, their grief, their exhaustion—so that when they came to see me, their own very real pain wasn't an additional burden I had to bear. Amber remembers:

Perhaps the difference between emotional and physical caregiving is this. When you are there physically, you cannot get emotional. You have to stay strong and present for whomever you are caring for. They look up to you as the one positive. If you let your emotions get in the way of the task at hand, it can go very badly. I never wanted Robin to see myself scared.

I had to keep family, friends and colleagues tuned in and up-to-date without scaring the daylights out of them. I put people into categories depending on how much detail I felt they should know. I never wanted to scare ANYONE.

With that being said, I did have an absolute meltdown in the elevator and a nurse just happened to hop in with me at the last moment. ALL of my bottled-up emotions finally came to a head and there we were. I was a crying mess while she held me and assured me everything was going to be all right. She said, "This is scary stuff, I'm not going to lie, but everything WILL be okay." She was a little angel sent in to comfort me. I then left the hospital and just started walking. I walked and walked crying and sobbing on the phone with my best girlfriend, Crystal. She was MY point person. The one person I knew I could tell ANYTHING to without freaking her out. It's important to have that go-to person for the caregiver that will listen to you while you just ramble and let everything out. She always *knew exactly what to say to make me feel better :). Sometimes saying nothing was just as perfect.*

The big fear was graft-versus-host disease. If my body (the host) began to reject Sally-Ann's cells (the graft) then the transplant was unsuccessful. The chart that doctor had shown me, the one that put my life expectancy at under two years, would all of a sudden be relevant again. But there were other concerns. The transplant and the high-chemo prep before it could temporarily damage my liver, lungs and heart. Heartbeat irregularities and rapid heartbeat are scary and common side effects. Other post-transplant problems include muscle spasms, confusion and cataracts.

Numbness and tingling in the hands and feet, due to nerve damage in the preparative regimen, was also a big concern. Fortunately, the numbness for me was temporary. Unlike the other symptoms, this damage can be permanent, and it scared the living daylights out of me.

Dr. Giralt was especially concerned about the cosmetic effects of certain infections. He kept saying, "With most patients, the goal is just to get them better. But I've got to get you better and back on TV." Believe me, in the days after the transplant, getting back on TV was the furthest thing from my mind. I just wanted to be healthy again.

After Katrina, my mother had urged me to celebrate all that we had gained in the months after the storm. She said, "It's been a time of reawakening to not only what we had that's gone, but what we can rebuild and do." In the hospital room, my one and only goal was to build a path forward, one that would allow me to come out stronger and more alive than before.

* * *

You learn so much when you have an extended stay in the hospital. You're so lonely and yet you're never really alone. Every two hours there's somebody coming and checking your vitals, or administering medicine, or doing this or doing that. I had thought—crazily—that an extended stay in the hospital would mean a great deal of rest. It did not.

From the patient advisement:

You will be weighed each day around 6 a.m. Most weight changes during transplant hos-

pitalization are due to fluid retention or loss. The inpatient team needs this information by the time they make the rounds to make important decisions. Your blood pressure, temperature, pulse, respirations, and blood oxygen level will be checked every four hours around-the-clock. No one likes being awakened at night, but these measurements are important. Any change may require a treatment change.

Post-transplant, my body and mind were so pulverized, I didn't even know how sick I was. Especially during the first few days after the procedure, when I was on dozens of medications and my blood cells were being rebuilt from scratch, I experienced moments of forgetfulness that frightened me. During those moments, I would try to think of Mom. My spells were not as dramatic as some patients experienced, but they were sad and confusing all the same.

One afternoon, a physical therapist came to my room and she said, "You like Motown."

I said, "How do you know that?"

She said, "You told me that at our last session."

I said, "Have we met before?"

She looked concerned and said, "Yes, I've been here before."

I said, "Wow. I don't remember."

But it was true. I love me some Motown, so we started doing yoga to some great old tunes.

From the patient advisement:

Exercise and activity: Once isolation begins, you may not leave your room unless you are going for treatment. However, activity is very important. Get out of bed at least twice a day and try to walk in your room every day to maintain your muscle tone and strength. Sit up in a chair as often as possible. You can also ask for a restorator bike that has pedals that can connect to a chair. It can help you keep active.

Eating was excruciating. I wouldn't wish that pain on my worst enemy. That was tough. I always fluctuated between 150 and 155 pounds, and I got down to under 120. Which was a little scary: thirty to thirty-five pounds just *gone* in a matter of weeks. But I know for some people, it's far worse. After a transplant, your throat feels as if you swallowed a blowtorch. Mine was so raw and so sore and so painful. And if you can't swallow, they've got to feed you. I would just cringe every time a nurse hung a bag of lipids on my IV pole. It looked like white out and it smelled so pungent, rancid and horrid, like something someone had thrown up.

I sucked ice to keep my mouth from going completely dry, but even that provoked a reaction. I remember once putting an ice cube in my mouth and thinking, "Oh, sweet relief." But it tasted so bad that I spit it right back out. Something was wrong. I thought it was covered in some kind of mold.

I said, "Who put fur on the ice?"

Everyone in the room looked so scared.

Amber very lovingly and patiently said, "Robin, there's no fur on it." But I was so sure that I had felt fur, and the frustration of not being able to enjoy even a simple ice cube was heartbreaking.

Some of the most frightening moments after my transplant were ones that I don't even remember. I think the brain has an incredible way of protecting us when our bodies need to heal. Amber has been my gatekeeper and my caregiver, but she also has held, with love and trust, some of the most painful memories of my journey:

There came a point during Robin's treatment when I was not allowing any visitors. I became the gatekeeper and the gate was CLOSED. During this week Robin began taking anti-fungal meds along with her pain meds, resulting in a very hallucinogenic state of mind. Thank goodness this week fell when Dorothy and Sally-Ann were not visiting. I would have hated for them to see their baby sis in this state. I bring this up because it can be very difficult to witness your loved one like this. Eyes barely open, head tilted back as if she was trying to get a better focus and all motor skills completely out the door.

Robin didn't know this at the time, but while I was "sleeping" on the sofa, I was actually watching her attempt to write and send out an e-mail. Dropping the Black-Berry several times followed by a slow-motioned glance over my way to see if I saw her. Of course I let on like I was sleeping. This went on for hours. It just broke my heart. She was trying so hard.

I remember saying to myself: "This is just a phase and it will pass." "Take a few deep breaths." "She WILL come out of this." And she did. But not until after having her room literally come to life, complete with a dancing elephant swirling in circles on her shelf and her giant flower mylar balloon that stayed attached to the ceiling spinning like a pinwheel above her. She had herself one trippy evening.

Lois Ann and Cathy were due to come in for the weekend and I worried about Robin's heavily medicated state. I warned the girls that she was quite out of it and not herself. I wanted to prepare them for the absolute worst while I hoped for the best. After we washed up and put on our gloves and masks, I did my "coded knock" and slowly opened the door. To my absolute surprise and in complete Robin fashion, our girl had rallied. She was wide-eyed and bushy-tailed and so excited to see us all. As if she hadn't seen me for a week. That's when she began to tell us of her party that she had in her room the night before. During that time I believe a nurse had walked in to take her vitals and found Robin at the edge of her bed conducting an interview. If only I had witnessed that!

From that point on Robin was making tremendous strides. That unrecognizable person was definitely in the past and Robin be-

gan putting the pieces of her old self back together. We hung the GI Jane poster on the wall of her new room that weekend. From that point on there was no looking back.

But the good news was that despite the pain and the discomfort, Sally-Ann's cells and my body were getting along. I kept asking when would I feel better. My doctors told me I would know before they did. That I would wake up and know something was different. It took several days after the transplant but it happened. One day my white blood cell count was 2.2 when it had been just 0.4 the day before. Both Dr. Giralt and Dr. Roboz were very excited, because they took it as a sign that my body was busy producing healthy cells. They also cautioned that my numbers could fluctuate. We needed consecutive days of numbers moving in the right direction. But we were off to a very promising start.

That day, I was also moved to a new room. That often happens during long hospital stays. Patients are discharged and better rooms become available. The new room was a corner with windows on both sides. So much more light came flooding in. It was perfect for this phase of my recovery. Funny how when you get sick, the things you might take for granted when you're healthy feel like an enormous gift from God. The sunlight did more than warm my body, it warmed my soul.

CHAPTER 22

Fourteen Laps a Day

When the journey is a long one you look for milestones along the way. Being cleared from isolation was a huge one. When my numbers cooperated I was determined to get out of that bed. I would take my robe and I'd walk the hall. Fourteen laps around the floor and nurses' station equaled a mile, and I'm very competitive; I set a goal of doing fourteen laps every day that I was able. Of course, the first day, I set out to walk the whole mile, but was totally exhausted after two laps. My friends Lois Ann and Cathy helped get me back to my room.

Lois Ann and Cathy were visiting from Northern California. Lois Ann is Southern, originally from my birth state, Alabama. Lois Ann is my take-charge friend, like "Okay, what are we going to do?" She was a great friend to have come visit as I began to try to walk around and build my strength, because I tell you, you've got a task? Lois Ann Porter is the one to help you get it done—and with such sweetness. It's really an art the way she manages to be so in charge and so tender at the same time. Plus, Lois Ann has the biggest belly laugh, this guffaw that I loooove.

After weeks in the hospital, even with everything going as well as could be expected, you're bound to get the blues. You just can't stare at four hospital walls for twenty-four hours a day and not feel the severity of your situation weigh in on you, just a little bit. Later, I also learned how much also weighed on my friends. Jo and Kim told me they vowed not to cry in front of me, but they often did when they left my room. I was moved when Kim told me: "Robin, I was terrified and had no idea what to expect. Your strength gave me strength."

I was buoyed every day by the prayers and messages of our viewers, friends of friends and people I know I'll never have the privilege to meet. If you've ever thought, "Should I send a card?

Does it matter?" I want you to know that the answer is "Yes!" The notes and messages we received not only lifted my spirits, they brought joy and hope to my family and my friends. Amber saw it firsthand:

Emotional caregiving is just as important. These are the people that can't make it to your hospital room but are there on the sidelines cheering you on. They send cards, gifts, e-mails, texts, you name it. They are the uplifters from beyond the outside world. Robin had MANY emotional caregivers. Reading through all the cards gave me something to do while on the rare occasions Robin was napping. As much as the cards were meant for her, they filled me with an incredible sense of comfort. Just like the nurse had told me, everything was going to be okay.

For the most part, everyone was pretty respectful of Robin, myself and the family. I think if you send a card, a gift, leave a voice mail or send an e-mail or text…do it without expectations. We had every intention to respond, and we did to most. But at times a simple thank-you seems like THE biggest task at hand when your loved one is hooked up to fifteen bags of meds and doing their best to stay alive.

For security purposes the hospital had this gentleman, Gregory, who would be out near my door and it was always nice because we'd talk about sports, we'd talk about the upcoming election, it was like my connection to the outside world, other than my friends. I would look forward to seeing him when I was able to leave the room. We usually took our walk very early before the hall became busy with activity. "Roshanda," my trusty mobile IV pole, was with me. Pushing it along helped me keep my balance. As I passed the nurses' station I would get big thumbs-up. The nurses were so encouraging.

One morning, while walking with Gregory, I saw this gentleman who had his IV pole, but he had on jeans and a shirt and loafers. I was wearing my slippers and robe. And I kinda looked at him and he said, "You can wear clothes if you want to."

What a surprise. I said, "I can get dressed? I didn't even know." So I asked Amber to bring me some clothes from home. And it was *amazing* how much better I felt. Put on my jeans, a T-shirt, my tennis shoes and do my fourteen laps.

But I would have never known if I hadn't seen another patient wearing street clothes in the hospital.

But don't let the laps fool you. There were days when I couldn't do fourteen laps, much less one lap. There were days when it would take all the energy I had just to swing my legs to the side of the bed and sit up straight. There were moments when the bathroom, which was merely ten feet away from my bed, seemed miles away, and as I felt the bone-weariness of Sally-Ann's cells trying to pump me back to life, I would wonder, "How bad do I need to go to the bathroom?"

Although it was my nature to talk to people and make friends, Dr. Roboz warned me that you have to have a little bit of tunnel vision as a patient. She urged me to "Focus on you, your disease, your experience, and be very careful even in walking around up on the unit. You've got to be careful. You want to make friends all the time, you want to hear their story, you want to be empathetic, you want to be sympathetic—but it's their story, it's not your story. And you can't assume that because the disease sounds the same or has the same letters, that it's behaving the same way for somebody else as it is for you."

Dorothy, Sally-Ann and Amber were the constants. Friends flew in from all over the country. My childhood pastor, Reverend Jemerson, and his wife, Jacqueline, came from San Antonio. It was comforting to see them both. They told me stories about my parents that I had never heard before. I did recall the time we were running late for church and our usual seats were taken. When Reverend Jemerson stepped to the pulpit and saw us on a different side of the church he stopped his sermon. He drew strength from seeing our family in a particular pew every Sunday directly in his line of sight. He politely asked if folks could squeeze in so "the Roberts family could sit in their proper place in the house of the Lord."

I was always happy to see my friends from ABC. Tory Johnson always came bearing wonderful gifts from her "Deals and Steals" segments on *GMA*. I was especially grateful to receive a comfy jacket that had zippers in the long sleeves and zippers just below the shoulders of the jacket. It was perfect for my PICC line. In fact, the woman who designed the jackets, called RonWear, came up with the idea because of her brother. In 2004, Deb Papes-Stanzak was caring for four family members who were receiving various kinds of infusion and dialysis treatments. Her brother, Ron, told Deb that he was tired of how cold he got during dialysis because of the short-sleeved shirts he wore to accommodate his port. Deb is a seamstress who has worked in the fashion industry. She sewed a zippered fleece jacket for her beloved brother, and RonWear was born. Let me tell you, it is the perfect gift.

My friends, ABC colleague Deborah Roberts, who is married to Al Roker, and Gayle King, who is an anchor for *CBS This Morning* (and yes, she's Oprah's BFF), happened to visit when my sisters were with me. Gayle is such a girly girl. Her fabulous high-heel shoes always make me smile. Dorothy had to ask: "How do you walk in those things?" Both Deb and Gayle traveled all the way to Mississippi for Momma's homegoing.

My sweet Diane came in her sweats, wearing her glasses. She gave me a toy lightsaber like the one from *Star Wars*. May the Force be with me.

The hardworking nurses were especially excited when Rich Besser, Sam Champion and Josh Elliott came to visit me. The nurses always seemed to wear a little more makeup on those days. Rich is about six feet five inches tall, so handsome and charismatic. What makes Sam and Josh so adorable is that they don't realize how adorable they are. They knew they couldn't bring me flowers, so they stopped by the hospital gift shop and brought me a big balloon shaped like a sunflower. They also got me these cute froggy slippers. When they showed a picture on the show of me wearing them, the slippers completely sold out. Oprah even got a pair.

* * *

I've had such an interesting career and I am so, so grateful for it. One thing morning television allows you to do is sit and talk to people from all walks of life. But you also get to go out and try things. A few years before my mother passed away, I did a segment on *GMA* called "In Their Shoes," in which I was aged by a group of Hollywood special effects artists from the age of forty-five to the age of eighty-five.

Tony Gardner does amazing movie transformations. He got his start working on Michael Jackson's "Thriller" video. The first step on my path took more than two hours as he covered me with a medical, flexible silicone to take molds of my face. Weeks later, they returned with more than ten prosthetics. Assembling more than a dozen pieces one step at a time. Assembling new

cheeks, ears, using seven different colors to create skin tones and wrinkles. I watched myself
slowly vanish and I began to see the outlines of
my grandmother in the mirror. I was starting to
look like Grandma Sally.

But it didn't end with the makeup. Boeing had
developed something called the "Third Age"
suit. It allows you to simulate arthritic pain in
your joints. With some 77 million baby boomers
turning sixty, Boeing is using the suit to redesign
planes for an aging population. Even getting
dressed with the suit on wore me out. Suddenly,
all of my joints ached. I couldn't stand up
straight. The smallest movements were a struggle. They smeared Vaseline on my glasses to mirror the effects of cataracts, and I went about my
day trying to complete simple tasks like crossing
the street and shopping for groceries. All of it was
hard, hard, hard in the body of an eighty-five-
year-old.

Ida Mae Astute/ABC

I remember looking at myself in the mirror during that segment and thinking, "The tall, confident athlete of my youth is gone."

In the hospital, it was as if the transplant had done the work of a talented team of movie makeup artists. When I looked in the mirror, I saw a shadow of myself, aged and worn in ways that I didn't recognize.

Now, when I look back at photos of me in my stark hospital room, I feel so much tenderness for the patient who looks like me, but isn't the me

I've known my whole life. I have lived my entire life in motion. Activity and athletics defined who I am, and I always welcome physical challenges. For as long as I can remember I've been fascinated with how fast I can run and how far I can throw a ball. I took great pride in earning a college basketball scholarship. I've run mini-marathons, taken part in triathlons. On GMA you've seen me climb into the pace car at the Indy 500. Shoot hoops with Shaquille O'Neal and play golf with Tiger Woods.

I had the same feeling each morning on the transplant ward as I had when I had done the segment on aging: Had I lost the most vital, recognizable part of myself? Was the tall, confident athlete of my youth gone? Just disappeared? As I ticked off each day in the hospital room, closed my nose to the smell of lipids and struggled to remember the names and faces of the physicians, therapists and nurses who came to care for me, I prayed that this altered state was just a temporary resting place: a necessary corridor on my way to a cure.

CHAPTER 23

Home

*W*hen I was born, Dorothy was four and Sally-Ann was eight. As they tell it, it was as if my mother had brought home a living doll from the hospital. Sally-Ann recalls being amazed by my curly hair and Dorothy remembered that once she tried to bounce me on the bed to see if I was as springy as a ball and she almost dropped me. They got the message pretty quickly from Mom and Dad, "Robin is not a toy."

And yet, here I was, decades later, feeling very much like a baby again. When I finally was able to return to my apartment, a month after checking into the hospital for my transplant, Amber and my friends had decorated my apartment with a big pink baby balloon that read IT'S A

GIRL. Dorothy was overcome with emotion, thinking about how she had also been there when I was brought home as a newborn fifty years ago.

It was a day of such mixed emotions. Because as happy as I was to be going home, I was petrified to be leaving the hospital and the watchful care of the transplant team. Such conflicting feelings: Yay I'm going home/Oh, my gosh, I'm going home?!

I had never taken for granted how many people watched out for me when I was hospitalized. I could push a button and someone came. If I got a fever, they knew what to do. But to be responsible for myself, to have to depend on Amber and whoever else was with me at the time, that was a whole different story. When my head nurse, Dena, came in to discuss the medications I'd have to take at home, she didn't have one sheet. She had *several* sheets. In the hospital, I knew I was on a lot of medication, but two pills in a cup here, a pill in a cup there. I was never actually counting. Seeing all of those pill bottles lined up on my dresser, I felt like I was watching someone else's life. This was my new normal. Again, shades of Mom.

I actually had a panic attack as I was leaving

the hospital. I waited just inside the main door of the hospital as the car was loaded with my bags. Standing there I saw people walking by, coughing. The wind was blowing pieces of trash in the air. I didn't want to go outside. I didn't want to leave the controlled environment that had been my home for thirty days. I said a small prayer, and wearing a mask and gloves I was escorted by a hospital staffer, Tonya, out the door.

After thirty days of isolation, I took my first breath of fresh air. It just washed over me. It was so overwhelming to just see the sky. I paused for a moment to let it sink in. With grateful tears in my eyes I looked skyward. I swear I could see my heavenly ancestors cheering me on.

It never felt so great to be home as it did that day. I immediately went into my living room, where large windows frame the Hudson River. I extended my arms high in the air, threw my bald head back and began pumping my fists. I kept saying: "Yes, yes, yes!"

I knew that some never make it home after transplant. Another reminder of how very blessed I am. I curled up on my couch, wrapped myself in a brown, fluffy throw and stared out the window at the water for hours.

From the transplant patient advisement:

Your home must be kept as free of dirt and dust as possible. However, you should not go to extremes. Do not repaint your walls or put down new carpets. In fact, you should not be around any renovations or construction. This includes those in process and those done within the past three months.... In general, try not to do any chores like dusting or vac-

*uuming for the first three months after [the]
transplant.*

Even though I was being allowed to go home, I
was still in a kind of quarantine. I would go back
to the hospital three or four times a week to have
my blood checked. My journey was far from
over. In transplant terms, I was twenty-one days
old. I'm sure some of you remember what it was
like to bring your baby home for the first time.
Your precious bundle didn't leave the house
much, and you were careful that anyone who
came into contact with your child was healthy.
The biggest concerns for me were infection and
dehydration. I discovered that drinking Penta
Water helped tremendously. It's chock-full of important electrolytes. My skin was also extremely
dry and scaly from the transplant. Soaking in a
warm tub with lavender Epsom salts was quite
soothing. My doctor told me my full-time job
was to eat, drink, move and stay away from
germs. And it did feel like a full-time job. I had
energy for little else.

When I first got home from the hospital, I
could hardly be by myself, because my balance
was way off and I was falling—a lot. I remember
once when Sally-Ann came to stay with me to

give Amber a break, she stepped out to see my neighbor and her dear friend Susan Taylor. Susan lives just one building over from me. Sally-Ann didn't realize that her phone was off and I kept calling her to come back. Somebody came to my door and I was almost like a little kid. I thought, "The last thing I want is to get an infection—should I answer the door?" It was someone wanting to make a delivery, and I remember saying, "Please don't come too close. There's nobody here." I struggled to put on gloves and a mask before opening the door, and I was just so scared.

Normally, when I'm home, I have a constant companion in KJ. It was odd being at home without her. I've had her for over fifteen years. I knew Jo and Kim were taking great care of her and we Skyped a lot, so I could see for myself. KJ had been such a comfort when I went through breast cancer. The chemo left me very achy, especially my knees. It was almost like KJ could sense that as she curled up with me on the couch and laid her sweet head on my knees.

For the first three months, there was a long list of foods I had to avoid because they could cause infection. No undercooked meat, raw fish like sushi, foods that might contain undercooked eggs like quiches or casseroles, raw honey, miso products, lettuce...the list went on and on. We also had to be very careful how the food was cooked. Cross-contamination was a real concern, so each item had to be prepped then cooked separately with an elaborate clean-down of the kitchen in between. We found that using separate cutting boards was essential. A red cutting board for meat. Green for veggies. When I got home, I was still not really eating. There's something post-transplant about the taste of metal and how it overpowers the food. So I used plastic utensils for the longest time. Protein shakes were also a go-to.

Mom came up a lot when I had breast cancer treatment. But now she wasn't here, so Dorothy and Sally-Ann tried to fill her role. But, sadly, no matter how hard they tried, a sister cannot be your mother, especially if your mother was a retired widow the way mine was. Eventually my sisters had to go back home to their spouses, to their children and to their jobs. I remember walking them to the door, and it took all my strength not to get down on the floor, grab my sisters by the ankles and beg them to stay. I just kept thinking: "Don't leave me; I don't want you to go. Please don't leave me; I don't want you to go."

I felt so bad. I didn't want to be putting my sisters through all that they had gone through with me, so I tried to be a big girl and I hugged them good-bye and I wished them safe travels. Then as soon as I heard the elevator door close, I crumbled on the floor and cried like a little child. Amber did all she could to comfort me. But, all of a sudden, I was four years old again and my sisters — my beautiful, smart, talented big sisters — were going through that front door and all I wanted was to be wherever they were. *"Don't leave!"* I wanted to shout. "Please. Take me with you."

CHAPTER 24

Everybody's Got Something to Give

*F*or as long as I can remember, I've used the same kind of day planner. It's eleven by seventeen inches, thin, with a black cover, and it's the simple low-tech way that I juggle my life. What was so striking to me after I came home from my transplant was that for the first time in my adult life, my day planner was completely empty. Nothing for me to do but take my medicine, rest my body, heal my spirit and get well.

My friend Bugs came to New York to cook for me for an extended period more than once. Her nickname is Bugs, but her real name is Michelle. I've known Bugs since we played basketball together in college. My attitude was, you always want to have a suitemate who lives nearby

EVERYBODY'S GOT SOMETHING

so you can go home and get a home-cooked meal.

The first dinner her mom cooked for me when I was in college was legendary. Bugs had done so much bragging about how well her mom could cook. But her mom was really nervous; she's Cajun, and she didn't really have black friends. Having me to dinner was a new experience. So she made food she thought I would like: barbecue ribs, potato salad, corn bread. But her mom was so nervous she burned the ribs.

We laughed about it later and I said, "What are you comfortable cooking?" She replied etouffee and I said, "Well, whoop up some crawfish etouffee." Bugs inherited her mother's talent for cooking. It brings her much joy. She came to both my parents' funerals. I went to her dad's. Thankfully her mother is still alive and lives close to Bugs and her husband, near Atlanta.

Bugs left her understanding husband, Darren, back in Georgia to come cook for me. I was a bridesmaid at their wedding, and now I finally forgive Bugs for the puffy powder-blue dresses she made us wear. Her only child, Michael, had recently left for college, so Bugs was experiencing a little empty-nest syndrome. I couldn't imagine having a stranger in the house during my fragile post-transplant time, so Bugs came to my rescue.

She came in and started making all of her specialties: chicken gumbo, cabbage rolls, *great* food that normally I would devour. I said, "Don't be offended if I don't eat. You go ahead and prepare it, and it may inspire me to try to eat." She also prepared all kinds of delicious soups and froze them so that I could have easy access to meals after she left.

Then I started watching the Food Network and ABC's *The Chew*. Someone had the great suggestion, I wish I could remember who it was, that when you don't have an appetite and the smell of food bothers you, watching food being made on TV can help. Watching it and not having to smell it really kind of sparked my interest in different types of food that I would want.

I couldn't go into the grocery store, because I wasn't allowed to go into any stores whatsoever, so I just relied on my imagination and tried to remember the things I liked to eat before the transplant. For example, I like watermelon, so I'd ask Bugs for some. And hopefully, it would taste like watermelon.

When I began to regain my strength, Bugs gave

me and Amber a few cooking lessons; teaching us the proper way to sauté vegetables, how to keep chicken moist, how simple it is to make homemade soup.

There's a photograph of Bugs teaching me how to cook on my own. I had to sit down because I couldn't stand long.

Bugs was such a gift during those days. Cooking is in her wheelhouse, and she put her life on hold to feed me when I literally couldn't feed myself. Everybody's got something, but it's also true that everybody, and I do mean everybody, also has something to *give*.

From the transplant patient advisement:

Most people find it takes time to regain their strength. It may be helpful to follow a regular exercise plan. When you begin to exercise, start with easy ones first. As you feel ready, ask your doctor how to increase your exercise. Do not play contact sports or ski until your platelet count is over 100,000.

I wasn't allowed to go to my gym, and I desperately wanted to exercise. A month in the hospital and loss of considerable weight left my body unrecognizable to me. My friends Lois Ann and Cathy set up a fitness Wii in the TV room. It was so much fun, playing simulated games of tennis, basketball, bowling. You'd be surprised how much of a workout that is. It felt great to move again. Bugs and I had some heated battles playing that Wii. We're both *very* competitive. It was another perfect gift.

Amber moved into my apartment, and for months she was my lifeline to the outside world. Her best friend, Crystal, took care of Amber's dog, Frances, a beagle and Australian mix, for a month until she had to travel. Then Amber's friend Stephen stepped in and took care of Frances for another two months. My family began to text Amber, because they knew she could answer their questions. They also used her as a second set of eyes. If I had told them "Everything's fine" once too often, they would call Amber to say, "Okay, what's really going on?" They knew that I might be able to talk on the phone and sound perfectly okay, but at the same time, I couldn't walk down the hall without pain.

Amber also played security guard when people from the media and entertainment world wanted to come and see me. In the first one hundred days after the transplant, I was allowed to be home, but the orders were clear: The risk of infection is great, so keep visitors to a minimum. Every room in the house had big industrial-size jars of hand sanitizer, and Amber made sure that everyone kept to the regimen.

From the transplant patient advisement:

You may have close physical contact with those in your immediate family. Do not have close contact with someone who has a cold or any signs of being sick. Wear a mask if you must be in the same room with someone who has a cold or is sick.... Take some precautions.... Do not touch the water in a vase of flowers unless you thoroughly wash your hands afterwards. Someone should change the water in the vases daily.

I remember so well doing a story about breast cancer thrivers and being shocked at how cancer can be a wedge in a relationship and just destroy it. I interviewed a young woman whose boyfriend said, "I can't do this. I'm out of here." I had to lean so heavily on Amber after the transplant. And I have to say the post-transplant months weren't easy for me or Amber. I made it tough on her because I needed her assistance, but I also had so much going on in my body that I couldn't always be clear. It was like, "Come here. No, go away. Why aren't you here?"

She was very good about being present, without getting in my space. I needed the comfort of having her close, but I just couldn't engage in regular conversation the way we normally do. She'd say, "Okay. I'm here, I'm going to sit right here with you. We can watch TV or we can listen to music. We don't have to talk, I'm here." And that was so incredibly comforting.

Anyone who's been a caregiver to someone battling a life-threatening illness knows how frustrating it can be. On one hand, you feel like, "I don't want to tell you what I need." And at the very same time, you feel like, "If you loved me, you would know what I need."

Of course, the caregiver is caught in the middle because he or she thinks, quite logically, "If you don't tell me, how will I know?"

Amber had planned for some time on returning to Northern California for her high school reunion. Quite a few times she said, "If you don't want me to go, I'll stay here with you." She had already sacrificed so much to be by my side nonstop, and I knew she was looking forward to seeing old friends and her family. I insisted that I'd be fine, and Bugs had agreed to come back to stay with me. Midway through Amber's visit back home I had to be readmitted to the hospital. I was devastated and scared. Amber asked if she should come back.

I said no. I admit I was being passive-aggressive with her. I wanted her to come back without me asking.

Amber had a little bit of a different take on things:

I was definitely in it for the long haul. I was there seven days a week, even when family and friends were there "to relieve me." I just needed that sense of being next to her. When the opportunity came to go to my twenty-year high school reunion, I felt this was it ... my break to be with family and friends. MY "south." MY touch of home that would finally comfort me, only the way your parents and longtime friends know how to do. My plans were set months in advance, and it was THE one thing I was looking forward to that did not relate to anything transplant. Robin gave me her blessing to go. Funny ... when I finally reached home, the topics of discussion were still transplant and, of course, Super Storm Sandy. Which had just hit that weekend before. Being away from Robin felt so far, talking about her made me feel so close.

I arrived early in the week and get in contact with my best high school girlfriends, Berta and Tina. All my worries seemed to have slipped away. I was transported back to such a blissful time. The simple pleasures of just hanging out together and catching up seemed so per-

fect to me. We found out there was a pre-
reunion gathering Friday night at our local
pizza joint, Skipolini's, followed by drinks at
the bar next door. The reunion would follow
that Saturday night. We rounded up a few
more friends and voila! The weekend was coming together.

I was out and about when I see a call from
Robin come through on my cell phone. My
heart raced with excitement. "She's calling because she wants to hear the sound of my
voice!" Not exactly. She was calling to tell me
she was being admitted back into the hospital.
I listened to her every word and waited until
she was finished. I then asked, "Do you want
me to come home?" She responded along the
lines of "You do what you would like." Well,
shoot, that doesn't help me one bit, does it? We
hung up with each other, and then the panic
set in.

What to do? Looking back, my reaction
should have been "Don't worry, honey! I will
be right there. I will switch flights and take
the next possible one out." But it wasn't. It
was more along the lines of "How can I make
this all work out?" She was looking for my loving reaction, and I was looking for a direct

*response on what to do. Communication was
clearly down.*

*I decided to forgo my reunion on Saturday
night and stay for the Friday-night pizza gathering. There were a handful of friends I was
going to miss seeing that I was really looking
forward to catching up with. Friday night was
a blast, and I really felt great about my decision. I headed back to New York first thing in
the morning and went straight to the hospital.
From what I remember, Robin was not happy.*

I had Bugs with me, but I wanted and needed
Amber.

Again, I admit I was being passive-aggressive with
her. I wanted her to come back without me asking. Bugs was a little out of her comfort zone
now. She's very nurturing, especially when it
comes to cooking, but taking the lead in my
medical care was an entirely different story. I was
used to Amber paying close attention to what the
doctors were saying and relaying the info to family and friends. Amber took meticulous notes,
when she wasn't playing Candy Crush on her
iPad. I would hear her on the phone with my sis-

ters using medical terms and breaking it down in easier ways to understand. I often thought: "How does she know all that?"

After a couple of tense phone conversations, Amber cut her trip short by a day or two. I was relieved to see her when she walked into my hospital room. But a short time later she left to have lunch with friends in town. I was furious. When she returned, we went at it. We were screaming so loudly at each other that I thought we were both going to get thrown out of the hospital.

In hindsight, both of us could see that as my lead caregiver, Amber wasn't taking very good care of herself. It's a mistake she now urges other caregivers not to make:

> *I so badly needed a break. Maybe if I would have taken time off from caregiving when family and friends came in, my reaction and thought process would have been different. But here I was feeling I made the right decision, only to return to a very upset Robin.*

> *I never took time off. Maybe a morning or two where I would come in later than usual, but it was never really time off. My suggestion would*

be to do just that and take some time for your-self. I know for many patients you have to relocate to a hospital that is out of town. Research the local gyms, yoga studios, whatever it is that you do in your everyday routine, and see if there is one near you. Something to clear your head and recharge your body. Otherwise you will totally burn out or, in my case, make very poor decisions that feel right in the moment.

She had been so selfless in caring for me for many months. Going to every doctor's appointment, with me every day in the hospital, putting her life on hold. She said she needed to be around her friends, that she had a life, too. I regret that I told her: "Well, you don't get to have a life right now!" I wouldn't have blamed her if she had walked out and never had come back. I've heard plenty of stories from others that their spouses, partners or significant others did just that. In some ways it's more difficult for the ones we love than for those of us going through a life-threatening illness. We are told to have one focus: Getting well. We are encouraged to be selfish, to put our needs first as we battle for our lives. Meanwhile our loved ones feel so helpless.

I know how lucky I am to have Amber in my corner and in my life.

I often think about my colleague Joel Siegel, who waged a valiant battle with colon cancer. He died right before I was diagnosed with breast cancer in 2007. Joel was our movie critic, and I remember being with him one year at the Oscars. Joel had an outburst or something, and it was very out of character. The Oscar people were upset and wanted to bar Joel from ever going there again.

Months later Joel was in our studio doing a segment on holiday movies. I said something about how it was kind of a tradition for my family to go to the movies on Christmas Day. Joel made some crack, which I took as a snide remark. Something like, "Wow, that's a *fun* family." I remember I was so angry and Diane said, "Robin, you don't understand, the medication that he is taking alters his behavior." At the time I thought, "Well, okay."

I'm here to tell you that moments like that come back full circle sometimes. Because there were medications I've taken that have had a similar effect on me. One time I snapped at Amber about something and she just looked at me and said: "That's not you, that's the prednisone talking." Bless her for knowing it was indeed the steroid that was affecting my behavior. There have been days when I've had to cut myself some slack, going, "Why am I acting this way?" Now I know some of the medication *will* affect your behavior, especially if you're someone like me, who rarely took even an aspirin before.

Amber was in the dark, like I was, about what a bone marrow transplant entails. She found a wonderful blog written by a man named Scott who was about six months ahead of me in the process. Scott is about the same age as I am. He didn't have any underlying health conditions. And he has a zest for life. Amber checked out his blog more than I did. It was as helpful to caregivers as it was for patients. When I had to go back into the hospital in April I remembered: "Oh, Scott, that's right, he also went back to work and then had to go into the hospital." I said, "Okay, all right. It does happen. It's not anything that's unusual. Oh, okay." Again, once you know that someone else has walked that path before you, it makes it a little bit easier for you. Thank you, Scott.

CHAPTER 25

Setbacks and Comebacks

*T*here's an old saying in sports: A setback is a setup for a comeback. In November 2012, I had my first setback. I developed what is called an opportunistic virus, cytomegalovirus, or CMV. The virus is common, especially in big cities like New York, where I live. It's a latent virus that many of us have, but our immune systems take care of it before it becomes a problem. But when I contracted the virus, it was day fifty after my transplant, and I didn't have an immune system to fight the virus off. I was admitted to the hospital and given intravenous drugs every twelve hours to knock the CMV out. The doctors estimated that it would take seven to ten days.

At first it had been my goal to make it to the

critical one-hundred-day mark without going back into the hospital, and I was disappointed to be readmitted. But as I always say, you have to change the way you think in order to change the way you feel. So I decided to see it as just coming back in for a tune-up. With Amber at her high school reunion in California, it was great that Bugs was back with me. My doctor even allowed her to bring food from home for me, since it was thanks to her good cooking that I'd finally started to get some much-needed meat on my bones. They didn't want me to lose that momentum. So Bugs and her cooking to the rescue once again!

I was so thankful that my big sister came up to see me when I was back in the hospital. I remember she was in the hallway getting prepped, going through the whole sterilization routine, and she had this big smile on her face. I just leaned out to look and I thought, "Sister Sally is coming to see me."

Sally-Ann remembers that she felt bad for Butch because he wanted to be there. We communicated a lot, especially on my private blog, but he just couldn't come to New York at the time. He was working for a new school district outside of Houston, and he couldn't get the time off. That's what I appreciate about my siblings. I don't live in the real world, they do. They keep me grounded.

It was unusual that Dorothy and Sally-Ann were able to be there as much as they were, because if you spend even five minutes in the transplant world, you hear the horror stories. People lose their jobs while they are fighting for their lives. Families fall apart under the stress and pressure of the costs and the caregiving. But we didn't have that—and thank God, because I really needed them.

Sally-Ann came up in November for my birthday. She didn't come because I had CMV; the trip had been planned already. And she asked me if she could do a taped interview with me for her TV station. It was sweet how folks in New Orleans were so concerned about me and Sally-Ann. We had the interview all arranged, and then I became ill.

I didn't know I was going to be in the hospital, but luckily I was getting better and I was going to get out soon, so I said, "Okay, let's do the interview."

Sally-Ann's camera crew came in and we all said hello. It was comforting that they were local guys. I had worked with the lead photographer,

Michael Rose, for years. I was far from camera ready. In fact, I was huddled in one corner of my room, holding on to an IV pole, getting a platelet transfusion as the camera was being set up. But I thought, "I promised Sally-Ann an interview, and I'm going to keep that promise."

I asked the nurse if we could take a break in the treatment. She agreed and we began. It was all going fine, the standard stuff about my transplant and my sister being my donor, when Sally-Ann hits me with this: "Robin, I have a birthday gift for you from our mother."

I said, "Excuse me?"

Sally-Ann smiled her big, sunshiny smile and takes out this beautiful cross. She says, "It's from Mother."

I said, "Our dead mother?"

And it was one of those moments when you have to laugh because I'd just had a platelet transfusion, I'm recovering from this awful virus, and my dear sister, my donor, my match, hits me with a "from the grave" birthday gift.

The camera was rolling and I was smiling, but what I was thinking, "Oh, Sally-Ann, I'm going to pop you."

I opened it and it was this beautiful cross, and I said, "Well, thank you." And I really meant it.

* * *

Still, you better believe that I teased Sally-Ann for months about that interview: *Oh no she didn't! She didn't pull out the dead momma birthday gift!* But she did, and what I love about my sister is that even when the chips were down—"CMV infection messing with my platelets" down—something zany like that interview can happen and we can laugh about it. Reminds me of the picture frame on my coffee table that says: "Family, we may not have it all together. But together, we have it all."

100 Days

*A*fter my transplant, all I wanted to do was get to one hundred days. It's a term you hear again and again in the transplant world: A hundred days. A hundred days. A hundred days. You get to the hundred-day point and your chances of survival increase dramatically.

I thought of my father often during the one hundred days when I lived in my apartment in near isolation. My apartment overlooks the Hudson River, and to the west of that is New Jersey, where my father was born and raised.

Trained in Tuskegee, Alabama, where I was born, the Tuskegee Airmen were America's first black military airmen. Their success rate during World War II was unmatched by any other fighter group. The brave pilots completed 1,578 missions, including escorting bombers, and they never lost one to enemy fighters.

I've always loved that my father was in the Air Force. I thoroughly enjoyed being a military brat. I have an old family picture that's my favorite. I'm about five, and my dad is in uniform. My dad was a quiet man, but he lit up when he talked about flying. "It's complete freedom," he used to say. "I guess it's what birds must feel. You go up, down, left, right, wherever your heart leads you."

I had a lot of time to sit at the window during my one hundred days, time to look at the birds and to sit with my wonderful memories of my father. My dad always used to say, "Daughter, recharge that battery. Recharge that battery, daughter." For one hundred days, that was exactly what I did. During my recovery I had a chance to rediscover who I am and also imagine who I could become.

I had an ambitious reading list for my one hundred days. Mellody Hobson and her now husband, George Lucas, sent me an amazing stack of classic films. I didn't anticipate that this forced isolation was not going to be a trip to the spa. I didn't read dozens of books or learn a foreign language. I didn't have the strength or the energy. One book that I did pick up again and again was one of my mother's favorites, *Streams in the Desert*, a book of Biblical devotions first published in 1925, a year after my mother was born. Something I read in *Streams* stayed with me during the toughest moments of my post-transplant recovery: "I walked a mile with Pleasure, she chattered all the way. But left me none the wiser, for all she had to say. I walked a mile with Sorrow and ne'er a word said she. But oh, the things I learned from her when sorrow walked with me."

I missed KJ and our walks by the river. That was

always my time to slow down and not think about my game plan for a moment. It was always a welcome respite. During my recovery, I fell back on an old family tradition: quiet time. Taking a few moments each day to be still, reading *Streams in the Desert*, meditating. Day after day, I recited the Prayer for Protection silently to myself: *"The light of God surrounds me, the love of God enfolds me, the power of God protects me, the presence of God watches over me.... Wherever I am, God is."*

I spent a lot of my one hundred days missing my mother. Even though she was on her aging journey when I was going through breast cancer, she was a great comfort. She would visit me often and even stayed at a nearby assisted-living facility the summer after I completed my chemo to be near me. She would often say, "I just want to lay my eyes on my baby."

When Mom wasn't here, she was always a phone call away. We talked on the phone every day. Her sweet voice was the best medicine. She would read her favorite passages from *Streams in the Desert* or sing to me if I had had a particularly difficult chemo treatment:

By and by, when the morning comes,
When the saints of God are gathered home,

We'll tell the story of how we've overcome,
For we'll understand it better, by and by.

It was so difficult to go through my transplant journey without her. I had never gone through any challenge in my life without her. Breakups, career woes, stubbed toes—Mom was always there to pick up the pieces, always there to let me know that I would understand it better, by and by.

As much as I wanted to, I didn't watch GMA every day when I was away. It was hard to watch the show and not be on. I'd fought so hard for us to be number one. I was wracked with guilt when I became ill again. We had all worked so hard, and now I was sidelined indefinitely. James Goldston, an ABC News executive, took me out to breakfast shortly before my medical leave. He assured me, like others had, that my return to good health was the number one priority. But he also said something that stayed with me. He said when I left it would be important to signal to the audience and to my fellow anchors to carry on with my blessing. He said something to the effect of: "Give them permission to have fun." During my absence there was an article written that stated Matt Lauer and others felt that when I was away the *Today* show would return to number one. Never happened. The most precious gift our beloved audience gave me was that they continued to watch *GMA*. They continued to make us number one.

One of my goals was staying well enough for KJ to come home. And that happy reunion came on my hundredth day. Amber and I were at home in Connecticut; Jo and Kim drove down from Maine with KJ. It was like one hundred Christmases. KJ came scampering through the front door, ran at full speed past me, racing wildly all through the house. I could hear her nails on the hardwood floors. All of us were just laughing, jumping up and down, and finally KJ stopped, her poor tongue hanging to the ground. I scooped her into my arms and started dancing with her. A sight for sore eyes. My sore eyes. In fact, we sat and stared at each other for a while. It was almost like neither one of us could believe we were finally seeing each other after four long months. She snuggled with me on the couch. Let the healing continue.

One hundred days was the goal, and I marked each day in a calendar of gorgeous beach photos, dreaming of the moment when I could be out there in the world again. There was no way to beat the clock, no fancy athletic moves to push the boundary of space and time. One hundred days is what a body needs to heal and accept the transplant, and my body was no different. One of my favorite stories tells of a butterfly cocoon. Someone sees the movement of the butterfly pressing against the wall of the cocoon and they think they'll help it along and just cut a little hole in the cocoon so the butterfly can come out with ease. But the butterfly dies soon after. There's a reason why it's beating its wings against the wall of the cocoon—to make it stronger. It doesn't serve the butterfly, in the long term, to come out too soon.

CHAPTER 27

Good Morning America

*J*anuary 8, 2013. Big Day! I had another long treatment day at the hospital. These visits usually took a few hours. First, they took my vitals, checking my blood pressure and taking my temperature. Then I stepped on the scale. I was still not gaining any weight, but at least I wasn't losing any more. Next my blood was drawn. Usually, I wait about half an hour for the results. I'm always on pins and needles waiting to hear the numbers. Those will determine the rest of my visit, hydration, medications, IVs. The story of my life, for now anyway.

On this visit, I saw both Sergio and Gail. Sergio told me that the bone marrow test I took the previous week showed no abnormalities—I was absolutely stunned. We all were. He was cautious to use the word *remission*. But everyone couldn't believe the progress I had made in such a relatively short amount of time. My platelets were still in the low 80s, but otherwise my numbers were improving. So much so that we could actually begin the discussion about when I could return to work. Dr. Giralt took the lead and came up with a game plan. He suggested doing a "mock" GMA in a couple of weeks, a kind of test run, then regroup and set a date to return to the anchor chair, probably late February.

My emotions were all over the place hearing this news. When Dr. Roboz and Dr. Giralt left the room, I broke down in tears. Amber climbed in the hospital bed with me and held me. My sweet nurse Lorraine took my hand. It was such a special moment.

As anxious as I was to return to work, I was incredibly nervous. I was thankful that the show had been doing well without me. Even though ABC News President Ben Sherwood, my executive producer, Tom Cibrowski, and everyone were telling me it was in part because viewers cared about me, I wasn't so sure. And why did I even care how the show was doing? I was alive—feeling more like my old self—more energy. Yet I was not overjoyed like I thought I would be—like I <u>should</u> have been?

My dear friend Kelly came over for dinner that night. It was great to see her. She was a young producer when we met years ago at ESPN. She's married to a great guy, Hussain, and now she's an excellent reporter for ESPN. It's not easy to go from producer to on-air talent, but Kelly is unique. And she has a wicked sense of humor.

She was as amazed as I was that going back to work was already on the table. I shared my concerns with her and she assured me that I would make the right decision with my doctors when the time was right. Even though I said we would not talk about Mom, we did—I couldn't stop crying. Mom adored Kelly. And Kelly loved Mom right back.

We recalled the time Kelly went to Easter service with us one year. Mom was delighted that Kelly was wearing a festive Easter hat. We pulled up in a cab to the Riverside Church. Mom enjoyed hearing Reverend James Forbes's sermons. We weren't the only ones. A large crowd was already waiting to get into the church. At the time Mom kept a collapsible cane in her bag. She whipped it out, and we were escorted to the front of the line. Kelly and I chuckled at the memory of that. Happy sorrow. But I knew I still hadn't allowed myself to fully grieve the loss of my beloved mother.

I would have to face those emotions before I could return to the anchor chair. For as long as I can remember, every morning after *GMA* I would go back to my dressing room and call Mom. She looked forward to my phone calls, and it was always a treat to hear how she felt about the show that morning. I don't care how old we are, we just want to make our parents proud. I wouldn't even have to say: "Good morning, Mom!" She knew I was calling and would launch right into conversation. Usually starting off with her delightful little laugh. I dreaded the thought of my first *GMA* back and not being able to call Momma.

Sergio, Gail and their nurses were preparing me physically to return to work. I also had help getting mentally prepared, thanks to my wonderful yoga instructor, Christine. I've been working with her for a few years. There's a small yoga studio as part of the gym in my apartment building. I had to take extra precautions, making sure my yoga mat was sanitized and that no one else was using the space.

Christine is a lovely soul, with dazzlingly curly

hair. She is talented, with hopes of being a full-
time actress one day. For now, she gets occasional work, also produces shows and has an in-
fectious spirit. She is patient because I'm not the
most flexible person in the world. But I soon discovered with Christine that yoga is about much
more than flexibility. It truly is a beautiful,
serene practice. Breathing. Being. Feeling. Resuming yoga with Christine was just what I
needed, for my body and soul.

A few days later, I got up early because a crew
was coming to film at my apartment for GMA,
detailing my return to the show. I hadn't done
live TV since the end of August, and I was more
than a little nervous. Elena had me looking
good. It felt odd to have makeup on again. Since
I didn't have any hair yet, Petula's job was much
easier. Just take the shine off my glistening, bald
head. Sitting under the bright lights waiting for
the show to begin, I could feel my heart pounding in my chest. But once I heard George's voice
in my earpiece I felt at ease. I shared what Sergio
had told me: no abnormalities in my bone marrow. I felt everything went very well. It was wonderful that everyone was so excited to see me.
They said I looked "radiant." I certainly felt that
way.

Later that morning, my ABC colleagues came to see me at home: Tom Cibrowski, our executive producer; Ben Sherwood, the president of ABC News; and James Goldston came to my apartment. James was the executive producer of *GMA* before Tom and had been promoted to senior VP of content and development at ABC News. James is delightfully British and is the one who finally convinced me to join Twitter. All three were excited to see me for the first time in months. We had talked a lot on the phone but seeing each other face-to-face again was powerful. I could tell they were all a little nervous, not wanting to spread any germs. They sat as far away as they could from me in my living room. They were thrilled that I was ahead of schedule, but they wanted to make sure that I didn't feel pressured in any way to return until I was ready. Every ABC executive had been consistent in telling me the only thing that mattered was my returning to good health. My job would be waiting for me. Again, something I wish everyone in my position experienced with her employer.

Ben had also been my executive producer at *GMA* before he left in 2006 to continue writing. His first novel was published in 2000; I love the title: *The Man Who Ate the 747*. It's about the crazy things we do for love. Ben's novel *Charlie St. Cloud* was made into a movie staring Zac Efron. And after Ben left ABC, he wrote a book I certainly relate to: *The Survivors Club*. It explores who bounces back and who doesn't in tough times. Everybody's got something. I was ecstatic when he returned to us four years later as president of ABC News. Ben is a strong leader but also refreshingly sensitive. And also very tall, standing six feet four inches. Even after Ben left ABC, we stayed in touch. Sitting in my living room, he told me I could do as much or as little as I wanted when I returned. He was laying out all these plans. Did I want to be considered as the new host of the game show *Who Wants to Be a Millionaire*? Did I have any interest in my own daytime talk show? I wasn't sure if I wanted to do any of that at this point in my life—but I would certainly consider it. First things first: returning to *GMA*.

Now it was time to engage Sergio's game plan. February 20 was the target date, exactly five months since my transplant. It would also be the week before the Oscars. It would be a huge psychological boost if I could return to the scene of the crime, so to speak. It was at the Oscars the year before that I knew something wasn't right. So returning would be my way of saying: "Take that, MDS!"

Before Sergio would even allow me to go into the studio for my first test drive, he wanted me to wake up at my normal time for a week. Not that there's anything normal about a 3:45 a.m. wake-up call. The first couple of mornings went fine but then not so much. I had become accustomed to sleeping until about 6:00 a.m. I would put on my froggy slippers that Sam and Josh had given me in the hospital and go into the kitchen to prepare breakfast. Usually just cereal with whole milk. Normally I use skim milk, but I was told to sneak in calories wherever I could. With my bowl of cereal I would prop up my feet on the coffee table in my living room and watch the show. During this time, my feelings about resuming normal life fluctuated: One minute I felt excited about returning to work, the next I wasn't so sure.

My goal was to work with Christine once or twice a week. Some days my energy would be low and I would feel better after a few downward dogs. My balance was still an issue, but I was beginning to see improvement. When I just wasn't up for a session with Christine, she would send me a thought-provoking poem or passage.

I was also well enough at this point to have more visitors come to my apartment. I spent a lovely afternoon with Deborah Roberts and her children, Leila and Nicky. They brought delicious Chinese food from Shun Lee: dumplings, chicken with broccoli, vegetable spring rolls. We sat around my dining room table catching up.

At the lunch at my apartment with Deb, I gave her daughter a small journal. I have watched Leila blossom into a beautiful, talented, intelligent young woman. I know the teenage years can be difficult, especially for girls. So I encouraged Leila to write down her thoughts, to document this wonderful journey she is on.

My family has always kept journals. Jotting down our thoughts, emotions, dreams, fears. I haven't been the most consistent in doing that. But found it to be very comforting during my recovery. This is an excerpt of my entry from January 21, 2013:

Very emotional day—Inauguration and MLK day. Thought about Mom a lot and cried. Remembering four years ago—Mom and Dot [Dorothy] in DC—Mom proudly wearing her old mink coat. It's hard to be on the sidelines on a big day like this. The Obamas looked so regal—so beautiful—so proud.

I know there's still much for me to do in this life. My mind is all over the place. Need to breathe deeply and know all will reveal itself in time. I've always been goal-oriented, always pushing myself in all areas. Just want to relax and not feel I need to have all the answers right now.

Before I knew it, it was "Test Drive" day at GMA. I got up early and went to the studio for the first time since August 30. I was incredibly nervous—Karen and Evelyn were there to shoot me for the prime-time special I was considering doing when I returned. I was excited to see many colleagues for the first time in almost five months, especially the studio crew. Stage managers Angie, Scott and Eddie always have the tough task of trying to rein us in along with the camera crew: Adrian, Gene, Scott, Mary and Steve. Steve's wife has successfully faced down breast cancer, and he always seems to know just what to say to me. Denise is both our senior broadcast producer and our resident fashionista. On the way to the set I always pop in her office to get her approval. Bobby, our technical director, looks so much like the actor who played Carlton on *The Fresh Prince of Bel-Air.* Whenever we need a good laugh, Bobby breaks out in the Carlton dance.

* * *

Everyone was excited to see me, too. I could tell many were nervous to hug me or touch me. I honestly think some of the crew feared they would never see me again. There were so many tears, so much joy. I was touched to see many #TEAMROBIN signs hanging everywhere. Rita, our sweet green-room coordinator, had one outside the green room where the show's guests gather every morning. It's still there, as is the #TEAM-ROBIN sign on Eddie's jib camera in the studio.

Diandre, my stylist, picked out a beautiful blue-and-black St. John dress for me to wear. Once I put it on and Elena and Petula worked their magic, I felt fine. Great, actually. Seeing myself in the mirror, except for the few sprouts on my bald head, I felt like my old self for the first time in a long time.

I went to the studio before the show started, blowing a kiss skyward to Mom and Dad. I watched from the sidelines for the first hour of the show and then retreated to my dressing room. I was feeling a bit tired. This was the most excitement and activity for me in quite some time.

After the show ended, I returned to the studio to sit in my anchor chair. The bright studio lights really bothered me. My skin was still very sensitive. There was copy in the teleprompter for me to read. It was very difficult. The treatment had affected my eyesight, leaving me with blurred vision, floaters. It's a temporary side effect of the transplant. My vision had improved since the transplant, but was still not totally back to normal. A frustrating reminder of what I endured.

Other than that, the test drive was a success. I have to admit that when Sergio first suggested doing this, I thought it was silly. I've been a broadcaster for decades. But Sergio was absolutely right. There was no way I could have done a live show that day. There were too many emotions, but I felt much stronger when I left than when I arrived.

A few days later, I met George, Sam, Josh and Lara at Loi, a restaurant near my apartment. The same restaurant where I was when Dorothy called to say Momma had taken a turn for the worse. I was meeting with the gang to shoot a spot for the prime-time special about my journey with MDS. I'm always so comfortable around them. We spend a lot of time with each other away from work. Even though it had been a while since we hung out like this, it was as if no time had passed at all.

George is the quietest of the five of us. Any downtime he has, he prefers to spend with his family at home. One time I asked his wife, Ali, if George was okay with the rest of us hanging out together so much. She assured me that George had no problem with that whatsoever, and hoped that no one took it the wrong way if he didn't always join our outings. When we are together, George fits right in, though it can be hard for him to get a word in edgewise sometimes.

Josh and Lara are the life of the party: funny, engaging, confident, but never cocky. Lara and her husband have two beautiful children. They live in Connecticut, and Lara is in a car by 4:30 a.m. headed to the GMA studios in Times Square.

Josh also lives in Connecticut. His sweet little daughter lights up his life. If we can't find Josh, it usually means he's having a tea party with his little girl. I admire how Josh and Lara juggle young children with such a demanding career.

Sam is so sensitive. When we all met at Loi, I

could tell he was still worried about me. He was very concerned about my weight or lack thereof at the time. I'm so thankful I was well enough to go to Sam's wedding a couple of months before. It was absolutely beautiful. A small affair at his apartment. Only his family and a few close friends. His husband Rubem's family is from Brazil so they Skyped in for the ceremony. When we took photos we held the computer so they could be included in the wedding pictures. I was touched that Sam and Rubem asked me to read the Elizabeth Barrett Browning sonnet "How Do I Love Thee."

I still had to go to the hospital once a week to have my numbers checked and to make sure I was staying hydrated. On one of my visits Sergio asked me: "Is there anything you want to do that you feel I'm not allowing you?" I said, "Well, yes, there is. I want to go to the Super Bowl in New Orleans." I thought he would say no right away, but instead he said he wanted to think about it.

Sergio called a couple of days later and said, "We didn't put you through all this to not let you live your life." He would not allow me to go to the crowded Superdome for the big game, but I could fly to New Orleans and go to Sally-Ann's Super Bowl party at her house.

I felt before I could go home to *GMA*, I first needed to really go home to the Gulf Coast. I still was not cleared to fly commercial, and I was so appreciative that Disney provided a private jet for me to fly home. My colleagues on the flight were also very appreciative. This was a rare treat for all of us.

Amber went along to keep a close eye on me. I couldn't overdo it. This was my first time being able to leave the East Coast since my transplant. My assistant, Sonny; my producer, Emily; and my attentive staff had Kleenex for me, hand sanitizer, water, gum—I think they were more nervous than I was. No one wanted anything to happen to me on their watch.

Again, there was a crew shooting a little video of me on the plane for the special. I was like a kid pressed against the window looking out, especially as we got closer to the Gulf Coast. This was home for me. The people who love me for being the daughter of Lawrence and Lucimarian Roberts. I know they are proud of me being a network TV anchor—but they would love me just the same if I were not.

When we landed, there was a wonderful surprise. A big delegation from my alma mater, Southeastern Louisiana University, was waiting for me. Students, cheerleaders and our mascot, Roomie—a big, fuzzy lion—were all there. It was so special to see all the signs that read SWAB-BIN' FOR ROBIN. I was just so thrilled that my school has conducted bone marrow drives to register donors. I was especially happy to meet the young woman who came up with the idea. Her father had a bone marrow transplant years ago, and his sister was his donor, too. Small world.

After the great reception at the airport, Josh, Sam and I headed to a catering place—Mendenhall. Sam had been tweeting pictures of our trip. It just so happens my doctor, Sergio, follows me on Twitter. He saw me hugging people at the airport. Sergio sent me a LONG e-mail cautioning me to cool it with the hugs, reminding me that I was still very vulnerable to infection.

He e-mailed me: "Stick with elbow bumping, Robin."

That's very hard for me to do, especially around people I love the most.

I had so much fun with my guys. We ate gumbo and po'boys, and the bread pudding was out of this world, so delicious. They had a brass band Mardi Gras theme, and we second-lined and danced all afternoon. Wonderful! Then we had a reception at one of Emeril's restaurants in downtown New Orleans. I was exhausted but very happy.

The next day, I got up early and hung out behind the scenes at *GMA*, which was broadcasting live near Jackson Square. NFL great Emmitt Smith and his lovely wife, Pat, were there. It touched me to see Emmitt wearing my bracelet! He even wore it when he was competing on the all-star edition of *Dancing with the Stars*. That meant a lot to me.

I also had a very nice visit with country music star Tim McGraw, who performed on the show, and his stunning wife, Faith Hill. We spent time on their tour bus catching up. Tim looked fantastic. He works out and runs, and it shows. Faith was adorable as ever—she's so cute with her braces. We talked and talked. I've known them both awhile. Both have appeared on my country music specials. They invited me to spend time with them in Nashville—I often say that I will, and hopefully this time I will. I get invitations like this frequently from celebrities who have become my friends. Usually when I do have free time, I just want to be at home with Amber and KJ.

The next morning we drove from New Orleans

to the Pass. It's about an hour's drive, one I've taken countless times, but this was different. It would be the first trip home since Momma's passing almost six months before. I don't think I ever felt such raw emotion. We first stopped at the Boys and Girls Club, the state-of-the-art facility in the Pass that my mom helped establish after Hurricane Katrina. The kids there had sent me many handmade get-well cards and wanted to see me. There was a large crowd at the Club to greet me. Did I say how much I love my hometown? The gym in the Club is dedicated to our family. When I saw the plaque above the gym door I broke down. My emotions were very much on the surface. Dorothy also stopped by the Club, and when she saw me she hurried away crying. Later I asked Amber what that was all about. She said Dorothy told her: "I can't believe how frail my baby sister looks." Amber assured her I was doing well, that despite my size I was getting stronger every day.

When we pulled up in front of Mom's house, I couldn't get out of the car. I just stared at our family home. How I used to love to walk through the front door and hear Mom's voice and then feel her squeezing my cheeks, kissing me—so happy to have me home.

Dorothy was with me when I walked in and inhaled the comforting, familiar aroma. I looked to the heavens and said, "Momma, I'm home," and Dorothy responded, "She knows." The last time I left the house after Mom's service, mere days before my transplant, I honestly didn't know if I would ever be back. I walked around the house just taking it all in. Looking at family pictures. Mom's little touches that made this house a home. And then I sat on her piano bench. Mom had bought the beautiful baby grand piano for herself after Katrina. It was a big deal for Momma to spend money on herself like that. She joked that she wanted to put a sign in the yard that read: I'M SPENDING MY CHILDREN'S INHERITANCE. That was more than fine with us.

I hesitated when it came to deciding whether or not to show me going home in my special. I thought it might be too much. I can't tell you how many people have thanked me for including it in the show. They, too, had felt similar emotions when they returned home for the first time after the death of a parent. It was somehow comforting to them to know they are not alone.

The crew set up to do a sit-down interview at the house with me and my siblings. Sally-Ann and Butch would be arriving shortly. I treated the crew to the most delicious po'boys on the Coast from Pirate's Cove. When we moved to the Pass it was located off Highway 90. I didn't like seafood when I was young, so I would get their roast beef po'boys dripping in gravy. Now I opt for the dressed shrimp po'boys from Pirate's Cove. The shrimp is crispy golden, cooked to perfection. Wash it down with a Barq's root beer—now that's what I call livin'!

Katrina wiped out the original Pirate's Cove on the highway, and for about eight years they were in a temporary location. The only seating: wooden picnic tables outside. I'm happy to report that in late 2013 Pirate's Cove finally moved to a permanent location on Menge Avenue. The Pass is coming back.

Butch, Sally-Ann, Dorothy and I sat in the family room in front of the stone fireplace we never use. It was the first time seeing Butch since Mom's funeral. With cameras rolling we talked about faith, family and friends. I had planned on staying the night at the house with Amber and going to our church in the morning, the church where we'd had Mom's homegoing. But emotionally I was not ready for that yet. One step at a time.

Super Bowl Sunday was Ravens versus the

49ers. I really didn't care about the matchup, though we were looking forward to Beyoncé and Destiny's Child performing at halftime. What mattered most to me was just being with family in Sally-Ann's home. We felt it was important for Mom's grandchildren and great-grandchildren to know that we are still together. A united family.

I was moved to tears by what each family member said to me: Rene, Bianca, Judith, Kelly, Jessica, Lauren—my sweet, beautiful young nieces.

Kelly, Sally-Ann's youngest daughter, was especially touching. She's normally very quiet, but she spoke so eloquently about how much I mean to her and to our family. Kelly was feeling overwhelmed surrounded by such unconditional love.

Jeremiah, Sally-Ann's son, expressed his emotions through a music video: He's so talented. He's living in New York City now, attending the New School for Drama.

Remember this name: Jeremiah Richard Craft. You'll be seeing it up in bright lights one day.

I was pleasantly surprised that I wasn't totally exhausted from my first road trip. It was uplifting to see my family—I've never felt closer to them.

When I got back to New York, I was a little more tired than before. I think the adrenaline of all the travel had worn off. I was grateful the trip went well with no complications. I had been a bit worried about that. I didn't yet fully trust my body. Since I was feeling relatively fine before I got sick, every twitch or pain made me worry.

February 5, 2013, was Mom's birthday. She would have been eighty-nine years old. I really thought she'd live into her nineties. Her mother and grandmother did, and they had such hard lives and not the best health care. I really think Momma was tired—tired of being strong—tired of being alone since Daddy died. I never knew anyone who was looking forward to going to heaven more than Mom. The previous summer, when I went to visit her in the rehab center after her stroke, I wheeled her out in the patio to get some sun. She closed her eyes and started calling out the names of people she was seeing: Daddy, her mom, my brother-in-law's mom, "Ma Dear." She seemed so happy. When I nudged her to open her eyes she seemed disappointed that she was still here and not in heaven with them.

After Mom's birthday, Amber and I snuck in a trip to Key West. We had always wanted to go to Key West in February, but we never could because of sweeps. February is an important month for ratings, when ad rates for the show are set. This year, 2013, was different, since I wasn't yet back on the air. The weather in Key West was perfect: no humidity, not too hot. Usually, people recognize me, but are very laid-back.

This trip was different. There were a ton of people coming up to me. They were so pleased to see me doing well, health-wise, and were excited about my return to *GMA*. ABC was running promos about my return: "Robin's back!"

While on vacation in Key West I started to think: "What's the rush?" I wanted to stay an extra week or two, because it finally felt like I was relaxing. People think a medical leave is vacation. Trust me, it's not. But being in Key West was.

A week later, I returned to New York and had some time to reflect. My second trip away from the doctors had gone well. I felt fine physically, but not necessarily emotionally. I really began to wonder if I should take more time before going back to work. No one was pressuring me; ABC had been incredibly patient. My medical team said it was totally up to me. I was medically cleared to return to the anchor desk. The "test drives" had gone well. There was still a small problem with my eyesight, but they assured me it would get better. I decided to stick with the schedule that we set.

On February 19, 2013, I had another routine doctor's appointment, just to get the final all clear to return to work. Dorothy, Sally-Ann and Sally-Ann's sister-in-law, Phyllis, had all flown in for my first show back. The night before my return to work, I couldn't get to sleep. It was just impossible. I was so excited and nervous. First-day-of-school jitters.

February 20, 2013. Finally, the day arrived.

The night before, my sisters had urged me, "Take your hands off the wheel, just let people love you." I was anxious about all the fanfare surrounding my return. Ben Sherwood, Anne Sweeney and other executives were there to greet me. They literally rolled out the red carpet for me. And a big red bow was wrapped around my anchor chair. We taped a special open with George, Sam, Josh and Lara huddled close to me.

Before I entered the studio, I looked up at the heavens and said good morning to my parents. It was the first time I was going to be back on air after Momma's passing.

Then I walked to home base, took a deep

breath and smiled. Then I said, "I've been waiting 174 days to say this: Good Morning, America."

One hundred and seventy-four days—WOW!

The date was so significant. I came back to GMA on February 20, exactly five months after my transplant.

President and Mrs. Obama taped a special greeting—so did Hillary Clinton, Oprah and country star and dear friend Brad Paisley; Buddy Valastro, the Cake Boss, made a delicious red velvet cake. Dr. Roboz and Dr. Giralt were interviewed on the show. When George and I ended our chat with them, I led a standing ovation for their nurses who were also in the studio. They are the unsung heroes. They are with you the most in the hospital and are the first to know when something the doctor prescribed is not working. During my comeback show, Sergio, Gail and the nurses kept a close eye on me the whole time. They nearly freaked out when I went outside during a commercial break to greet the large crowd. I could hear their voices in my head: "Be careful of the germs. The risk of infection is still great. Stick with elbow bumping, Robin."

But how could I not go outside and say thank

you? Thank you, and you, and you! Thank you for being here. Thank you for caring. Thank you for not forgetting about me.

Mandisa, one of my favorite singers, was our special musical guest and sang her hit song "Stronger." The lyrics are so powerful:

> *When the waves are taking you under*
> *Hold on just a little bit longer*
> *He knows that this is gonna make you*
> *   stronger, stronger*
> *The pain ain't gonna last forever*
> *And things can only get better*
> *Believe me*
> *This is gonna make you stronger*
> *Believe me, this is gonna make you*
> *   stronger.*

Dorothy, Sally-Ann and I—the Sisters Three—had been holding it pretty much together until Mandisa brought down the house. Dorothy in particular lost it. She is by far the most sensitive of the three of us. She's the middle child. It pains Sally-Ann and me that Dorothy is sometimes overlooked just because her two sisters are on TV. We are as proud of Dorothy as she is of us. She makes some of the jewelry that I wear on *GMA*.

All in all, I thought the show went well, but I realized I still had a long way to go, both physically and emotionally. To this day, I still can't put on any weight because my metabolism is out of whack and will be for a year.

I was exhausted after the show. I was also so relieved my return was behind me. Afterward I had a lovely brunch with Amber, Dorothy, Sally-Ann and Phyllis at Sarabeth's near Central Park. It was a chance for me to catch my breath, though I still didn't have much of an appetite and was quieter than usual. Everyone else did most of the talking. I realized I was more tired than I expected, plus I was taken aback by the number of people who wanted to take pictures with us when we left the restaurant.

After brunch, when my sisters left for the airport, I didn't break down and cry like I did the last time. Then I cried like a baby, like a two-year-old pleading for them not to go. I remember that I even rubbed my eyes like a bawling two-year-old. No tears this time; getting stronger, I guess. I hope.

February 21, 2013 was day two back at GMA. A member of the crew, Jerry, said yesterday felt like "welcome back" and that today was more like "welcome home." It was more normal; it was actually the day I was looking forward to more than the day before. I was craving normalcy, whatever that is these days. It was pretty much business as usual. I felt a little more comfortable in the anchor chair. I just wished I could see the teleprompter better.

George, Lara, Sam and Josh were so incredibly supportive. They've shown our viewers how to care for an ill coworker. The show must go on, but my colleagues made me and *GMA* viewers feel as if I was there with them every day of my medical leave—that I was never far from their thoughts and hearts. They totally had my back.

And, of course, I know that my angels are always watching out for me, too. Before my medical leave, each morning, I would blow a kiss before walking out onto the set. "Morning, Daddy, watch over Momma." Now, I blow two kisses. Before I say good morning to America, I say, "Morning, Daddy. Morning, Momma. I love you."

CHAPTER 28

Back in the Game

I spent most of 2012 fighting for my life and then amazingly, miraculously, I began to get better. I went back to work on a very part-time basis, but it felt so good to be back in that chair. It was still a struggle to keep my weight up, and I was still on too many medications to count, but all signs indicated that the transplant was successful. I had traveled so far on a combination of faith and science. As Dr. Giralt said when he inserted my chest with millions of Sally-Ann's stem cells, "Let God do His work and it will work."

As taking care of my health began to be less of a full-time job, other thoughts and concerns came flooding in. More than anything, I became aware that I had not fully grieved for Mom, and the wide range of emotions that I felt for her was almost dizzying. I recall going into her bedroom the day after she passed away and screaming, "Why did you leave me now?" I was so angry and scared. I'm not angry anymore—just incredibly sad. Not a day has gone by that I have not thought of her.

I began thinking that I should book an appointment with Dr. A, my therapist. She and I had last seen each other after I had beat breast cancer. I thought I'd be thrilled with treatment being over, but I became depressed. There was no one to check on me on a regular basis after I'd seen a doctor every week and gone through chemo and radiation for almost a year. But it turns out that the sadness I felt was common in patients who've undergone extensive treatments.

When I went to see Dr. A, she agreed that I had a wellspring of delayed grief and emotions concerning my mom. She also understood the transplant regimen and the intense recovery after: It took every bit of mental and physical energy I had to make it through the last few months. But after a couple of sessions with Dr. A, I became so emotional that I decided to wait awhile before seeing her again. I realized I still wasn't quite ready to deal with the hurricane of grief that was tied up in losing Momma. She assured me that I would know when the time was right.

It was helpful that I already had a history with Dr. A. I first started seeing her after my dad died in 2004. Seeing a therapist is not a sign of weakness but rather an acknowledgment that you don't have all the answers and you need help finding them. Plus I like the idea of a totally objective person. When you tell your problems to a friend, you may leave some things out because you're embarrassed by what they might think. I find with a therapist you can be truly transparent. At times Dr. A has wanted to prescribe antidepressants for me, but I've always rejected the idea. I don't think they're wrong. They help millions of people. It just hasn't felt like the right choice for me. I would rather meditate, exercise, eat healthy and get proper rest. And thankfully, that worked for me.

Many days I never left my apartment. I would use the time to catch up on e-mails and send thank-you notes. I was so thankful for the viewer who sent me thank-you notes with stamped envelopes. If you are wondering what gift you can give a friend or loved one at home on a medical leave, thank-you notes with stamped envelopes will be much appreciated. Since eating out was still dicey, Bugs inspired me to cook more at home. I saw what joy it brought her. I would make something simple like turkey spaghetti or broiled pork loin with roasted veggies. Amber has a lot of wonderful qualities; cooking is not one of them. So she also benefited from Bugs motivating me to get busy in the kitchen. I do set a mean table, complete with burning candles.

At the end of my first week back, Michelle Obama came to the studio for an interview. It was great to see her. She looked fab as usual with her new bangs. Petula had picked out a hairpiece with bangs when I returned to *GMA*, but it looked too much like Mrs. Obama—I didn't want people to think I was copying her. So unlike when I had breast cancer, this time I decided to forgo the wig.

The interview with Mrs. Obama went well; it centered around her health initiative with kids. Master chef Marcus Samuelsson was also part of the interview. He is a genius in the kitchen.

After the interview we headed to the airport to travel to LA for the Oscars.

It was the first time I'd traveled that far after the transplant. I was a little nervous about being on the Red Carpet with so many people. But mentally I knew it would be a tremendous boost. One year ago at the Oscars I knew something wasn't right, and here I was, back again at the Oscars. Almost like staring down MDS and saying, "You didn't beat me!"

I had a limited role on the Red Carpet special. I wore a velvet cobalt-blue Marc Bouwer creation. The year before he dressed me in a slinky, white sequined gown. I found out at the last moment I would be able to return to the Oscars. And Marc came through for me. I interviewed Robert De Niro and his lovely wife, Grace, on the Red Carpet. I also chatted up the glamorous and talented Halle Berry. She was rockin' a gown worthy of being a Bond Girl. It was a chance to thank her for the long camel cashmere robe she sent me. Disclaimer: I thought it was a long sweater. It was just so beautiful, I assumed it was meant to be worn out. Amber, who is much more fashion savvy than I, thankfully pointed out to me that it was actually a robe.

Sometimes people would caution me, not my doctors, but my friends and coworkers. They would say, "You're doing too much. You're doing too much."

I just wanted to say, "Oh, people, come on,"

because inevitably they would refer back to someone they loved and an illness they had. They would say, "When my son or daughter _____ [fill in the blank] went through this..."

Everyone's different. I just know, for me, it wasn't so much a goal of "I want to be back in that anchor chair." It was more: I wanted to be well enough to return to my job, to the things that I love to do, to the places that I love to go, to the people that I love to spend time with. It was really that simple.

In hindsight, traveling to New Orleans and Mississippi, to Key West and then to LA for the Oscars in the five months after my transplant was a bit ambitious, but that's still the only speed I know—full steam ahead. I didn't go through all I did to sit on the sidelines—I wanted back in the game! Put me in, coach, I'm ready to play. Or so I thought.

CHAPTER 29

Noncompliant

*I*t was early April, Final Four weekend, which meant Key West. My first vacation after my return to work. I had just filled in for Kelly Ripa on *Live! with Kelly and Michael.* I adore Kelly and Michael Strahan is the bomb diggity. He plays "Lovely Day" by Bill Withers in his dressing room before the show. It certainly is a lovely day with Kelly and Michael. I wasn't feeling that well when Amber and I headed to Key West. Usually when we land, we hop in our rented convertible, cruise Duval Street and then stop at the gas station and pick up Dion's Fried Chicken. But I was feeling so bad I just wanted to crawl into bed. Amber kept trying to get me to go to the doctor. I said, "No, no, no. I don't want to ruin your vacation. I don't want to ruin my vacation. I'm not sick. I'll be fine. It will pass. It will pass."

But it didn't pass. Beth, one of my friends from Atlanta who also is one of the owners of our home in Key West, got to town a few days later. Like Amber, she was worried. I had brutal coughing spells. My toes would even curl and cramp, because I was just coughing so hard. I lost a lot of weight, went down to a rail-thin 115 pounds. A friend of Beth's, Kim, flew in from Seattle to join us. We all grabbed a bite to eat in town and rode our bikes back home, as we always did. Kim and I made it back first, I doubled over coughing. Kim simply said: "I really don't know you, but you shouldn't mess with your lungs." Amber and Beth had been after me for days, but a virtual stranger finally got my attention.

Tom Cibrowski, my executive producer, called me in Key West. I could barely put two words together without coughing. He immediately called Rich Besser, who called Gail Roboz. I had been e-mailing with Gail but not actually talking with her. She called me and asked what in the heck was going on. She could hear the difficulty I was having breathing and insisted I go see a doctor right away. Beth has been going to Key West much longer than I and is the honorary mayor there. She made some quick calls and got me in to see a doctor. We had no idea even where the hospital was in Key West, but we managed to find it. Everyone there could not have been nicer. They drew my blood and took chest X-rays. In our bathing suits we waited for the results. The doctor brought me and Amber into his office and called Gail. Even I could see how cloudy my chest X-ray was. I had "walking pneumonia" and needed to get back to NYC ASAP.

It was a bit of a mad scramble to fly out of Key West and back to my hospital in New York. Dr. Giralt and Dr. Roboz made alternate arrangements for me to be treated in Miami, just in case. By the time I arrived in New York, I literally crawled down the hall of the emergency room. I was just waving the white flag and saying, "Okay. Okay. Okay."

At one point, I was just so angry. I feared that my illness was much worse than my doctors were letting on. I'd heard so much about your body rejecting the graft, the dreaded graft-versus-host disease. I feared my body was rejecting Sally's cells and that my medical team was keeping something from me. Dr. Giralt and Dr. Roboz let me know, in no uncertain terms, that they wouldn't hide important information from me and that moreover, there was nothing to hide. Dr. Roboz said, "It's just that these viruses are very painful and not a lot of fun. No, everything else is fine." I just had to start believing that it would be okay, and I did, slowly.

My illness in April was a real hurdle. But I have no regrets about going back to work when I did. I know it was very important for me — emotionally and psychologically — at that moment. Yes. I could have stayed at home and the illness in April still could have happened. My doctors were very quick to point this out. It was not a result of going back to work. I hadn't been over-doing it. It was just one of those freak things. We all have these dormant viruses in us, and our bodies usually fight them off. These dormant ones decide to poke their head out and they see clear sailing and go to town.

I also had to admit to myself that I was... what is the word? "Noncompliant." I wasn't taking all the prescribed medications I should have been taking. I got a little cocky, felt I was doing okay and I didn't want to take some of the medication. Especially one that was a thick, neon-yellow liquid. Yuck!

We should have done a piece on the show, because this happens with all kinds of people with all kinds of illnesses. You think that you're okay, you stop taking your medication, you stop doing everything by the letter because you think, "I'm well." No, you're not. You're well because you're taking your medicine.

I'm willing to admit that I'm not perfect and the reason is because the mess that was my health in April has a message. I know that there are people who are reading this book who are on blood pressure medications, diabetes medications and so on, and sometimes you get a little bit comfortable and you start to taper off. But this is what my story is about: You can be cooperative and intelligent and aware—and you're also human. It's so easy to say, "You know what, I feel fine. These doctors are just being conservative. This stuff tastes yucky, I don't want to eat this." Right? How many times have you personally finished a course of antibiotics? Hardly ever. All of us are like, day three, day four—yeah, I'm good, I've got it.

Wrong!

Let me be clear. I learned my lesson. I now take every last drop of whatever it is that they tell me to take when it comes to my medication, and

I've been better for it. Haven't been hospitalized since April 2013. (Knock on wood.)

April was a horrible, horrible month. I was in the hospital for about a week, and it was the wakeup call I really needed. All I wanted to do was pick up the phone and call Mom. But I can't call Mom anymore. Again and again, it comes to me. I'm a grown woman but when I am sick, when any of us are sick, we want our mommies.

CHAPTER 30

Taking the Stage

*A*lthough I could hardly imagine it when I was crawling down that hospital room corridor, little by little, I began to get better. I was still on a part-time schedule at *GMA*, appearing two to three times a week. When I wasn't working, I rested. I took my medicine. My trainer, Angel, adjusted my workouts according to my strength and endurance. And I finally began to gain weight. As my body got stronger, so did my spirit. By summer, things had begun to come full circle. The summer of 2012 had been such a rope-a-dope.

Do you remember the Rumble in the Jungle with Muhammad Ali and George Foreman? The year was 1974 and the two greatest boxers in the world were set to fight in what was then known as Zaire, now called the Democratic Republic of Congo. Foreman was favored to win because of his powerful punching ability, but Ali had secretly been perfecting a technique, where he would lean against the ropes of the boxing ring and while it looked like Foreman was just pulverizing him, the ropes were actually absorbing the majority of the blows.

The summer I was diagnosed with MDS was full of so many punches, I didn't know how I was ever going to stand up tall in the ring again. You know what I was up against. I announced my diagnosis and began pre-treatment. My mom suffered a stroke, and the ravages of aging began to take her down. My sister Sally-Ann was a perfect match for me, and that saved my life. My sister Dorothy ran point on the care of our aging mother. My mother died in my arms, then just a week later I began the most aggressive, brutal regimen of chemotherapy I had ever known. Then I had a bone marrow transplant—and began the count of a hundred days. Every day ahead of me brought with it the risk of an infection that could kill me. Every day behind me meant that like a newborn baby in her first few weeks of life, I was getting stronger. Somehow I made it. It might have looked as if life was beating me senseless with challenges and tragedies and loss, but God was holding me the whole time. He was the ropes that took the brunt of the blows. As the poet Nikki Giovanni so powerfully wrote, "Not more than we can bear... more than we should have to."

When I got the news that ESPN, my old home team of esteemed and beloved colleagues, had decided to award me the Arthur Ashe Award for courage, the first thing I did was thank God. Thank God that he had given me, bit by bit, the strength and the courage and the good fortune to be a thriver, more than a survivor, of a terrible disease once more. The second thing I did was pick out a beautiful red dress, a dress that to me said with its vibrant color, "I celebrate life!" The third thing I did was up my time in the gym with Angel, so that I could look good in said dress, designed by Wes Gordon. It was June 2013, and the award show would be held in Los Angeles in July, just a few weeks away.

It's called the ESPYs, and the acronym stands for Excellence in Sports Performance Yearly award. In the world of sports, it is the equivalent of the Oscars. Everybody gets dressed up and comes to see who will be named the best female athlete, the best male athlete, the coach of the year, the top paralympic athletes and the most outstanding in the collegiate ranks. The men and women in the room have pulled off so many awe-inspiring acts of physical greatness. World-class athletes that we're used to seeing in uniform are now in their Sunday best. Movie stars share the stage, and the audience is filled with musicians and luminaries of the sports world. It's my favorite kind of crowd: brilliant, eclectic and diverse.

For me, it's always a thrill just being at the ESPYs, in a room with the world's premier athletes. But this past year, I wasn't there to observe or even to present, which is always an honor as well. I was there to receive the Arthur Ashe courage award. Arthur Ashe was a dear, dear friend of mine. He taught me the importance of using the platform we've been blessed to be given to be of service to others. He showed all of us that by his selfless acts off the court. The award spoke to what my momma always said: Make your mess your message. Find the meaning behind whatever you're going through, because everybody's got something.

Michelle Obama sent her regards to me by videotape, her beauty and sincerity radiating from the big screen. Tom Cruise narrated the video tribute to me. LeBron James introduced me to the crowd: "I just want us to think about one thing, as all athletes here—male and female. When there's a time that we're working out or…when we feel like we have adversity that hits us, and we start to think, 'I can't.'…Let us just think about this moment. This is an unbelievable woman and I'm honored to be in this position. I'm honored to present the Arthur Ashe Award for courage to the most beautiful, strong woman I've ever been around, Ms. Robin Roberts."

Even before I got on the stage, I was blown away by the star power in that venue. How did I get here? I'm just a little girl from Mississippi, sitting here with my siblings and Amber, and I'm just grateful to be alive. My knees were knocking. I'd love to say I was sitting there all calm, cool and collected, but my heart was pounding. Arthur was such an important person in my life. I was at the press conference with him announcing this very award. Fast-forward twenty years, I'm standing there holding it. So many things were flashing through my mind. I knew that in two more commercial breaks, I'd be up. And I was thinking, "How am I going to navigate the stairs in this dress?" Luckily, my studly GMA cohort Josh was such a gentleman and escorted me to the stage.

I thanked Michelle Obama for her warm words, then I thanked LeBron James for graciously adding to this immense honor. My momma was from Akron, Ohio, and she loved herself some King James. I knew she was smiling down on us at that moment. Then I looked out to the crowd and I spoke from the heart:

It's a moment I couldn't even begin to dream of when I began my career. You heard me, I just wanted to be the best sports journalist that I could be. I wanted to be a pro athlete. That's what I really wanted to be. I wanted to be a pro athlete. But there's something—wait a minute, what is it called again? oh yes, ability—you must have. So I am in awe of your vast accomplishments and to be in your company tonight. And in the company of some old, dear friends at ESPN.

I realize there are many worthy of holding this honor. Others who have exhibited far more courage, strength and resilience. It's humbling for me to represent you tonight. I draw strength from you. You give me the courage to face down any challenge, to know that when fear knocks, to let faith answer the door.

Those of us who are fortunate to overcome some form of illness or adversity are often told that we are strong. I didn't find that strength on my own. It's a quality that grew with every kind word of support, every prayer, every tweet, every e-mail, every phone call.

I gained strength from the doctors and nurses who checked on me, long after their shift was over. From those I knew and others I may never know, who took time out of their busy lives to reach out and let me know they were thinking of me [and] praying for me, every step of my journey.

Through it all, I've learned that strength, true strength, isn't when you face down life's challenges on your own. It's when you take them on by accepting the help, faith and love of others. And knowing you are lucky to have those....

My family and dear friends, their unconditional love brings me to tears....My big sister Sally-Ann, my donor, I wouldn't be standing here. Heck, I wouldn't be standing anywhere if it were not for you. And I thank you for that.

Throughout the ceremony, whenever the camera panned to my sister, she pointed to the sky as if to remind us that she wanted no praise, but to give it all to the Lord. In the weeks and months after the awards, sister Sally pointing skyward became an image and a touch point that people referred to again and again.

It's very easy to spot Sister Sally, she's always the one who's like, "Yes, Jesus. Yes, Lord. Yes."

Yes, Jesus. Sister Sally will set you free.

I remember when Jim Valvano was the first recipient of the Arthur Ashe courage award. I was standing backstage . . . the next presenter on after Jimmy V when he accepted the honor with an inspiring speech that touched us all and still does. That night, in establishing the V Foundation for Cancer Research, Jim said, "We need your help. I need your help. We need money for research. It may not save my life. It may save my children's. It may save someone you love."

I've been blessed to achieve things in life I could have never imagined as a little girl growing up in Mississippi. But most of all, I've never imagined that I'd be standing here, twenty years after Jimmy V's speech, and say that because of everyone who has responded to his challenge, because of all the donations, research and support, mine is one of the lives that's been saved.

But other than my family taking selfies with celebs on the red carpet, the most hilarious moment involved my sister Dorothy. The night before the ESPYs, ESPN treated my family and friends to a big steak dinner. Dorothy had declared, more than once, that the steak was delicious and ginormous. I didn't realize that she took her leftovers back to the hotel and put it in the fridge in her room. Then the next day, on the flight from LA back to Mississippi, she boarded the plane with those leftovers. When we spoke on the phone, Dorothy proudly said, "I ate off of that steak for four days." That's my family: From walking the red carpet to praising the Lord onstage with LeBron James to eating cross-country leftovers, we know how to have a good time and we always keep it real.

The day after the awards, I received a very special gift from Tom Cruise. He arranged for me to fly a P-51 Mustang, the exact same type of plane that my beloved father had flown in World War II. It was as if my friend who arranged this experience had cast an invisible lasso to my past that tied me palpably and memorably to my father's career as a fighter pilot, at a time when men like him were still treated like second-class citizens the moment their feet hit the ground.

About ten years ago, *Good Morning America* did a fantasy segment and invited all of our on-air team to live their wildest dreams: Mine was to fly a plane like my father had, to fly—not walk—in his shoes, as he had in the 1940s. My wish was granted. The producers arranged for me to have eight hours of training at Moton Field in Tuskegee, where my father and his fellow soldiers had trained. And as I made my way down that tarmac toward the plane, I could literally feel the spirits of all those brave young men who had walked this road before me. They were called the Tuskegee Airmen, but at eighteen, nineteen, many were barely old enough to shave. Young men who couldn't vote, couldn't attend the same schools or even drink from the same water fountains as the white recruits, and yet they saved thousands of lives without regard to race. My father and his fellow Airmen broke the color line in the sky decades before they could break it on the ground.

My father was still alive when we taped that segment, and I had been doing TV for a good long time. He was not easily impressed by the bells and whistles of fame and he remained, throughout his entire life, the strong and silent type. The day that I taped my *Good Morning America* fantasy segment was a different story. Dad, who was usually reserved, was ablaze with energy and conversation that morning. He wore his red blazer because that was what the Airmen wore. When that old AT-6 aircraft came chugging down the runway, it was hard to tell who was more excited, me or Dad. Then when I got into the plane and put my hands on the gear, shifting the nose upward, and the plane took off from the ground, I will never forget the expression on my father's face. He had lived to see me fly a plane the way he had as a young man. I had always been a daddy's girl, but that moment cinched it forever.

My father passed away the next year, suddenly and unexpectedly. This year will mark ten years without him, and I still miss him every day. Lawrence Roberts retired as a full bird colonel from the military, and while it's a funny term—"full bird colonel"—it's fitting for my dad. He was an eagle: proud, strong, with wings that were strong enough to carry our entire family all the way around the world then safely back home. Because my dad was a pilot, an eagle, there's nowhere I feel closer to him than when I'm in the sky. I'm never nervous flying, even when it's a turbulent ride, because I know that no matter what, the spirit of Daddy is near.

I was already on cloud nine after the ESPYs, but the next day when I went out to the airport to receive Tom's gift, the opportunity to fly a genuine Tuskegee Airmen plane, I was beside myself. In the *Good Morning America* fantasy segment, I had flown an AT-6, which was the plane my father had trained on before the war. But this plane, the one that Tom owns and keeps in meticulous condition, was a P-51 Mustang, and it was *exactly* the same as Dad's, right down to the red-painted tail that had made the Tuskegee Airmen famous.

It's been said that life is not measured by the amount of breaths we take, but the moments that take our breath away. As I stood on the tarmac, I felt like I was five years old again. There was no music, but I did a little swaying happy dance. The kind of dance that a kid might do if you announced that unexpectedly, there was no school. And oh yeah, veggies have been outlawed. And you were taking them to the amusement park where you fully expected them to ride all the rides and eat as much candy as humanly possible. Being up in that plane, in the same make and model that my father flew was like getting a chance to high-five Daddy in heaven. My heart was pounding, my blood was racing. I was *soaring*, literally and figuratively. Thank you, Tom.

CHAPTER 31

Still Freakin' Blessed

*W*hat I have wanted for most of this past year
sounds very simple. I just wanted to feel better
the next day than I'd felt the day before. It had
been so long since I'd felt normal, whatever normal is. Just feeling normal again was such a gift.

In August 2013, I sat in again for Kelly Ripa
and did her show with Michael "Lovely Day"
Strahan. There was a $400 million jackpot in
the New York Powerball, and everyone was talking about it. Michael asked me what I would do
with so much money. And I just couldn't answer
the question. Of course, there are people I could
help and even more causes I could support. I
know that money can do good and make a difference. But for me, now and for the rest of my life,

the only jackpot that I've got my eye on is perfect health. I just want to be well.

You can't put a price tag on that. I would give every dime I have, I would give everything I own, just to be at full health again. My physical and mental well-being has been my primary focus, my only focus.

I had the opportunity to interview Oprah when Lee Daniel's *The Butler* came out, and as always, we did more talking during the commercial break than we did on the air. Off camera, she asked me, "So how are you? How are you, really?"

I told her that, "I can honestly say now I'm doing really well." I was saying it before, but I meant it now.

She said, "You came back in February."

I said, "I know, but I was willing myself into that chair. That was 90 percent willpower."

I was medically cleared. I want people to understand that I didn't do anything beyond doctor's orders. I followed doctor's orders. Physically, yes. Physically my numbers were at a place that let me come back. A big part of me wanted to resume my life.

Dr. Giralt says, "All of these things were carefully planned. We try to identify what's an individual's North. You want to try to never take away somebody's North because you leave them without hope. Robin's North is her ability to be out there and communicating with people. Putting her in Saran wrap and locking her in a room so she wouldn't get an infection would have led to depression and worse things. We felt we had to start letting her go out. The risks were well worth the mental benefits that she got. We were exposing her to a healing power that no medicine could have, and that was the perception that she was going to get back to her regular life and the things that made her thrive."

But it wasn't really until last May and June that I started to turn the corner. I think it had more than a little something to do with the weather. I'm a summer girl. I think it's a Southern thing. I love the warmth and being able to take KJ for longer walks and getting out in the fresh air. I was so appreciative of how *comfortable* I felt being out and not being so scared that I had to wear a mask or gloves.

Since I've been feeling better, I have Skyped and talked with many people going through cancer and, more specifically, facing a bone marrow transplant. It's usually the loved one who contacts me, not the patient. Family and friends are searching to do whatever they can to help in any way they can and they reach out to me, especially when the patient mentions my name to them.

Oftentimes I'm the only one they know who has gone through this. I usually do most of the listening because they know I truly understand them, that I understand their fears, questions and hopes.

Recently, I got into an e-mail conversation with a man whose young daughter was at a nearby hospital awaiting a transplant. Somehow he'd gotten my direct address, and we began e-mailing back and forth. It was a Saturday afternoon, and he wrote to tell me that she'd been taken off of the transplant list because she had bacteria in her blood. It was such a long e-mail, full of random thoughts, and at the end, he said, "I'm sorry, I'm rambling." He said, "It's the weekend and the hospital is so quiet."

As my mother would say, "Oh, mercy." I remember that. At that moment, it all came flooding back to me. How quiet it was on the weekends in the hospital. How the regular staff was gone and the friends who stopped by on their way to and from work were running around doing their weekend things. The days seemed endless and the nights seemed reaaaaaaaaally end-less. I could understand what he was feeling, and I was happy to be able to share that lonely, quiet moment with him.

I am so committed to sharing my journey, and I pray that it's helpful, but what just rips my heart out is that there have been many times that I get a follow-up call months later and learn that someone I've spoken with didn't make it. Amber always knows when it is one of those days.

The other day, Amber called, and she could tell from the tone of my voice something was wrong. She said, "What's the matter?"

And I said, "There was a little boy that I talked to, it was after Hurricane Sandy, and he was in the hospital in New Jersey, and I Skyped with him."

It was really funny, because I couldn't get Skype to work, and he was about eleven years old and he's talking me through Skype. He asked, "Now did you push this? Now do this."

Then boom, he comes up on my screen. He's got a Jets jersey on, and I have a Saints one on. We had such a good time talking and it was re-ally sweet. And now he's gone. It's just not fair.

There was a gentleman and his wife. I talked to them on the phone, and just six weeks later the person who had arranged the call sent me an e-mail: "I just wanted to let you know that he's passed away, but he really appreciated it and his wife appreciated the phone call." All I could think was, "Wow."

But I have to believe that our conversations are part of a ripple effect, a good that comes out of all the bad that is this disease. All these people, my fellow thrivers, touch my life, and I hopefully make some small impact on their journeys, and none of our lives are ever exactly the same.

*　*　*

During my agonizing round of high-dose chemo followed by the absolute gut-wrenching post-transplant recovery, I had stared at a picture of Hawaii on my hospital room wall. Once I'd reached my hundred days, once I'd gotten back to work, I thought, "How do I thank my friends for all that they've done? How do I thank Bugs for her great Cajun cooking? Lois Ann and Cathy for repeatedly traveling cross-country from California? How do I thank Jo and Kim for taking care of KJ? How do I thank Scarlett for squeezing my hand when the fear of death was knocking at my door, and how do I thank Julie for helping me write my last will and testament?"

I thought about sending them something engraved and fancy from a place like Tiffany. Then I remembered Kim's fiftieth birthday in Tuscany. My fiftieth birthday in Turks and Caicos. And I thought of places we hadn't all gone together like Hawaii, and the picture my friends had so lovingly taped to the hospital room wall. The gift I wanted to give couldn't be wrapped. I wanted to take my friends to Maui.

One of my favorite edicts is "Make one day, day one." We spend so much of our lives wishing and hoping. And I get that not everybody has the means or the ability to make their dreams come true at this very moment. But if there's one thing that spending a year fighting for your life against a rare and insidious bone marrow disease will teach you, it's that time is not to be wasted. If you can, let the darkest moments of my journey inspire you. You want to start exercising? Make one day, day one. Get up today and start walking. Because there were days when I couldn't even get out of bed. You want to start eating healthier? When you're walking down the aisles of the grocery store, skip the junk food and buy a bag of salad. Think of all the days and days when I couldn't even chew food and my only nourishment was a foul-smelling bag of lipids being fed to me by IV.

As I've gotten better, this is a message I must preach to myself. For so long, my friends and I had said, "One day, we'll all go to Hawaii." But for most of 2012, I didn't know if I was going to live long enough to see that magical island again, much less do something as luxurious as go on vacation with my friends. But somehow I survived. And while not everyone could come, most of my inner circle were able to join me for a trip that was as much about gratitude as it was about mai tais and palm trees. Hawaii was my way of saying, "Thank you. Thank you for loving me through this." It was also a sunshine-filled message to my own battered soul. I had made it. I had made it. One day was now day one.

Afterword

A New Year

For Momma

Dear Momma,

December 31, 2011. I was sitting with you in the family room. You were in your comfy recliner in front of the TV. *Dick Clark's New Year's Rockin' Eve* was on the tube. When we bought this house in 1975, you insisted on having a fireplace built in the family room. A beautiful stone fireplace that we never used. But you always wanted a fireplace, so a fireplace we had. That was you, Momma. You'd get your mind set on something and that was that.

I sat at my laptop, helping you put the finishing touches on your memoir. All that

was left was to write the acknowledgments. I
was touched that you referred to me, Butch,
Dorothy and Sally-Ann as the loves of your
life. But you didn't stop there. You kept firing
away, name after name. You thanked your
friends, your doctors, every nurse that had
ever taken your temperature, every home
health-care worker who had ever crossed our
door. You gave shout-outs to church members, neighbors who had long moved away,
even the postman. I remember innocently
suggesting that you didn't have to thank *everyone*. I will never forget your response. You
turned and looked at me, straightened your
glasses and smiled. You said, "Oh, honey,
you can't put a limit on gratitude."

You can't put a limit on gratitude. As the
new year would unfold, I would learn just
how true your words would prove to be.

Now it is almost New Year's 2014 and I
am putting the finishing touches on a book I
never expected to write.

Momma, for fifty-two years, you filled me
up with your own Lucimarian brew of love,
a love that made me as strong as the oak
trees that surrounded my childhood home.
Strong enough to fight for my life, not once

but twice. Strong enough to survive the worst storm that could ever blow my way—losing you. Losing Daddy was so hard. When your four grown children came home to comfort you after his death, it was you who comforted us, by asking us to crawl in your lap. At almost every age, your lap and your arms were my safety net. I leapt, in my life, and with my heart wide open, because I knew that you would always be there to catch me. Actually, you inspired me to take chances and knew if I fell that you'd be there to pick me back up.

How did you know, Momma? How did you know that I could hold your hand as you took your last breath, kiss your sweet face good-bye and still be standing? I didn't know. But somehow you knew. You filled me with love and trusted that your love would see me through. And it did. And it has.

You told me, as you finished your book, that you can't put a limit on gratitude. I promise that I will not skimp on my own acknowledgments. I will not leave out a soul.

But as I close this chapter of my life, as I put MDS in the rearview mirror and I begin—day by day—to fully inhabit the land of the well and forget what it was like to be shipwrecked in the land of the sick, I want to make sure that my gratitude for you is crystal clear. Your devotion, your faith, your kitchen-table wisdom were the never-waning weapons in the arsenal in the fight of my life.

Thank you, Momma. Miss you, Momma. Again and again, every day of my precious life, I love you and I thank you.

Acknowledgments

As Momma said: You can't put a limit on gratitude. So this could take a while.

I was humbled when I was approached by pub-
lishers to share my story. At first I was uncertain
if I wanted to write another book. While many
encouraged me to write it shortly after my return
to the anchor chair, Jamie Raab at Grand Central Publishing told me to take my time. Thank
you, Jamie, for believing my story would have
an impact whenever I decided to share it. From
our first phone call I knew you were the one.
Your spirit is contagious. I'm drawn to authentic
souls like yours. My thanks to you and your stellar team at Grand Central.

As a journalist I write for a living. Writing a

book is totally different. Thank you, Veronica Chambers, for your literary expertise and friendship. You were instrumental in helping me bring my words, my story, to life. You gently pushed me to reveal more about my journey than I ever have. I'm grateful for the amount of time you spent with me in my home in New York and the Pass. Time with me meant time away from your precious family. Thank you, Jason and Flora. I hope Flora gets that puppy she wants. In the meantime she can walk KJ anytime.

I literally fall on my knees and thank the good Lord for directing me to Dr. Sergio Giralt and Dr. Gail Roboz. They were the team captains of my dream team of nurses, technicians and all the health-care professionals who were my angels. For thirty days at Memorial Sloan-Kettering you were there for me 24/7. Every patient there was under your watchful, caring eyes. The nursing staff at MSKCC are rock stars and are led by Holly Wallace and Kathy Choo: Dena Barnes, Julie Kleber, Theresa Mathews, Chelsea Mintz, Jenny Tran, Katie Kilroy and Tonya Samuel; nutritionist Tatanisha Peets and your staff; music therapist, Taryn Thomas; physical therapist Lauren Liberatori; security guards Manny Rosa and Gregory Amour; my outpatient nurses

Sheila Kenny, Lorraine Jackson and Gloria Coffey; my outpatient physical therapist, Sharifa Gayle...thank you all for making me laugh and wiping away my tears. Thank you, Jeanne D'Agostino, for fiercely protecting my privacy.

At New York–Presbyterian: physician's assistant, Maureen Thyne; nurses Jessica Markis and Judy Murphy; medical technicians Virginia Hernandez and Anna Castillo; security staff Mark Warren, Sergeant Andrew Pottinger, Officer Susan Franov and Crystal Dones; patient services: Ellen Hawa...thank you for my continued great care, and thank you to Takla Boujaoude for also protecting my privacy.

Diane Sawyer and Richard Besser...my early guiding lights on this journey. You both made me truly believe that this, too, shall pass.

I know it was not only my medical team who saved me but all the prayer lists I was blessed to be placed on. From Apple Springs Baptist Church in Texas to First Presbyterian in Hartford, Connecticut, to Old Town Presbyterian in Bay Saint Louis, Mississippi. I've never adequately been able to express what everyone's prayers around the world have meant to me. I truly felt them all, and I return them to you hundredfold.

I'm grateful for the connection I have with people, especially those who watch GMA every morning. Often someone will say: "You know, Robin, we could be best friends." And I feel that way, too. If I lived in your town, we'd probably hang out, have lunch. I'd like that. I never take for granted that you invite me into your homes every morning. Thank you.

I'm grateful to everyone at N. S. Bienstock for your guidance and friendship. Peter, Paul, Richard, Carole, Jonathan, Janine...I'm energized every time I'm in your presence. You make me believe that anything is possible in my career and in my life.

I found out this past year that my apartment building in NYC is more like a neighborhood. Appreciate the notes slipped under my door, the offers to walk KJ and the best building staff in the city. To my longtime neighbors in Farmington, Connecticut, the Picorillo family, thanks for bringing in my trash cans from the curb when I'm not at home. I wouldn't be able to keep my home there were it not for my longtime personal assistant, Pam Guglielmino. Don't know how you do it, Pam. Nothing is too small or too big for you to tackle, all while raising four beautiful children.

Even though I've lived on the East Coast for almost twenty-five years, I will always be a Southern girl and the Pass will always be my home. My thanks to the entire Mississippi Gulf Coast for embracing the Roberts family. We love y'all right back.

My friends at the V Foundation for Cancer Research. Like Jimmy V said, "Don't give up, don't ever give up." And my new friends at Be the Match. You truly have helped me make my mess my message.

When it comes to ESPN and ABC/GMA...I need a second volume to thank everyone. Bob Iger, Anne Sweeney, George Bodenheimer, John Skipper, John A. Walsh, Ben Sherwood, Tom Cibrowski, James Goldston...and if I start naming all the anchors and correspondents who are dear friends, as Momma would say, "Oh, mercy!"

My fellow GMA anchors: George, Josh, Lara...you along with Sam had my back and I have yours. You make getting up at 3:45 a.m. an absolute joy because I know I get to spend my mornings with you. The entire GMA staff/family is second to none. The original #TeamRobin: Emily, Sonny, Karen, Elena, Petula, Diandre, Sharde...I love you all.

Before I thank my inner circle, a nod to Amber's: Crystal, Stephen, Todd, Alex, Bret, Sloan, Alana, Alan and Kalid. You took care of your girl so she could take care of hers.

To my second family: Jo, Kim, Lois Ann, Cathy, Jel, Scarlett, Linda, Julie, Bugs, Nancy, Denise, Carol, Beth, Sandy. There's a toast I like to say: "To friends who are family and to family who are friends."

It's one thing to love your family but to actually like them is simply priceless. Butch, Sally-Ann, Dorothy…you are the greatest gifts Mom and Dad ever gave me. It's a gift that keeps on giving, with all your children and grandchildren and—can't believe I'm saying this—great-grandchildren. Ron and Cynthia, you are the perfect fit for our family.

Amber, thank you for giving me your blessing to share what you mean to me and to my family. You shy away from the spotlight, but I'm proud that many now know what I've always known…you are a phenomenal, beautiful woman in every way. Bless you for selflessly being the wind beneath my wings.

Thank you, Momma, thank you, Daddy, for GIVING me wings and encouraging me to fly high. I miss you both so much. Not a day goes by that I don't think about you. I draw upon the lessons you lovingly taught me about faith, family and friends. You taught me to be true to myself. Momma, I remember what you said, "God loves you because of who God is, not because of anything you did or didn't do." As always, Momma, you get the last word.